European Governance and Supranational Institutions

What drives the political and legal enforcement of member state compliance within the European Union?

European Governance and Supranational Institutions examines the role of the European Commission and the European Court of Justice in compliance politics, tracing development since the 1970s and describing strategies for strengthening the EU's enforcement system. The author shows how supranational institutions have played an independent role in the creation of a European enforcement system, which is exceptionally effective compared to that of other international organizations.

This book makes important theoretical and empirical contributions to the study of European governance. Drawing on principal–agent theory, Tallberg uses a novel principal–supervisor–agent model, specifically designed to explain strategic interaction in the enforcement phase of international cooperation. Charting previously undocumented processes, the book unveils the dynamics of EU compliance politics. It will appeal to all those interested in the European Union and international relations theory.

Jonas Tallberg is Research Fellow at Lund University and the Swedish Institute of International Affairs.

Routledge Advances in European Politics

1 **Russian Messianism**
Third Rome, revolution, Communism and after
Peter J. S. Duncan

2 **European Integration and the Postmodern Condition**
Governance, democracy, identity
Peter van Ham

3 **Nationalism in Italian Politics**
The stories of the Northern League, 1980–2000
Damian Tambini

4 **International Intervention in the Balkans**
A critical evaluation
Edited by Peter Siani-Davies and Stephanie Schwandner-Sievers

5 **Widening the European Union**
The politics of institutional change and reform
Edited by Bernard Steunenberg

6 **Institutional Challenges in the European Union**
Edited by Madeleine Hosli, Adrian van Deemen and Mika Widgrén

7 **Europe Unbound**
Enlarging and reshaping the boundaries of the European Union
Edited by Jan Zielonka

8 **Ethnic Cleansing in the Balkans**
Nationalism and the destruction of tradition
Cathie Carmichael

9 **Democracy and Enlargement in Post-Communist Europe**
The democratisation of the general public in fifteen Central and Eastern European countries, 1991–1998
Christian W. Haerpfer

10 **Private Sector Involvement in the Euro**
The power of ideas
Stefan Collignon and Daniela Schwarzer

11 **Europe**
A Nietzschean perspective
Stefan Elbe

12 **Europe, Globalisation and Sustainable Development**
Edited by Brian Baxter, John Barry and Richard Dunphy

13 **European Union Council Presidencies**
A comparative analysis
Edited by Ole Elgström

14 **European Governance and Supranational Institutions**
Making states comply
Jonas Tallberg

15 **European Union, NATO and Russia**
Martin Smith and Graham Timmins

European Governance and Supranational Institutions

Making states comply

Jonas Tallberg

Routledge
Taylor & Francis Group
LONDON AND NEW YORK

First published 2003
by Routledge
11 New Fetter Lane, London EC4P 4EE

Simultaneously published in the USA and Canada
by Routledge
29 West 35th Street, New York, NY 10001

Routledge is an imprint of the Taylor & Francis Group

Typeset in Sabon by
BOOK NOW Ltd
Printed and bound in Great Britain by
Antony Rowe Ltd, Chippenham, Wiltshire

British Library Cataloguing in Publication Data
A catalogue record for this book is available from the British Library

Library of Congress Cataloging in Publication Data
Tallberg, Jonas
European governance and supranational institutions : making states comply / Jonas Tallberg.
p. cm.
Includes bibliographical references and index.
1. Law–European Union countries. 2. Sanctions (Law)–European Union countries. 3. Law enforcement–European Union countries.
4. Europe–Economic integration. I. Title.
KJE971.5 .T35 2003
341.242′2–dc21 2002155707

ISBN 0-415-31137-3

To my mother and father

Contents

Illustrations

Figures

Tables

Acknowledgments

My work on delegation, enforcement, and compliance in European governance and international cooperation has developed in, and profited from, a number of research milieus, to which I extend my deepest gratitude. Lund University has offered a stimulating academic environment for the completion of this book, as well as cheerful colleagues and generous autonomy. The Centre for Advanced Study, Oslo, presented me with excellent conditions for productive research in the spring of 2000, within the program on Explaining International Regime Effectiveness. The Swedish Institute of International Affairs, Stockholm, has provided a peaceful working environment and an inspiring proximity to the world of policy-making. Brief periods at the Forward Studies Unit of the European Commission and the Policy Planning Group of the Swedish Ministry for Foreign Affairs have also contributed to my understanding of European governance.

This book presents the full theoretical and empirical version of an argument that I have published portions of elsewhere. An abridged account of the state liability account in Chapter 6 originally appeared in "Supranational influence in EU enforcement," *Journal of European Public Policy* 7 (1): 104–21 (2000). Chapters 5 and 6 develop empirical accounts first presented in "The anatomy of autonomy," *Journal of Common Market Studies* 38 (5): 843–64 (2000). Parts of Chapter 4 develop a theme originally discussed in "Compliance and post-agreement bargaining," *European Journal of International Relations* 4 (4): 371–408 (1998). Some of my conclusions are adapted from those I first drew in "Delegation to supranational institutions," *West European Politics* 25 (1): 23–46 (2002). Finally, the figures and tables appearing in Chapters 3 and 4 are reprinted from my article "Paths to compliance," *International Organization* 56 (3): 609–43 (2002). I gratefully acknowledge the respective permissions of Taylor & Francis (www.tandf.co.uk), Blackwell, Frank Cass, Sage and MIT Press to use this material. For constructive comments and generous encouragement to turn the original dissertation at Lund University into a published book, I thank, in particular, Karen Alter, Bo Bjurulf, Tanja Börzel, Elisabeth Corell, Ole Elgström, Kjell Eliassen, Jon Hovi, Christian Joerges, Christer Jönsson, Ronald Mitchell, Mark Pollack, Olav Schram Stokke, Alec Stone Sweet, Mark Thatcher, Arild Underdal, Oran Young, and Michael Zürn.

I gratefully acknowledge the financial support of the Anders Otto Swärd Foundation, the Bank of Sweden Tercentenary Foundation, the Crafoord Foundation, the International Chamber of Commerce, Lund University, Nordisk Forskningsutdanningsakademi, the Royal Swedish Academy of Sciences, the Siamon Foundation, the Swedish Institute, the Swedish Institute of International Affairs, and the Swedish Ministry for Foreign Affairs.

Finally, I wish to thank my wife, Kalina Tallberg Lindahl, for her advice, encouragement, and love. I dedicate this book to my mother and father, Ingegerd Tallberg-Broman and Tommy Tallberg, who have been a dependable source of support, and whose intellectual curiosity I admire.

Jonas Tallberg
Lund and Stockholm

Abbreviations

Coreper	Committee of Permanent Representatives
DG	Directorate General
EC	European Community
ECHR	European Court of Human Rights
ECJ	European Court of Justice
ECSC	European Coal and Steel Community
EEC	European Economic Community
EFTA	European Free Trade Association
EMS	European Monetary System
EMU	Economic and Monetary Union
EP	European Parliament
EPC	European Political Cooperation
ERDF	European Regional Development Fund
EU	European Union
Euratom	European Atomic Energy Community
GATT	General Agreement on Tariffs and Trade
IAEA	International Atomic Energy Agency
ICC	International Criminal Court
IGC	intergovernmental conference
IMF	International Monetary Fund
IR	international relations
JHA	Justice and Home Affairs
MEP	Member of the European Parliament
NTB	non-tariff barrier
P–A	principal–agent
P–S–A	principal–supervisor–agent
QMV	Qualified Majority Voting
SEA	Single European Act
TEU	Treaty on European Union
UK	United Kingdom
UN	United Nations
US	United States
VAT	Value Added Tax
WTO	World Trade Organization

1 Introduction

When, where, and how are the European Union's (EU's) supranational institutions able to advance their own political agenda?[1] This question is one of the central bones of contention in the study of European governance. Historically, theories of regional integration have offered competing answers, depicting the EU's supranational institutions as either "engines of integration," independently driving European cooperation, or "obedient servants," effectively controlled by national governments. In recent years, scholars dissatisfied with these rival accounts have turned to institutional theory for the means to explain variation in supranational influence over time, institutions, and issue-areas.

This book makes two distinct contributions to the study of European governance. First, it explores the role of the EU's supranational institutions in post-decisional compliance politics. As opposed to existing research, which is heavily focused on the agenda-setting phase of EU policy-making, this book examines the influence of the European Commission and the European Court of Justice (ECJ) in the enforcement of state compliance. It traces the evolution of non-compliance with EU rules 1978–2000, and it describes the supranational institutions' strategies for strengthening the EU's enforcement system in response to these developments. The study explicitly links all the levels in the EU compliance game: the Commission and the ECJ at the supranational level, member governments at the national level, and domestic courts and litigants at the subnational level.

The empirical analysis demonstrates that the EU's supranational institutions have played an independent role in the development of a European enforcement system that is more constraining than national governments ever intended. Dissatisfied with existing means of enforcement at the European level and with governments' reluctance to delegate more powerful instruments, the ECJ and the Commission independently created and perfected a system of decentralized supervision, whereby individuals and national courts are engaged to monitor and enforce state compliance. This system of decentralized supervision is now an integral part of European governance. The EU's supranational institutions have influenced the course of European integration, not only by introducing new issues to the policy agenda, as is often argued, but also by securing a higher degree of compliance with the policy decisions that indeed are taken.

The second contribution is the presentation of a novel principal–supervisor–agent (P–S–A) model, designed specifically to capture strategic interaction between governments and supranational institutions in the enforcement phase of international cooperation. The model rests on core tenets of principal–agent (P–A) analysis, developed explicitly to address questions of delegation, control, and autonomy in economic and political affairs. Yet the P–S–A model moves beyond existing applications in EU studies and International Relations (IR) theory, by adapting the P–A framework to the strategic relationship in post-decisional compliance politics.

The P–S–A model offers effective theoretical tools capable of explaining the major developments in EU enforcement. It points to the "dilemma of credible commitments" in the delegation of supervisory functions to international institutions, it isolates the institutional and informational sources of supranational discretion, and it identifies governmental control mechanisms that constrain the scope for supranational influence. The model explains why delegation of enforcement powers by necessity involves the granting of discretion, which then may be used by supranational institutions to pursue independent political agendas. The model also suggests why the EU as a strategic context is comparatively more open to supranational maneuvering by the ECJ than by the Commission.

The empirical and theoretical arguments in this book carry implications beyond the European context, for general debates in IR on delegation to international institutions and determinants of state compliance. Increasingly, the design of international governance structures involves the delegation of powers to more or less independent institutions. Most notable is the growing delegation of powers of monitoring, dispute settlement and enforcement in the areas of trade, human rights, and the environment. This study suggests that P–A analysis provides powerful theoretical tools for explaining the sources and effects of these developments.

Furthermore, the EU case generates evidence that challenges existing divisions in the ongoing IR debate on the most effective means for combating non-compliance. Whereas so-called enforcement and management theorists stress the effectiveness of coercive and problem-solving strategies respectively, the EU case demonstrates the complementarity of the two approaches. Today, the EU boasts the most effective international system for making states comply. The combination of problem-solving and coercive strategies in a "management-enforcement ladder," operated by the EU's supranational institutions, is the key source to this effectiveness.

The debate

One of the distinguishing features of the EU in comparison to other international organizations is the degree to which its member governments have delegated powers and functions to the central institutions of the EU. In simplified terms, the Commission has been delegated the essential tasks of initiating and developing proposals for new EU policy, executing EU policy within some clearly specified domains, and ensuring member state compliance with EU rules as the "guardian of the treaties."[2] The ECJ has been delegated the function of interpreting the treaties and ensuring that EU law is applied correctly in the member states. And the European Parliament (EP) enjoys delegated powers in the legislative process through which EU policy is created, in the budgetary process through which the EU budget is shaped and adopted, and in the control and supervision of the Commission.

These functions and powers delegated to the Commission, the ECJ, and the EP – commonly referred to as the supranational institutions of the EU – have been the subject of fierce academic debate since the inception of European integration (for overviews, see Hansen 1969; Puchala 1972; Hix 1994, 1998; Caporaso and Keeler 1995; Caporaso 1998). The two dominating theories of regional integration – neofunctionalism and intergovernmentalism – have traditionally offered the most distinct and influential conceptions of the institutions' role in the integration process. In recent years, however, scholars dissatisfied with the competing claims of these theories have turned to institutional theory in general, and P–A analysis in particular, for tools to explain variation in the autonomy of the supranational institutions.

In the 1950s, 1960s, and early 1970s, the first wave of neofunctionalists and intergovernmentalists debated whether the delegated powers actually conferred a role on the supranational institutions in European cooperation. The early neofunctionalist literature addressed mainly the supranational institutions indirectly in its attempt to advance a theory of regional integration (Haas 1958, 1964, 1967; Lindberg 1963; Scheingold 1965; Nye 1971; Lindberg and Scheingold 1970, 1971). The central claim of this literature was that regional integration would proceed through a process of spill-over from one sectoral domain to the other, as societal demands for European policies were encouraged and translated into concrete proposals by the supranational institutions, the Commission in particular. The supranational institutions were considered highly instrumental to the progression of European integration.

Conversely, early intergovernmentalist scholarship turned sharply against this picture of the supranational institutions as engines and facilitators of European integration (Hoffmann 1966, 1982). Grounded in classical realist conceptions of anarchy and power politics, early intergovernmentalism posited that national governments had not, and were unlikely to, endow the supranational institutions with powers that would grant them a true role in European politics. The authority of the supranational institutions was perceived as limited in scope, conditional on member state approval, reversible if proven unacceptable in its results, and unlikely to be extended to domains of key importance to national interests.

When the study of European cooperation was reinvigorated in the second half of the 1980s in response to the relaunch of the integration process itself, the point of contention in the neofunctionalist–intergovernmentalist debate changed. In the contemporary debate, the source of disagreement is not whether the institutions fulfill essential functions in European governance – all now agree they do – but whether they only fulfill the functions delegated to them by member states, or have developed roles for themselves that go beyond those that national governments intended. In causal terms, do the supranational institutions solely produce effects on European integration as desired by EU governments, through the competences they have been delegated, or do they also exercise an independent causal influence that goes beyond what is intended?

Modern-day neofunctionalists generally contend that the supranational institutions enjoy substantial autonomy from national governments in the exercise of their powers (Sandholtz and Zysman 1989; Sandholtz 1992, 1993; Burley and Mattli 1993; Cram 1997; Stone Sweet and Sandholtz 1997). As a consequence, they contend that the institutions are capable of independently driving European integration further and in other directions than member states wish. The Commission is considered causally important as an agenda setter and policy entrepreneur that identifies policy problems, mobilizes support from transnational interests, exploits openings in the political opportunity structure, and calculates strategically how to achieve "more Europe." The ECJ, for its part, is seen as having successfully engineered a process of legal integration, which goes far beyond member governments' original intentions when designing the European legal system.

Intergovernmentalist scholars, by contrast, assert that member governments remain firmly in control of the process of integration (Keohane and Hoffmann 1991; Garrett 1992, 1995; Moravcsik 1991, 1993, 1998, 1999). They assert that the supranational institutions do not enjoy autonomy in any real sense of the term, and are not capable of exerting independent causal influence. On the contrary, these institutions function as passive devices facilitating intergovernmental bargaining. The Commission's supposed influence as agenda setter and policy entrepreneur is illusory, since the Commission simply fulfills functions entrusted to it by, and in the interests of, member governments, drafting its proposals with a view to what would be acceptable in the capitals of the major European states. Similarly, intergovernmentalist scholars contend that the ECJ has acted autonomously only with the consent of member governments, that its legal system is consistent with the interests of national governments, and that it tends to tailor its rulings to the preferences of the major member states.

Since the mid-1990s, the study of European cooperation has gradually surrendered the previous preoccupation with grand theories of regional integration to the benefit of middle-range theorizing about specific aspects of European governance.[3] The most pronounced trend in this literature is the increasing recourse to forms of institutional theory, often divided into rational choice institutionalism, historical institutionalism, and sociological institutionalism (Hall and Taylor 1996; Peters 1999; Aspinwall and Schneider 2000). Privileging the institutional structure of political interaction in the EU, institutional analysis specifies how changes and variations in this structure affect the behavior of actors operating under it.

On the question of supranational influence, institutionalist contributions share the ambition to move the debate beyond the competing claims of neofunctionalism and intergovernmentalism, and to demonstrate the merits of institutional theory (e.g. Pierson 1996; Pollack 1997, 2003; Alter 1998a; Armstrong and Bulmer 1998; Tallberg 2000a; Aspinwall and Schneider 2001; Tsebelis and Garrett 2001). This literature addresses the puzzle of variation in supranational influence, which the dominant theories of regional integration have proven unable to account for. Why are the EU's supranational institutions able to advance private agendas in some cases, but not in others? What are the factors that determine the degree of autonomy for an institution, and why are some institutions more autonomous than others?

Principal–agent analysis, as developed within rational choice institutionalism, has emerged as the dominant theoretical tool for conceptualizing and explaining variation in supranational influence (e.g. Pollack 1997, 1998, 2003; Alter 1998a; Franchino 2000; Schmidt 1998, 2000; Tallberg 2000a, 2002a; Thatcher and Stone Sweet 2002). The analytical core of P–A theory is the principal–agent relation, which in its simplest version arises whenever one party (principal) delegates certain functions to another party (agent). P–A theory posits that this relationship is inherently problematic, as conflicting preferences and information asymmetry induce the agent to pursue its own interests rather than those of the principal – to "shirk" in P–A vocabulary. Yet the principal may seek to prevent or reduce such shirking by engaging in monitoring of the agent's actions and by threatening the imposition of sanctions if undesired behavior is detected.

In the standard application of the P–A imagery to EU politics, member states are conceived as principals that have delegated certain powers to supranational agents for the purpose of solving particular functional problems. The degree of discretion or autonomy enjoyed by the institutions in this relationship is then explained by the extent to which governments have established credible and effective control mechanisms, capable of preventing, deterring, or undoing independent supranational maneuvering. Next to existing work by rational choice institutionalists, the explanatory potential of P–A theory is best illustrated by the recourse made to these conceptual tools by intergovernmentalists and neofunctionalists in search of theoretical additions enabling them to address variation in supranational influence (see Moravcsik 1995; Stone Sweet and Caporaso 1998).

The orientation of the study

This book differs from existing studies of supranational influence through its focus on post-decisional compliance politics. So far, research on the influence of the EU's supranational institutions has been concerned almost exclusively with the capacity of these organs to engage in political or judicial policy-making. By contrast, the supranational institutions' enforcement functions have generally been overlooked, although policy-making in the EU would be of little value if compliance with EU rules could not be secured. Slightly simplified, existing research on supranational influence has examined the Commission's authority to initiate and execute policy, while neglecting its third traditional function, to enforce policy. Similarly, studies of the ECJ's autonomy have been preoccupied with its function to interpret the treaties, but have paid little attention to its second traditional task of ensuring compliance with EU rules.[4]

Theoretically, this study draws on the analytical tools and insights of P–A analysis. P–A analysis offers a number of advantages to scholars who are willing to subject the question of supranational influence to careful empirical examination:

1 By acknowledging the initial primacy of member states and then investigating their degree of control over the supranational institutions, P–A analysis offers a neutral theoretical language which does not a priori discriminate against the claims of either neofunctionalism or intergovernmentalism;
2 P–A analysis permits open-ended empirical analysis of the degree of autonomy in the relationship between member states and supranational institutions; and
3 P–A analysis encourages the formulation of conditional generalizations about supranational influence, as it recognizes the likelihood of variation across time, issue-areas, and institutions.

Yet, for P–A theory to provide a powerful explanation of supranational enforcement influence, it must be adapted to the strategic relationships in post-decisional compliance politics. The roles that member states and supranational institutions play vary depending on what aspect of the EU policy process is under scrutiny. For the purposes of capturing strategic interaction in EU enforcement, I develop a triangular P–S–A model (see also Tallberg 2000b). The addition of a supervisor to the cast of actors is familiar from economic P–A theory, where it is recognized that the principal, for the purpose of enhancing control over the agent's actions, may engage a supervisor whose role it is to gather information about the agent's activity.

In the P–S–A model presented here, national governments (principals), for the sake of self-commitment, assign to the Commission and the ECJ (supervisors) the task of enforcing compliance with EU law, as delegated to the individual member states (agents). Member states are thus conceived of as both principals and agents, who at t_0 collectively reach decisions in intergovernmental bodies, and at t_1 are expected to individually carry out the adjustments necessary to realize these decisions. The supranational institutions function as supervisors engaged by national governments for the purpose of monitoring actual member state behavior and enforcing compliance with EU rules. This configuration reflects the roles of member states and institutions as laid down in the treaties and as exercised in practice.

The member states' act of collective self-commitment transforms the original P–A relation into a P–S–A relationship. But, whereas the delegation of supervisory powers to the supranational institutions ameliorates the problem of state non-compliance, it also creates a new dilemma. The supranational institutions have interests as well, which may lead these organs to conduct their enforcement operations in ways other than those desired by member governments. Engaging the Commission and the ECJ as supervisors does not therefore solve the problem of shirking *per se*. Rather, it replaces governments' concern with one form of shirking – state non-compliance – with another – supranational influence. Instead of one, we now have two P–A-like relationships, namely, that between supervisor and agent and that between principal and supervisor. Both of these relationships are characterized by conflicting interests and information asymmetries, and in both, the scope for autonomous action is determined by existing means of monitoring and sanctioning.

When confronted with an inventory of interests, information, monitoring, and sanctions in EU compliance politics, this model yields three sets of novel and theoretically coherent hypotheses about supranational influence. The first set pertains to the conditions that induce the Commission and the ECJ to pursue private enforcement agendas, the second to the scope for supranational influence, and the third to the forms of supervision that the institutions are likely to promote.

I assess the explanatory power of the P–S–A model in the light of the Commission's and the ECJ's efforts to develop the EU's enforcement system in the 1980s and 1990s, against the backdrop of non-compliance problems associated with the EU's internal market. The aim to complete the internal market between 1985 and 1992, through the elimination of all barriers to the free movement of goods, people, services, and capital in Europe, was the most ambitious target the European Community (EC) had ever set itself. The internal market program – as agreed upon by the European Council in June 1985 and later formalized in the 1986 Single European Act (SEA) – called for extensive legislative efforts on the European level and required far-reaching changes in national regulatory practices.

Recognizing that the internal market and its rules would amount to little if member states did not correctly implement and apply the measures set out in the program, the Commission and the ECJ embarked on a crusade in the early 1990s to strengthen EU enforcement. The enforcement-enhancing actions followed three parallel tracks:

1 efforts to improve the enforcement potential of existing, delegated means at the centralized EU level;

2 attempts to induce the delegation of new and more far-reaching enforcement powers at the 1991 and 1996–7 IGCs; and
3 concerted action to independently boost the supervisory potential of decentralized enforcement through national courts.

These three parallel tracks effectively constitute three cases with internal variation across key elements of the P–S–A relationship. The supranational institutions sought the same outcome in all cases, yet the constraints and opportunities they confronted in this process varied between the cases. The three strategies conformed to alternative ways of exerting independent influence, each involving specific conditions for government control: exercising delegated powers contrary to the preferences of member governments, inducing the delegation of powers that member governments would not have conferred in the absence of supranational maneuvering, and single-handedly creating new means beyond the confines of the treaties.

In the empirical analysis, I assess the degree of supranational influence in these three processes and analyze the factors facilitating and impeding member state control.

These processes have only partially been documented before, and never in a comprehensive fashion or for purposes of assessing supranational influence.[5] Existing works in political science and law signify a compartmentalized rather than integrated understanding of EU enforcement. The Commission's use of the infringement procedure at the centralized EU level is viewed as distinct from the ECJ's development of decentralized enforcement through national courts. The orientation of this book reflects another perspective – one where EU enforcement is viewed as a coherent strategic setting, where these two levels of supervision are understood in relation to each other. The development of EU enforcement since the early 1980s cannot be properly explained unless it is recognized that the Commission's and the ECJ's actions at both levels are driven by the same logic. The choices the institutions make reflect their understanding of the effectiveness of EU supervision as a whole, not just either centralized or decentralized enforcement.

This study presents new empirical data on patterns of non-compliance in the EU 1978–2000, the Commission's exercise of its enforcement powers at the centralized EU level, the Commission's role in encouraging decentralized enforcement through national courts, the supranational institutions' joint efforts to induce governments to delegate more far-reaching enforcement tools at the 1991 and 1996–7 IGCs, and member states' response to the ECJ's creation of the principle of state liability. The empirical analysis is based on extensive primary material, drawn from three main sources: official documentation from the Commission, the ECJ, the EP, member states, and IGCs; unofficial documentation from the Commission to which I was granted access on the condition that I only refer to these documents as internal Commission memos; and about thirty interviews with national and supranational officials involved in EU enforcement, national implementation, and IGC negotiations.

Empirical P–A analysis is associated with analytical pitfalls that only can be safeguarded against through a careful selection of research strategies. The problem that warrants attention is the notion of rational anticipation, which can make it exceedingly difficult to determine whether agents/supervisors act completely autonomously or are effectively controlled by principals (e.g. Weingast and Moran 1983; McCubbins *et al.* 1987; Moe 1987; Pollack 1998, 2002; Stone Sweet and Caporaso 1998). The essence of this problem is the possibility that agents may rationally anticipate the reactions of their principals, such as the imposition of sanctions, and therefore choose to adjust their behavior in line with the principals' interests *ex ante* so as to avoid these punishments. Agents may therefore seem to act autonomously, since principals do not exercise any overt control, while they are in fact perfectly controlled through the threat of sanctions. Indeed, the more effective the principals' control mechanisms, the less overt sanctioning there should be.

While recognizing the analytical problems posed by rational anticipation, the P–A literature also points to process-tracing and counterfactual analysis as methodological means for overcoming this potential pitfall (Pollack 1998). I employ both strategies in this study. By investigating and explaining the process by which initial conditions are transformed into outcomes, process-tracing isolates the mechanisms which link causes to effects (George and McKeown 1985; King *et al.* 1994: 224–8). In the context of P–A analysis, careful empirical process-tracing makes it possible first to determine the actors' true interests and then to trace the subtle influences principals, supervisors, and agents exert upon each other.

Counterfactual analysis is useful as a control strategy in cases where agents seem to have escaped the control of principals. Counterfactual thought experiments typically try to picture what the outcome would be in an imaginary case, in which everything is identical to the actual case, but the presumed causal factor is absent (Fearon 1991; Tetlock and Belkin 1996). Suspected cases of supranational influence must pass a demanding counterfactual test (Moravcsik 1995). Could the same outcome now credited to the supranational institutions also have resulted from member state actions in the absence of these institutions? Only if it is unlikely that member states would have stepped in to fulfill the same function and produce the same outcome, can it be established that the supranational institutions actually exerted an independent causal influence.

The argument

This study shows that the EU's supranational institutions are central in making states comply. Yet the Commission and the ECJ have fulfilled not only the supervisory functions delegated to them by member governments.

Historically, the EU's supranational institutions have exerted an independent influence by moving the European system of enforcement beyond governments' original intentions when first delegating supervisory competences. Most importantly, the Commission and the ECJ have engineered a system of decentralized enforcement, where societal actors monitor and sanction non-compliance. The EU's supranational institutions are thus capable of transforming European governance, not only by introducing new policy issues, but also by implementing independent enforcement agendas that ultimately secure an unusual degree of compliance with EU rules.

The findings of the empirical chapters in this book lend extensive support to the conceptualization of post-decisional compliance politics as a strategic environment where states' control mechanisms define the scope for independent supranational enforcement actions. Where member governments could readily observe, interpret, and intervene, and where unwanted actions that nevertheless occurred could be countered with sanctions, the Commission's and the ECJ's scope for supranational influence was restricted. By contrast, the supranational institutions were capable of implementing their own enforcement agenda where few means existed to actively monitor their actions, and where sanctions were either lacking or difficult to apply.

When the supranational institutions embarked on the crusade to boost EU enforcement in the early 1990s, they did so against the backdrop of growing non-compliance. Three forms of compliance problems were particularly prominent and worrying: non-compliance in the legal implementation of directives, in the actual application of EU rules, and with ECJ judgments. If the internal market were to be realized, non-compliance would have to be contained. Recognizing the limits of existing enforcement means, the Commission and the ECJ pursued three parallel avenues aimed at reinforcing Community supervision.

First, the Commission attempted to improve the effectiveness of existing powers through a fivefold set of measures aimed at enhancing the enforcement capacity of the infringement procedure at the centralized EU level: internal reforms that streamlined the handling of cases, a shift to a firmer enforcement policy, the encouragement of complaints to the Commission, the development of a shaming strategy, and the intensification of compliance bargaining. While strengthening EU enforcement, these efforts did not qualify as supranational influence. Nothing indicates that governments were opposed to effective use of the infringement procedure, and the procedure as such offered ample room for improvements without necessitating a supranational transgression of delegated competences. That said, it is evident that the Commission operates with a significant degree of autonomy within the infringement procedure. Anxious to secure credible commitments, governments have refrained from establishing control mechanisms that would allow them to interfere in the Commission's handling of infringement cases.

Second, the Commission sought to induce the delegation of new means of enforcement at the 1991 and 1996–7 IGCs; first, by the introduction of sanctions against non-complying states, and then by more time and resource efficient procedures for the imposition of these sanctions. On both occasions, the Commission's attempts to maneuver EU governments into accepting its preferred proposals failed. The IGC format granted governments an extreme form of monitoring, which in turn generated a more even distribution of information about the consequences of alternative proposals. Fearing the detrimental implications for national sovereignty of the supranational proposals, member governments either settled for less consequential alternatives or forced the Commission to dilute its suggestions.

Third, the Commission and the ECJ collectively sought to shift the gravity in EU enforcement toward greater reliance on decentralized supervision through national courts. Exploiting its judicial independence and the absence of intrusive government control, the ECJ strengthened the remedies available to individuals. Most notable was the creation of new decentralized sanctions through the introduction and expansion of the principle of state liability – a form of sanction that governments had explicitly rejected at the 1991 IGC. Member state attempts to punish the ECJ by revising its powers and refusing to apply the principle at the national level were of varied, but altogether limited, effectiveness. In parallel, the Commission launched policy programs that supplemented the ECJ's efforts by raising the awareness of EU rights and law among citizens and in the legal professions. These initiatives were carefully monitored by member governments, with predictable effects on supranational autonomy. Where the Commission did not adapt its proposals to government preferences *ex ante*, member states sanctioned the programs *ex post*. Yet the combined effect of the ECJ's new case law and the Commission's policy programs was to reinforce a system of decentralized supervision whose development and institutionalization governments had sought to prevent or undo on numerous occasions – a true case of supranational influence.

These results challenge established positions on supranational influence in European governance. First, the EU's supranational institutions may exert an independent influence, not only by introducing new issues on the policy agenda, but also by securing a higher degree of compliance with the policy decisions that indeed are taken. The source of this influence is the dilemma of credible commitments. Governments delegate supervisory powers to supranational institutions for purposes of strengthening the credibility of their commitments. Yet this act of self-commitment is only meaningful to the extent that the institutions enjoy extensive discretion and, accordingly, governments refrain from establishing intrusive control mechanisms. Since the supranational institutions have interests too, they will exploit this discretion in order to pursue their own political agenda. Supranational influence is thus a logical, if unwanted, effect of governments' desire to secure collective commitments.

Second, as predicted by P–A theory, governments' mechanisms for controlling the institutions condition the scope for supranational influence. The phenomenon of independent supranational effects on European integration is more complex than either neofunctionalism or intergovernmentalism would predict. Most notable are the patterns of variation between alternative strategic settings in European governance, and between the Commission and the ECJ. It is most difficult for the EU's supranational institutions to advance private agendas at IGCs. Intergovernmental conferences entail a high degree of agenda control for governments and a more even distribution of information, thus reducing the institutions' capacity to promote supranational proposals. Conversely, the Commission and the ECJ enjoy particularly extensive discretion in their pure enforcement functions, where they are typically relieved of intrusive control mechanisms.

It is equally clear that the Commission generally is more constrained in its actions than the ECJ. Ultimately, this is an effect of the two organs' main institutional functions, which shape EU governments' control mechanisms (Tallberg 2000a, 2002a). The Commission's core function as policy initiator forces the institution to seek informal contacts with member governments in the preparation of new legislation. This grants governments insight into internal Commission policy formulation and an ability to shape the outcome by signaling their preferences. Moreover, governments can always either dismiss the Commission's initiatives in the Council or relegislate, should the institution be insufficiently attentive. By contrast, the ECJ's position as constitutional court renders impossible any close control of its interpretation of EU law. Even if member governments may signal their preferences by submitting observations and arguing their cases before the ECJ, they cannot prevent it from handing down unwanted judgments, and possess no other means than treaty revision to undo interpretations based on the treaty. The ECJ has learned to exploit diverging member state positions for the purpose of pursuing agendas it knows governments cannot undo.

The argument in this book carries important implications for ongoing debates in IR on delegation to international institutions and determinants of state compliance. Instead of regarding the EU as a *sui generis* case, from which little can be learned, I consider it an important point of comparison, capable of generating lessons for general theoretical debates.

First, the growth of governance beyond the nation-state is one of the most pronounced political trends in recent decades. Increasingly, the design of international governance structures involves the delegation of decision-making powers to institutions that are organizationally and, to varying extents, politically independent from the founding states. Whereas this study validates the advantages of P–A analysis in the study of European governance, it is now time to recognize that P–A theory is equally relevant for addressing delegation and agency in international governance in general.

The EU is not the only case where governments have set up and delegated functions to international institutions, simultaneously creating potential control problems. Secretariats, courts, and dispute-settlement bodies of international organizations generally enjoy certain duties of representation, initiation, regulation, implementation, supervision, and rule interpretation. What makes the supranational institutions of the EU special in this comparative perspective is the range of the powers delegated, not the act of delegation itself.

Yet IR scholars have been slow to recognize the usefulness of P–A analysis in explaining patterns of delegation and agency in international governance. Even if much theorizing about international institutions originates from a functionalist understanding of international cooperation, P–A theory *per se* is only beginning to inform this literature (e.g. Alter 2002b; Kahler 2002; Martin 2002). P–A analysis is likely to be particularly useful for analyzing variation in the delegation of alternative functions between different international institutions. The relationship between functional demands for delegation and concerns for national sovereignty is an area in need of further exploration.

Agency problems, too, can be effectively addressed through P–A analysis, yet serious gaps in control are not likely to be as prevalent in other international organizations as in the EU, in view the unusual discretion accorded to the European institutions. The primary lesson that can be drawn from this study for the general IR debate pertains to the previously noted dilemma of credible commitments. Delegation of supervisory competences, by necessity, involves the granting of a certain discretion to international institutions, since monitoring, enforcement, and rule interpretation would be of little value if controlled by governments. We are therefore more likely to find autonomous institutions with independent influence among international courts, monitoring bodies, and dispute-settlement organs which help secure state commitments, than among institutions that provide technical expertise, engage in regulation, or implement intergovernmental agreements.

Second, the question of what determines compliance with international regulatory agreements has gained an increasingly prominent position on the research agenda through the burgeoning literature on international regime effectiveness and international legal systems. The contemporary debate is framed in terms of two alternative perspectives on compliance: the enforcement approach and the management approach. The two perspectives present contending claims about the most effective means of addressing noncompliance in international cooperation. Enforcement theorists characteristically stress a coercive strategy of monitoring and sanctions (e.g. Downs *et al.* 1996). Management theorists, by contrast, embrace a problem-solving approach based on capacity building, rule interpretation, and transparency (e.g. Chayes and Chayes 1995).

The EU case challenges this conception of enforcement and management as competing strategies for achieving compliance (Tallberg 2002b). The EU compliance system consists of both centralized, active, and direct "police-patrol" supervision, conducted by the EU's supranational institutions, and decentralized, reactive, and indirect "fire-alarm" supervision, where national courts and societal watchdogs are engaged to induce state compliance. At both these levels, the operation of the EU compliance system rests on a combination of enforcement and management mechanisms.

In the EU, the combination of compliance mechanisms takes the form of a highly developed "management-enforcement ladder" – a twinning of cooperative and coercive measures that step by step improve states' capacity and incentives for compliance. Simplifying slightly, this ladder consists of four stages:

1 preventive capacity building and rule clarification that reduce the risk of violations due to incapacity or inadvertence;
2 forms of monitoring that enhance the transparency of state behavior and expose violators;
3 a legal system that permits cases to be brought against non-complying states and that further clarifies existing rules; and
4 deterrent sanctions as a final measure, in case states refuse to accept the rulings of the legal system.

What is particular about the EU's combination of enforcement and management in a comparative perspective is the operation of these functions by independent supranational institutions and empowered societal interests. As opposed to most international regimes, where the signatories themselves play a central role in executing enforcement and management functions, the EU has supranational institutions in charge of capacity building, monitoring, rule interpretation, and sanctioning, with assistance from transnational societal interests. This supranational organization serves the EU's compliance system well, and makes it exceedingly effective in inducing compliance.

The plan of the book

This book is composed of seven chapters, including the introduction. Chapter 2 introduces P–A analysis and lays out the P–S–A model developed specifically to explain strategic interaction in EU enforcement. Chapter 3 provides the necessary framing for comprehending the supranational institutions' campaign to strengthen EU enforcement, by showing how member state non-compliance threatened the realization of the EU's internal market. Chapters 4–6 present the three cases, each focusing on one of the strategies pursued by the Commission and the ECJ for purposes of strengthening EU enforcement: enhancing the capacity of existing means of supervision at the centralized EU level, inducing the delegation of new and more far-reaching enforcement powers at the 1991 and 1996–7 IGCs, and independently shifting EU supervision toward decentralized enforcement through national courts. Chapter 7 concludes the book by summing up the findings and examining their implications for the study of European governance and international cooperation.

2 Principals, supervisors, and agents in EU enforcement

This chapter introduces the theoretical logic of P–A analysis, and presents the P–S–A model developed specifically to explain strategic interaction in EU enforcement. The chapter is divided into three sections. In the first section, I describe the development of P–A analysis within rational choice institutionalism, and depict its use within economics and political science. The second section provides an in-depth introduction to the generic P–A model, explaining its logic and key components. In the third and final section, I present the triangular P–S–A model, and isolate three basic sets of hypotheses about the conditions that lead the EU's supranational institutions to pursue private agendas, the scope for supranational influence, and the forms of supervision that the ECJ and the Commission are likely to promote.

Rational choice institutionalism and P–A analysis

Principal–agent analysis forms part of what in political science is often referred to as the new institutionalism in rational choice theory. Below, I outline the central features of rational choice institutionalism, describe how P–A analysis originated in the new institutional economics, and trace the importation of this analytical construct into the study of politics.

The new institutionalism in rational choice theory

The political science literature of today is replete with references to the "new institutionalism," which became one of the most prominent academic catchwords in the 1980s and 1990s. While the frequent use of this term reflects a renewed interest in institutions – which again have risen to the top of the research agenda – it does not refer to a unified body of thought. Rather, at least three different analytical approaches can be distinguished that are all described as the new institutionalism: historical institutionalism, sociological institutionalism, and rational choice institutionalism (Hall and Taylor 1996; Immergut 1998; Peters 1999; Aspinwall and Schneider 2000).

Rational choice institutionalism encompasses a quite diverse body of literature that addresses a multitude of empirical phenomena employing a highly varied theoretical toolbox, but which has a common ground in the assumptions of rational choice theory and the importance attached to institutions.[1] Like all forms of institutional analysis, rational choice institutionalism seeks to provide answers to two primary questions, namely, how institutions shape political, economic, and social behavior, and how institutions originate, persist, and change.[2]

The new institutionalism in rational choice theory is distinguished by four notable features (Hall and Taylor 1996). First, this brand of institutionalism relies on the behavioral assumptions of rational choice theory. In simple terms, actors are assumed to have a fixed set of preferences and to behave instrumentally so as to maximize the attainment of these preferences. Second, rational choice institutionalists tend to see politics as a series of collective action or contracting dilemmas. In the absence of facilitating institutional arrangements, individuals acting to maximize the attainment of their preferences may produce collectively sub-optimal outcomes, and contractual problems may prevent mutually advantageous exchange from taking place. Third, rational choice institutionalism emphasizes the role of strategic interaction in the determination of political outcomes. An actor's behavior is deeply affected by strategic calculations about how other actors are likely to behave. Institutions structure and shape these interactions and their outcomes, for example, by providing information about other actors' behavior. Fourth, rational choice institutionalists present a distinctive, functional response to the question of how institutions originate and persist. In simple terms, institutions emerge and survive because they fulfill important functions for the actors affected by these institutions.

P–A analysis in economics and political science

This study draws on a strand of rational choice institutionalism that emerged in the mid-1980s, when political scientists recognized the wider applicability of, and decided to import, the analytical tools of agency theory, as developed within the "new institutional economics."[3] Agency theory was centered on the P–A relationship and the problem of shirking. The P–A relationship was posited to arise whenever one actor (principal) engages another actor (agent) to perform a task on its behalf. The economic agency literature typically considered the relations between shareholders and corporate executives, between managers and employees, and between retailers and suppliers to be examples of the P–A relationship.

New institutional economists suggested that such contractual relationships would be subject to shirking, or free-riding, on the part of the agent, since agents often have private interests that diverge from those of their principals, and know more about their true performance than the principals do. As P–A analysis has developed within the new institutional economics, the primary analytical focus has been the result of shirking, so-called agency costs, which include the costs of monitoring the behavior of the agent and the loss resulting from undetected shirking. Embracing a comparative perspective to institutional design, this largely mathematical and non-empirical literature has been preoccupied with the question of how such agency costs can be minimized through alternative contractual arrangements.

While developed in relation to economic phenomena, the analytical tools of agency theory were neither by nature nor by definition restricted to the economic domain. On the contrary, they were highly generalizable. Politics is replete with hierarchical, contractual relationships, as Terry Moe noted in an article written for the purpose of introducing political scientists to the new institutional economics:

> Democratic politics is easily viewed in principal–agent terms. Citizens are principals, politicians are their agents. Politicians are principals; bureaucrats are their agents. Bureaucratic superiors are principals; bureaucratic subordinates are their agents. The whole of politics is therefore structured by a chain of principal–agent relationships, from citizen to politician to bureaucratic superior to bureaucratic subordinate and on down the hierarchy of government to the lowest-level bureaucrats who actually deliver services directly to citizens.
>
> (Moe 1984: 765–6)

The 1980s witnessed the gradual incorporation of analytical tools from the new institutional economics into rational choice institutionalism in political science.[4] The empirical, political domain, where rational choice institutionalists have most forcefully applied the P–A model, and where the scientific debate has come to be framed in terms of principal control or agent autonomy, is legislative–executive relations in the United States (US). The central question in this debate has been the extent to which the US Congress is effectively in control of the regulatory agencies to which it has delegated extensive administrative authority (e.g. Weingast and Moran 1982, 1983; McCubbins and Schwartz 1984; Weingast 1984; McCubbins *et al.* 1987; McCubbins and Sullivan 1987; Moe 1987, 1990; Kiewiet and McCubbins 1991; Epstein and O'Halloran 1999).

Advocates of the "runaway-bureaucracy thesis" have maintained that Congress (principal) has largely lost control of the regulatory agencies of the executive branch (agents). The US Congress has allegedly had few or no mechanisms for overseeing the agencies' administrative compliance with legislative goals, permitting the executive branch to develop policy in directions that deviate from legislative intentions. Emerging in response to the runaway-bureaucracy thesis, the "congressional-dominance school" has challenged the proposition that Congress has abdicated control to bureaucracies. Just because there are few direct means of oversight, this does not mean that control is non-existent. Congress's supervision is instead indirect, reactive, and decentralized: Congress has established a system whereby citizens and organized interests can monitor and challenge violations by regulatory agencies.

The literature on legislative–executive relations in the US constitutes the singularly most important application of P–A theory in the study of politics. The debate between the two contending perspectives, and the less extreme and more nuanced P–A analysis that was produced in its aftermath, recognized the problems inherent in political delegation, identified the means of political control, and helped specify the conditions under which political agents can escape the supervision of political principals.

The study of European governance is the contractual paradigm's most recent frontier in political science. Building on the work of rational choice institutionalists in American politics, students of European governance are turning increasingly to P–A analysis in order to explain the sources and effects of the EU's institutional features. Studies of delegation, autonomy, and control in the relationship between EU governments and supranational institutions dominate this literature (e.g. Moravcsik 1995; Pollack 1997, 1998, 2003; Alter 1998a; Stone Sweet and Caporaso 1998; Franchino 2000; Schmidt 1998, 2000; Tallberg 2000a, 2002a; Thatcher 2001). Yet it is becoming increasingly common in the study of European politics to frame delegation to national and EU regulatory agencies, central banks, and courts, as well as delegation within parliamentary democracies, in P–A terms (e.g. Egan 1998; Bergman 2000; Bergman *et al.* 2000; Majone 2001; McNamara 2002; Stone Sweet 2002; Thatcher 2002; Wilks 2002).

The growing interest in these theoretical tools is related to two developments. First, institutions, whether broadly or narrowly defined, have gained a more prominent position on the research agenda of EU studies. To a greater extent than before, researchers study the individual institutions of the EU and the institutionalization of politics and policies in Europe. This does not simply reflect an academic fad, but is the product of deep changes in the structure of the EU and its mode of governance. A central component of this transformation in governance is the increasing tendency of states, executives, and parliaments to delegate powers to non-majoritarian institutions at the national or European level (Thatcher and Stone Sweet 2002).

Second, rational choice theory has emerged as one of two main meta-theoretical orientations in the study of the EU, the other being constructivist. Ranging from actor-centered theories, to theories of strategic interaction, game theory, and formal modeling, applications based on rational choice have become everyday commodities in EU studies. The growing use of rational choice methods reflects a demand for theories with firm micro-foundations, linking individual action to collective outcomes. But it also reflects the conviction among many scholars that European governance, too, can be explained using general political science theories. The EU might be a *sui generis* phenomenon, but aspects of it are sufficiently general and comparable not to require *sui generis* theories and methods.

The P–A model

In this section I provide a comprehensive introduction to the generic P–A model. I begin by presenting the model in its simplest version, after which I focus in detail on each of the model's main components and on the ways it may be extended and elaborated. Throughout the overview, I draw on the P–A literature in both economics and political science.

The P–A model in short

In the seminal article where the P–A imagery was first introduced, Stephen Ross describes how this relationship arises "between two (or more) parties when one, designated as the agent, acts for, on behalf of, or as representative for the other, designated the principal, in a particular domain of decision problems" (1973: 134). The principal and the agent thus enter into a contractual arrangement, in which the principal chooses to delegate certain functions or decision-making authority to the agent, in the expectation that the agent will act in ways that produce outcomes desired by the principal.

The so-called P–A problem is the result of a simultaneous presence of information asymmetry and conflicting interests. First, information asymmetry prevails because agents generally know more about their interests and actions than their principals do. Second, what is optimal for the principal is not necessarily optimal for the agent. While the principal would prefer the agent to perform the functions it has been delegated in accordance with the principal's preferences, the agent may have private interests at heart.

When information asymmetry and conflicting interests coincide, the agent will shirk – that is, pursue its own interests at the expense of the principal's – to the extent that such behavior is not rendered disadvantageous by the principal. The essence of the principal's problem is therefore the construction of an incentive structure that will induce the agent to act as the principal would prefer. The literature on agency and delegation points to two means that the principal may employ: monitoring and rewards/sanctions. Monitoring is required to overcome the information asymmetry and to detect shirking on the part of the agent. Rewards or sanctions, in turn, induce the agent to faithfully fulfill its functions, by raising both the gains from compliance and the costs of shirking. Together, monitoring and rewards/sanctions determine the agent's incentive structure: the more extensive the monitoring mechanism and the greater the reward or the fiercer the sanctions, the less likely it is that the agent will try to shirk. Yet, since both monitoring and rewards/sanctions are costly and consume considerable resources, it is unlikely that the principal will invest in such measures to the degree that shirking and non-compliance can be fully eliminated.

Information and interests

Information and interests are the two fundamental building blocks of the P–A relationship. In simple terms, the degree to which the principal and the agent share the same information and the same interests determines the extent to which shirking becomes a problem. If the principal possessed the same information as the agent and their interests were identical, there would be neither room nor reason for the agent to shirk. Conversely, if the principal could not access any of the information held by the agent and their interests were highly contradictory, agency shirking would certainly be ubiquitous. In the P–A model, it is assumed that the relationship, at a first analytical stage, is subject to some degree of both information asymmetry and conflicting interests, which the principal at a later analytical stage may attempt to compensate for and align through monitoring and rewards/sanctions.

While the degree of asymmetry may vary, any act of delegation is likely to establish a relationship where information is unevenly distributed. As John Pratt and Richard Zeckhauser put it: "In most social and business relationships, the parties have different information available to them" (1985a: 4). Consider a few examples from the economic and political world. Stockholders generally know less than management about the appropriateness of corporate decisions. Employers rarely have the information to determine whether employees have performed at the top of their capacity. Politicians tend not to know as well as responsible bureaucrats whether government agencies really meet the goals set by legislators. Voters generally do not know as well as politicians whether elected representatives have in fact done their utmost to realize the programs they campaigned on.

The P–A literature distinguishes between two analytically distinct forms of information asymmetry: hidden action and hidden information (e.g. Holmström 1979; Moe 1984; Arrow 1985). Asymmetries from hidden action result when the behavior of the agent cannot be readily observed by the principal. Rather, as Gary Miller points out, "what [the principal] observes is some output that is determined by factors that include the [agent's] effort, but also a variety of uncertain other events" (1992: 121). While the agent knows what role its own efforts play in the outcomes produced, the principal does not hold the information necessary to separate the effects of the agent's actions from the effects of exogenous factors. Asymmetries from hidden information, on the other hand, are an integral part of those relationships of delegation where authority is conferred on an actor because of its superior knowledge or information. A classic example of this form of information asymmetry is the doctor–patient relationship, where the patient (principal) engages the doctor (agent) precisely because of the doctor's superior medical knowledge, and consequently is unable to determine whether the doctor's actions and orders are correct.

Turning to interests, a principal who enters into a contractual arrangement with an agent expects the agent to behave in ways that produce outcomes desired by the principal. But the agent has interests, too, that it acts to attain, and once engaged, the agent's actions may be driven by logics other than those dictated by the principal. While the shareholders of a firm want to maximize profit, the manager may want to collect a higher wage; while the employer wants the employees to work as hard as possible, the employees may prefer leisure; while the politicians want to see certain policies implemented, bureaucrats may be more concerned with expanding their organization; while the voters want their elected politicians to pursue the policies they have campaigned on, the politicians may also have private and party interests at heart.

Conflicting interests are a defining feature, not only when delegation entails transferring decision-making authority to an already existing agent, such as an employee or a politician, but also when it involves the setting up of an entirely new organization. Moe provides an excellent account of why the creation of a new organization, an administrative agency in this case, does not prevent conflicting interests from arising:

> Once an agency is created, the political world becomes a different place. Agency bureaucrats are now political actors in their own right: they have career and institutional interests that may not be entirely congruent with their formal missions, and they have powerful resources – expertise and delegated authority – that might be employed toward these "selfish" ends. They are new players whose interests and resources alter the political game.
>
> (Moe 1990: 143)

When information asymmetry and conflicting interests coincide, the agent has both the motive and the opportunity to pursue its own private agenda. Agent shirking can take a variety of forms, for example, not pursuing a matter hard enough, pursuing it overzealously, or pursuing other issues than those delegated. The sole defining characteristic is that the agent acts in a way that conflicts with the attainment of the principal's interests.

The contractual framework: monitoring and rewards/sanctions

Principals are not helpless in the face of agent shirking. The principal can mitigate this problem and induce the agent to better fulfill its delegated functions by designing a contractual framework that consists of monitoring and incentive mechanisms. By attacking the problem of shirking at its root – information and interests – the principal can alter the incentives the agent faces, make compliance a more attractive option, and deter the agent from shirking.

Monitoring affects agent behavior by making it less likely that shirking will go unnoticed. The elimination of both the hidden action and hidden information types of shirking requires, however, that both the agent's actions and information be monitored. To reduce the problem of hidden action, the monitoring mechanisms must uncover the agent's actual behavior. Similarly, to ameliorate the problem of hidden information, the principal must find means of tapping the agent's information about its true capacity. What form monitoring takes naturally depends on the context of the particular P–A relationship. The economic literature stresses, for example, economic auditing and means for measuring employees' productivity, while the political literature points to measures such as hearings, judicial review, and budget review. Nevertheless, certain general analytical distinctions can be made as to the various means of monitoring.

In an influential article, Mathew McCubbins and Thomas Schwartz (1984) introduce the distinction between "police-patrol" oversight, which is centralized, active, and direct, and "fire-alarm" oversight, which is decentralized, reactive, and indirect, allowing the principal to intervene only in those instances when the system signals the occurrence of shirking. McCubbins and Schwartz's argument pertains to legislative–executive relations in the US, but the distinction is equally applicable to other empirical domains.[5] In the US context, "police-patrol" oversight refers to Congress's own investigations:

> Analogous to the use of real police patrols, police-patrol oversight is comparatively centralized, active, and direct: at its own initiative, Congress examines a sample of executive–agency activities, with the aim of detecting and remedying any violations of legislative goals and, by its surveillance, discourage such violations.
>
> (McCubbins and Schwartz 1984: 166)

By contrast, "fire-alarm" oversight refers to the feed-back Congress receives from constituency groups affected by the performance of government agencies:

> Congress establishes a system of rules, procedures, and informal practices that enable individual citizens and organized interest groups to examine administrative decisions . . ., to charge executive agencies with violating congressional goals, and to seek remedies from agencies, courts, and Congress itself. . . . Congress's role consists in creating and perfecting this decentralized system and, occasionally, intervening in response to complaints.
>
> (Ibid.)

Monitoring does not come for free. To set up and operate the kind of monitoring mechanism required to fully eliminate agent shirking would be "either impossible or prohibitively costly" (Holmström 1979: 74). In economic terms, it is only rational for the principal to invest in monitoring to the point where the marginal benefits of better compliance equal the marginal costs of running the mechanism. In other words, the level of monitoring that is optimal in terms of reducing shirking is seldom optimal in an economic perspective. In general, therefore, "principal–agent problems do not have first-best solutions that guarantee perfect compliance" (McCubbins *et al.* 1987: 243–4). Yet certain forms of monitoring are less costly than others. One of the main advantages of "fire-alarm" oversight is that it provides principals with more monitoring for the same price, since the costs are predominantly borne by the "fire-alarms" providing this service (McCubbins and Schwartz 1984).

Rewards and sanctions affect agent behavior by making compliance more profitable and shirking more costly if detected. By structuring incentives through rewards and sanctions, the principal aligns the agent's interests with its own and induces behavior that better corresponds to the aims of delegation. Rather than positing, as neoclassical economics does, that the productivity determines the reward, the P–A model conjectures that the causality is the reverse: "[T]he specific system of rewarding which is relied upon stimulates a particular productivity response" (Alchian and Demsetz 1972: 778–9).

The economic literature tends to stress rewards as incentive mechanisms, whereas political analysis emphasizes sanctions.[6] For economists one of the main theoretical advantages of the P–A model is the possibility of studying how reward systems, such as pay schedules, should be structured in order to yield the greatest possible effort from the agent. These kinds of rewards and fee schedules are less common in the political world, where the threat of sanctions constitutes the primary incentive mechanism. Political sanctions include reorganizing agencies, cutting an organization's budget, refusing reappointment of personnel and re-election of politicians, overriding administrative shirking with new legislation, and challenging agents in court (McCubbins and Schwartz 1984: 166; Weingast 1984: 155–6; McCubbins *et al.* 1987: 248–9). Just like monitoring, political sanctions have their price: "[M]ost of the methods for imposing meaningful sanctions also create costs for political principals" (McCubbins *et al.* 1987: 252). The costs of sanctions limit both principals' actual recourse to these instruments and the credibility of the threat that sanctions would be used if agents decided to shirk.

In reality, the P–A relationship is seldom a one-shot operation, where all relevant contracting action is concentrated to an *ex ante* stage, and where the agent's *ex post* behavior is a direct consequence of how successful the principal was in providing sufficient monitoring and incentive mechanisms. Rather, P–A relationships tend to be dynamic and interactive, subject to bargaining and revision by the parties (e.g. Pratt and Zeckhauser 1985a: 21; Holmström and Tirole 1989: 123; Sappington 1991: 59–61). The delegated functions and decision-making authority may be up for renegotiation, and perhaps more importantly, the principal may choose to revise existing means of monitoring and rewarding/sanctioning in light of unsatisfying agent behavior. In that sense, the more general new institutionalist argument that unintended and sub-optimal consequences of institutional design can be corrected at later stages applies also to dynamic P–A relationships:

> Once the unanticipated consequences are understood, those effects will thereafter be anticipated and the ramifications can be folded back into the organizational design. Unwanted costs will then be mitigated and unanticipated benefits will be enhanced. Better . . . performance will ordinarily result.
>
> (Williamson 1995: 216)

Extending the P–A model

So far, the account has been exclusively concerned with the basic, two-actor P–A model of delegation. Yet few relationships of delegation in the real world involve only one principal and one agent. Whereas the introduction of more actors reduces the parsimony of the original two-actor model, not acknowledging the existence of other actors often results in an even greater loss of explanatory power. New actors can fundamentally change the nature of the game; for instance, by making monitoring easier and sanctioning more difficult. Often, therefore, the original model is extended either horizontally, by introducing multiple principals or multiple agents, or vertically, by adding supervisors or depicting chains of principals and agents.

When a principal delegates functions to more than one agent, this has implications for each agent's incentive to shirk, as well as for the principal's means of monitoring. An agent faces even greater incentives to shirk when it works as part of a team of agents, if the principal can only observe the output of the group as a whole (Alchian and Demsetz 1972: 779–81; Arrow 1985: 46–7). The agent not only faces the ordinary incentive to shirk, but also a free-riding incentive to let the other agents produce the collective good. Yet the existence of multiple agents carries certain monitoring advantages as well. The principal may, for example, encourage one or many of the agents to monitor and provide valuable information about the others.

> [S]imply because information is costly to the principal doesn't mean that it is costly to everyone. It may happen that the agents themselves are in good positions to monitor or advise each other. In reality it is common to find incentive mechanisms that involve agents monitoring each other.
>
> (Varian 1990: 85)

In politics, the system of institutional checks and balances serves this purpose (Kiewiet and McCubbins 1991: 31–2). To the extent that agents fulfill similar functions, the principal can also gain additional information about their efforts by comparing relative performances (Sappington 1991: 54).

The primary theoretical consequence of multiple principals is the likelihood of competing demands on an agent and the subsequent increase in the agent's discretion. Multiple principals generally means multiple wills. In some systems, such as those resting on a separation of powers, competitive multiple-principal arrangements are even built into the design (Moe 1984:

768; McCubbins *et al.* 1989: 439). The implication of competing preferences among the principals is potentially greater autonomy for the agent, since principals may disagree about the inappropriateness of the agent's actions and about the need to impose sanctions. The key factors influencing the agent's capacity to shirk and escape sanctioning in a setting of multiple principals are therefore the principals' preferences and the decision rules for sanctioning agents (Pollack 1997: 112).

Turning to how the original P–A model can be extended vertically, the most common addition is to acknowledge the frequent use of a supervisor in real-world delegation (e.g. Alchian and Demsetz 1972: 781–2; Tirole 1986; Holmström and Tirole 1989: 112–13). To enhance control over and information about the agent's actions, the principal may engage a supervisor, whose role it is to gather more information about the agent's activity than what would otherwise be available to the principal. Yet, while mitigating the original problem of shirking, the engagement of a supervisor also creates a new one. As Douglass North points out, a third-party enforcer or supervisor constitutes a kind of agent as well: "The enforcer is an agent and has his or her own utility function, which will dictate his or her perception about the issues and therefore will be affected by his or her own interests" (1990: 58). Since the supervisor, too, has been delegated authority by the principal, it is subject to agent-like problems as well. Just like the agent, the supervisor knows more about its own actions than the principal does, and just like the agent's interests, those of the supervisor are likely to diverge from the preferences of the principal. Consequently, the principal will have to monitor, and possibly sanction, the supervisor as well.

Finally, one single actor can be at the same time both a principal and an agent. Both business and politics can be conceptualized as a chain of P–A relationships, where all but the ultimate principal and agent occupy dual roles: shareholders–executive managers, executive managers–middle managers, middle managers–employees; or, voters–politicians, politicians–senior bureaucrats, senior bureaucrats–junior bureaucrats. Few would dispute that such chains of principal–agent relationships are the best conceptualization of what delegation looks like in reality. Yet, because of the difficulty involved in performing multiple-level P–A analysis in a systematic manner, it is still rare for studies to engage in this form of analysis.

A P–S–A model of EU enforcement

This study develops the original P–A model into a triangular P–S–A model by adding a supervisor to the case of actors. This is a direct theoretical consequence of the shift in empirical focus from the pre-decisional phase of agenda setting to the post-decisional phase of enforcement. The roles that member states and supranational institutions play vary across the phases of the EU policy cycle, and in the enforcement of compliance, member states are best characterized as both principals and agents, while the Commission and the ECJ function as supervisors. By providing a more correct identification of the strategic context in EU enforcement, the P–S–A model yields greater explanatory power than the ordinary two-actor model. In this section, I develop the main components of this P–S–A model. I begin by summarizing the general logic of the model, before I turn to the nature of the interests, information, monitoring, and sanctions in EU enforcement, and to the implications of the model.

The P–S–A model

The P–S–A model presents a strategic setting where the member governments of the EU (multiple principals) assign to the Commission and the ECJ (supervisors) the task of enforcing compliance with EU law, as delegated to the individual member states (multiple agents). Member states are thus conceived of as both principals and agents, who at t_0 collectively reach decisions in intergovernmental bodies, and at t_1 are expected to individually carry out the adjustments necessary to realize these decisions.[7] The supranational institutions, for their part, function as supervisors engaged by national governments for the purpose of monitoring actual member state behavior and enforcing compliance with Community rules.

The delegation of supervisory powers to the Commission and the ECJ constitutes an act of collective self-commitment. In rational choice terms, compliance with EU rules is a collective action dilemma, where each state at t_1 has an incentive to free-ride what was agreed upon at t_0, but where such widespread non-compliance would undermine the purpose of cooperation (Olson 1965; Axelrod 1984; Oye 1986). Much like Ulysses tying himself to the mast for the purpose of resisting the Sirens' calls, EU governments attempt to escape this dilemma by setting up an institutional structure that renders non-compliance less attractive and ameliorates the problem of free-riding. The anchor in this strategy is the supervisory powers delegated to the Commission and the ECJ.

Member states' act of collective self-commitment transforms the original P–A relationship into a P–S–A one. But, whereas the delegation of supervisory powers to the supranational institutions ameliorates the problem of state non-compliance, it also creates a new dilemma. National governments engage the Commission and the ECJ to perform certain well-defined enforcement functions – no more, no less. Yet the supranational institutions have interests as well, which differ from those of national governments, and which consequently may lead the institutions to conduct their enforcement operations in ways other than desired by member states.

Engaging the Commission and the ECJ as supervisors does not therefore solve the problem of shirking *per se*. Rather, it replaces governments' concern with one form of shirking – state non-compliance – with another – supranational influence. Instead of one, we now have two P–A-like relationships subject to the problem of shirking, namely, that between supervisor and agent and that between principal and supervisor. On the one hand, the Commission and the ECJ have taken over the burden of enforcing compliance. And on the other, member states are anxious to ensure that the Commission's and the ECJ's actions do not deviate from the mandate given.

Whereas conflicting interests provide agents and supervisors with the motive to shirk, information asymmetry furnishes the opportunity. Member state principals do not know as much about the supranational supervisors' enforcement efforts as the Commission and the ECJ do. Likewise, the supranational supervisors do not know as well as the member state agents what measures have been taken to comply with EU rules.

The scope for shirking in these two P–A-like relationships is determined by existing means of monitoring and sanctioning. The more extensive and credible member states' control mechanisms are, the less likely it is that the supranational institutions will attempt and manage to conduct enforcement in ways other than desired by EU governments. Similarly, the more powerful the Commission's and the ECJ's means of monitoring state behavior and sanctioning non-compliance, the more limited is the scope for inadequate implementation and unsatisfactory compliance.

These actors are involved in a dynamic and ongoing relationship, where the member states and the supranational institutions may revise their means of supervision, and national governments renegotiate the delegation of powers to the supervisors, in light of past experience. Since monitoring and sanctions do not come for free, however, it is unlikely that state principals will invest in, and the supranational supervisors be delegated, enforcement powers sufficient to fully eliminate non-compliance. Both principals and supervisors therefore search for methods of supervision that enable the most extensive enforcement for a given set of resources.

This is the P–S–A model in stylized form, expressing what standard P–A theory would consider as the typical problems, key factors, and logical consequences of conceptualizing EU governments and supranational institutions as principals, supervisors, and agents. In this stylized version, the model is not specific to EU enforcement *per se*, but would isolate the same problems, factors, and hypotheses in all instances where states delegate enforcement functions to international institutions. The stylized character of the model also means that it must be specified further, if it is to generate context-specific hypotheses about supranational influence in EU enforcement. Below, I identify the nature of actor preferences, information asymmetries, monitoring means, and sanctioning instruments in the EU context.

Interests and information in EU enforcement

The member states and the supranational institutions hold two distinct and partly conflicting sets of preferences with respect to compliance and enforcement.

The preferences of the supranational institutions

There is near consensus in the literature on European governance that the preferences of the Commission and the ECJ are best described as highly pro-integrationist (e.g. Pescatore 1983; Peters 1992; Grant 1994; Hartley 1994; Ross 1995; Garrett and Tsebelis 1996; Majone 1996; Cram 1997; Pollack 1998).[8] In a broad sense, the supranational institutions seek "more Europe." In the policy-making field, more Europe is generally synonymous with a broader and deeper decision-making competence for the supranational institutions themselves, and for the EU as a whole.

The Commission's pro-integrationist preferences are bound up intimately with its role as prime mover of European integration. As "[i]ts destiny and prestige are connected to the promotion of advances in European integration" (Ross 1995: 14), the political agenda of the Commission "has been, and probably always will be, broadly federalist" (Grant 1994: 65). When the Commission fulfills its three functions as policy initiator, policy executor, and policy enforcer, it does so with the furthering of European integration as its overriding objective. Like most organizations, the Commission considers a strengthening of its own position to be the best way of furthering its stated goals. But, as Giandomenico Majone notes, rather than attempting to maximize its budget, "what the European Commission attempts to maximize is its influence, as measured by the scope of its competences" (1996: 65). The more extensive the scope of the Commission's competences, the greater its influence in EU policy-making, and the better its chances of moving European integration forward.

As opposed to the Commission, the ECJ was not created as a political institution whose purpose it was to push European integration ahead. Yet few would disagree with the assertion that the ECJ has been of the utmost importance in driving the integration process forward, and most would agree with Judge Pierre Pescatore's famous statement that the ECJ has acted on the basis of "une certaine idée de l'Europe" (1983: 157). In an attempt to summarize the main elements of these pro-integrationist preferences, Trevor Hartley (1994: 86) identifies as distinctive goals the strengthening of the EU and especially its federal elements, the increase in the scope and effectiveness of Community law, and the enlargement of the power of the supranational institutions.

The pro-integrationist preferences of the Commission and the ECJ also hold true in the post-decisional phase of European policy-making, where "more Europe" takes the shape of adequate compliance. The European project can only be achieved through a high level of member state compliance and through proper implementation of policy programs. As the Commission and the ECJ emphasize in virtually all reports and judgments on compliance, policy-making initiatives are of scant value, and the concept of a "Community based on the rule of law" amounts to little, if member states routinely flout legislation and fail to comply with ECJ judgments. In line with the competence-maximizing objectives of the supranational institutions, the Commission and the ECJ consider enhanced enforcement means to be a potent solution to the compliance problems that plague member states' application of EU rules.

The preferences of EU member states

Member states' preferences are complex and cannot as easily be reduced to a single overarching objective such as "more Europe." Instead, member states hold three parallel and partly competing preferences.[9] These preferences reflect member states' various roles in EU enforcement, as expressed in the P–S–A role configuration.

First, as principals, governments want to see the policy proposals agreed to in the Council implemented properly and complied with. When EU governments agree on new rules in intergovernmental decision-making bodies, they do so with a purpose. Regardless of what policy domain the specific rules pertain to, they signify a desire among member governments to see the EU's undertakings develop in some specific way. Even if not all decisions have the support of all governments, intergovernmental decision-making rests on the expectation of member states' subsequent implementation and compliance. It is this preference for compliance over non-compliance that has led member governments to equip the Commission and the ECJ with enforcement powers.

Second, as principals, member governments are anxious to protect state sovereignty. Despite far-reaching integration, European governments see national sovereignty as a positive value that is intimately bound up with the unity, identity, and raison d'être of the state. In the tug-of-war over decision-making competence in the EU, member governments carefully protect national prerogatives, and to the extent that governments pool or delegate decision-making authority, this is done reluctantly in the expectation of greater problem-solving efficiency (Moravcsik 1998). Majone recognizes this, asserting: "[M]ember states strive to preserve the greatest possible degree of sovereignty and policy-making autonomy" (1996: 61). In the area of enforcement, this concern with state sovereignty is expressed in the desire to restrict the supranational institutions' enforcement weapons to the minimum necessary, and to ensure that the institutions do not exceed their competences.

Third, as agents, member states prefer to soften the adjustment demands of new EU policies on national political, economic, and administrative structures. Modifying national practices to EU rules is often anything but smooth, automatic, and costless; passing new legislation within the time limits set in the Council frequently puts strains on the legislative machinery; bureaucratic structures are often rigid and hard to change; and introducing new rules generally challenges those with interests vested in existing procedures. Proper implementation and subsequent compliance therefore tend to involve substantial economic, political, and administrative costs and strains, making non-compliance an attractive option.

All EU member states hold all three kinds of preferences, and in this sense, their preferences are fixed and stable. It is essential to note, however, that the relative intensity of the different preferences may vary across member states and across time. The relative weight attached by member states to each preference at any given point in time remains an empirical question, which can only be determined through close observation. This variation in the intensity of preferences has important implications for the likelihood of further delegation of enforcement means to the Commission and the ECJ, as well as for government principals' ability to sanction the supranational supervisors.

The distribution of information in EU enforcement

In the absence of monitoring mechanisms, information asymmetry prevails on both the principal–supervisor and supervisor–agent sides of the equation. That information asymmetry is a real problem for both government principals and supranational supervisors, and not just a theoretical assumption, is evidenced by the setting up of various control mechanisms. Put differently, why would member governments establish forms for monitoring the Commission and the ECJ, and why would the supranational institutions set up mechanisms for overseeing implementation and compliance, if these relationships were not initially characterized by information asymmetry?

The information asymmetry in these relationships can take the shape of both hidden action and hidden information. Asymmetries may result either because government principals cannot observe the Commission's and the ECJ's enforcement activities, or because they do not possess the information and knowledge to determine whether or not the behavior they indeed witness is in line with the supranational mandates. In the absence of control mechanisms, the full range of the Commission's enforcement actions is not perfectly observable to member states. Whereas the Commission's formal initiation of infringement proceedings is both highly visible and comprehensible, informal enforcement actions are not as readily observable or understandable in terms of intentions and effects. In the case of the ECJ, the enforcement actions are highly transparent in the form of court judgments. Yet the history of European legal integration shows that member states have had certain difficulties decoding the ECJ's apolitical legalese and identifying the long-term implications for EU enforcement of the ECJ's judgments.

Similarly, asymmetries may arise either because the supranational supervisors do not have the full capacity to oversee how EU rules are implemented and applied nationally, or because they do not have the knowledge and information necessary to tell whether the observed implementation is the most appropriate. It is extremely difficult for the EU's supranational institutions to fully observe how member states apply European rules on the ground even with extensive monitoring means, never mind without. And when the institutions are capable of identifying national actions, they may not have the information necessary to ascertain whether or not a state's implementation measures in fact constitute compliance for lack of knowledge of the national legal context.

Monitoring and sanctions in EU enforcement

What conflicting interests and information asymmetry make possible, monitoring and sanctions can prevent. This general conclusion from P–A theory applies to both sides of the P–S–A relationship in EU enforcement.

The supranational supervisors' control of member state agents

In the treaty, the High Contracting Parties delegate to the Commission to "[e]nsure that the provisions of this Treaty and the measures taken by the institutions pursuant thereto are applied" (Art. 211, ex. Art. 155), and to the ECJ to "ensure that in the interpretation and application of this Treaty the law is observed" (Art. 220, ex. Art. 164).

To provide the Commission and the ECJ with the means to fulfill these supervisory responsibilities, government principals have equipped the institutions with certain concrete enforcement powers. Primary among these powers is the Commission's right to initiate infringement proceedings against non-complying states under Article 226 (ex. Art. 169) and the ECJ's right in such cases to determine whether or not member states are in compliance. Besides these powers at the centralized EU level, an additional instrument has been created at the national level through the ECJ's transformation of the preliminary ruling procedure under Article 234 (ex. Art. 177) into a means of enforcement.

These two forms of supranational enforcement constitute the Commission's and the ECJ's primary tools for making states comply. In Chapters 4–6, I examine in detail how these powers have been used and developed since the early 1980s. Here, I confine myself to a brief introduction of the main features of these two enforcement structures. Both contain elements of monitoring as well as sanctions, but differ as to the particular means employed. In their respective profiles, these forms of centralized and decentralized supervision conform to McCubbins and Schwartz's (1984) distinction between "police-patrol" and "fire-alarm" oversight.

When the Commission and the ECJ enforce member state compliance through the centralized infringement procedure, they exercise centralized, active, direct, and resource-demanding "police-patrol" oversight. The Commission actively and systematically collects and assesses information on member states' compliance with EU rules. This involves ensuring that EU legislation has in fact been incorporated into national law, and that these national legal measures reflect the intentions of the original directives. In-house monitoring by the Commission also includes the collection of information on possible infringements from sources on the outside, such as official journals, news media, experts, companies, and individuals in the member states.

If the Commission detects a suspected infringement, it may initiate an infringement proceeding against the member state in question under Article 226. As a rule, the formal opening of an infringement proceeding is preceded as well as followed by informal consultation and bargaining between the Commission and the member state for the purpose of finding mutually acceptable solutions in line with EU law. If member states do not adjust their non-compliant behavior during the course of the proceedings, the cases are finally referred to the ECJ for a decision. If the ECJ rules against member states, and these choose to neglect the judgment, a renewed infringement proceeding can be initiated under Article 228 (ex. Art. 171). Since 1993, Article 228 has been equipped with the threat of financial sanctions, proposed by the Commission and decided by the ECJ.

In the EU, the Commission and the ECJ conduct "fire-alarm" oversight through the decentralized enforcement structure initially established in the 1960s, when the ECJ, through the principles of direct effect and EU law supremacy, transformed the preliminary ruling procedure, and thereby individuals and national courts, into instruments of enforcement. Whereas this transformation in itself is generally considered an instance of ECJ activism and supranational influence, that is history, and for the last four decades, decentralized action in national courts has been an established part of EU enforcement.

The basis of decentralized enforcement is the possibility for citizens, companies, and organizations to sue national governments in national courts for failure to comply with EU rules. If a national judge finds that the legal situation of the matter is sufficiently clear, it decides the question of compliance on the basis of EU law. If a national judge finds it difficult to determine whether or not a state is in compliance, it must or may refer the matter to the ECJ for a preliminary ruling, depending on whether it is a higher or a lower national court. The ECJ's ruling does not formally decide the issue before the national court, but its interpretation is generally sufficient to establish whether or not an infringement of EU rules has occurred. Since 1991, individuals can obtain financial compensation if a national court finds that a member state has violated the individuals' EU rights.

Through this decentralized enforcement structure, the supranational institutions engage individuals and companies as enforcement tools, which monitor member state behavior and sanction non-compliance. The role of the ECJ and the Commission in this form of "fire-alarm" oversight consists in providing the framework necessary for this decentralized structure to function properly. This is done, among other things, by delivering preliminary rulings on potential cases of infringement, laying down principles and conditions for actions in national courts, and informing citizens of the possibility of turning to national courts when they see their rights infringed.

Member state principals' control of the supranational supervisors

Member states possess a range of mechanisms for controlling the supranational institutions and their enforcement actions. The particular instruments of control differ substantially between the Commission and the ECJ. Grouping existing control mechanisms into a number of general categories allows us to distill what these differences consist of (for good discussions, see Pollack 1997; Alter 1998a; Stone Sweet and Caporaso 1998).

To actively monitor the Commission and the ECJ is one of two primary ways in which member governments oversee the supranational institutions. The terms participation- and observation-based monitoring are used here to differentiate between two distinct forms of monitoring with alternative conceptual and empirical properties. Participation-based monitoring refers to the ability to observe and actively intervene in the execution of an action, whereas observation-based monitoring refers to the ability to observe an action without the possibility of forcing a change of outcomes in this process. The distinction captures one of the main differences in the means available to member governments for monitoring the Commission and the ECJ.

No means exist for participation-based involvement in the ECJ's decision-making process. Even if member governments may submit observations and argue their cases before the ECJ, they are not involved in the actual decision-making of the ECJ and cannot prevent it from handing down a particular judgment. The Commission's initiation of infringement proceedings is relieved of participation-based monitoring as well. Yet, to the extent that the Commission engages in enforcement-enhancing actions in its functions as policy initiator and executor, it is subject to participation-based monitoring. Policy proposals require the consent of national governments in the Council, and the Commission cannot perform its executive tasks unless governments grant their approval in the so-called comitology committees. The monitoring of supranational actions at IGCs is a special case, since member governments' exclusive control of the agenda entails that both the Commission and the ECJ are subject to an extreme form of participation-based oversight.

The second way in which national governments can monitor the supranational institutions is through *ex post* institutional checks and judicial review. These forms of monitoring constitute an example of the strategy of letting agents (or in this case supervisors) monitor each other, familiar from general P–A theory. Again, the Commission is the more intensely monitored institution. As Mark Pollack puts it: "[A]lmost every EC institution besides the Commission plays a role in monitoring and checking the Commission's behavior" (1997: 116). Institutions that provide checks on the Commission's actions include the EP, the ECJ, the Court of First Instance, the Court of Auditors, and the European Ombudsman. A special form of institutional check is the ECJ's power to review the legality of the Commission's actions under Articles 230–2 (ex. Art. 173–5), which allow member governments, the Council, and individuals to bring actions against the Commission "on grounds of lack of competence, infringement of an essential procedural requirement, infringement of this Treaty or of any rule of law relating to its application, or misuse of powers" (Article 230). The ECJ, by contrast, is relieved of institutional checks and conducts, rather than being the object of, judicial review.

The first of four possible ways of sanctioning the supranational institutions is the rather blunt instrument of cutting their budgets and dismissing or refusing to appoint their personnel. Member governments can exercise this form of control by refusing to provide the organizational resources necessary for the institutions to adequately perform their general enforcement functions, or by cutting the budget of specific enforcement-enhancing measures.

A second form of sanction is the possibility of overruling a Commission or ECJ decision through new legislation. The Commission's actions are most susceptible to this form of *ex post* correction, since member governments can always relegislate. Yet, in practical terms, this is made more difficult by the Commission's exclusive right to initiate new legislation, and the requirement that governments must reach a sufficient level of agreement on new legislation. In the case of the ECJ, only decisions based on secondary legislation, such as a directive or a regulation, can be reversed by governments enacting new legislation. Again, the normal legislative procedures and decision-making principles apply, making this sanction more difficult to apply in practical terms.

The third and most drastic form of sanction against the supranational institutions is to alter their mandates through treaty revision. Pollack (1997: 118–19) denotes this alternative the "nuclear option" – exceedingly effective, but difficult to use. In their capacity as principals that have delegated certain powers to the supranational institutions, member governments always have the option of altering the scope and conditions of these powers. By renegotiating the treaties, member states can reduce the competences of an institution, whose actions stray too far from government preferences, or counteract unwanted legal development. If member states want to reverse an ECJ ruling based on primary law (the treaty), the only option open is a revision of the treaties. Yet revising the treaties requires that national governments first agree unanimously at an IGC, and that this revision is then ratified in all member states.

A fourth and final form of sanction against the supranational institutions is for member states to unilaterally decide not to comply with Commission decisions or ECJ judgments. National governments and courts can refuse to acknowledge new and enforcement-enhancing principles handed down by the ECJ, or refrain from cooperating with the Commission in the execution of its enforcement functions. Unilateral non-compliance allows member states to avoid adjustments stipulated by unwanted ECJ or Commission decisions. But, as opposed to other forms of sanctions, non-compliance does not remove the source of discontent and may become the object of infringement proceedings and court action at both national and EU levels.

Hypotheses generated by the P–S–A model

The P–S–A model generates three primary sets of hypotheses about supranational influence in EU enforcement. The first set pertains to the conditions that induce the Commission and the ECJ to pursue private agendas in EU enforcement, the second to the scope for supranational influence, and the third to the forms of supervision that the Commission and the ECJ are likely to promote. I begin by clarifying the theoretical status of these hypotheses and the power of empirical evidence to confirm or disprove them.

Models, hypotheses, and empirical evidence

The analytical purpose of the P–S–A model is to generate hypotheses, which can explain and predict supranational influence in EU enforcement better than alternative theoretical formulations. In a deductive model, such as this one, abstraction and simplification are the primary means for reaching this objective. "A *model* is a simplification of, and approximation to, some aspect of the world" (King *et al.* 1994: 49; see also Friedman 1953). When constructing the model, the theorist attempts to reduce the massive complexity of "the world out there" by only abstracting those features with most bearing on the problem at hand. The model specifies how these distinguishing features relate to each other analytically, that is, how a given set of values on these variables by necessity, and through a logic that is both internal and deductive, translates into a specific outcome (Snidal 1986).

The P–S–A model generates two kinds of hypotheses: general and specific. General hypotheses are derived from the P–S–A model in its stylized version. These hypotheses are always true in a theoretical sense, that is, they follow logically, given the assumptions and the specified relationships of the model. Whether they also hold true empirically depends on whether the model correctly isolates the key elements of EU compliance politics as a strategic environment. "Models are never literally 'true' or 'false,' although good models abstract only the 'right' features of the reality they represent" (King *et al.* 1994: 49). If the empirical evaluation does not confirm these general hypotheses, the model has not succeeded in correctly isolating the most essential features of the strategic setting. While true in a theoretical sense, the model is flawed as an approximation of reality.

Specified hypotheses build on general hypotheses, but result from an assessment of the empirical values on the key variables of the model in a particular political context, in this case EU enforcement. Specified hypotheses are thus context-dependent, expressing what the P–S–A would predict, given what we know about preferences, information, monitoring, and sanctions in EU enforcement. Unlike general hypotheses, specified hypotheses can be literally false if the assessment failed to identify the correct empirical value on a key factor in the model.

Incentives for supranational influence

In keeping with general P–A theory, the P–S–A model generates the expectation that conflicting interests and information asymmetries function as inducements for the EU's supranational institutions to pursue private enforcement agendas. Both elements are present in the EU context, yet the supranational preference of compliance carries certain specific implications. The supranational institutions' over-arching interest in the post-decisional phase is to ensure adequate compliance with EU rules. As opposed to most other preferences, such as private gain and political influence, which can be maximized indefinitely, compliance is a goal with a finite value. Consequently, if existing enforcement means are sufficient to secure good compliance, the Commission and the ECJ have little reason to pursue private enforcement agendas. If, on the other hand, existing means prove wanting and compliance problems are pervasive, the supranational institutions face strong incentives to independently strengthen EU enforcement.

Scope for supranational influence

The core question addressed by the P–S–A model is the scope for supranational influence, once the institutions have been induced to move enforcement beyond government preferences. The model generates the expectation that the Commission's and the ECJ's capacity to pursue private interests is determined by member states' means for monitoring and sanctioning the actions of the institutions. The more extensive these control mechanisms are, the more reduced the scope for supranational influence.

The inventory of member states' means of monitoring and sanctioning provides certain indications as to where the control apparatus may be particularly weak, and thus where the scope for supranational influence is likely to be the greatest. Control mechanisms vary across forms of supranational activity, as well as between the Commission and the ECJ. First, the Commission and the ECJ are comparatively less subject to control in the exercise of existing competences than at moments of treaty revision, and are therefore more likely to exert supranational influence either by employing delegated enforcement means in ways not intended, or by strengthening enforcement through their non-enforcement competences. Second, the ECJ is comparatively more relieved from member state control, and is therefore more likely than the Commission to succeed in exercising supranational influence in EU enforcement.

The existence of multiple principals in the EU context generates specific expectations about the use and credibility of government sanctions. The imposition of collective sanctions against the supranational institutions most often requires the support of all governments, and in some cases only a qualified majority. This makes collective sanctions a difficult instrument to use, given variations between governments in the relative importance attached to national sovereignty and proper compliance. By contrast, sanctions that can be executed unilaterally, such as non-compliance with supranational decisions, are not conditioned by institutional decision rules and the distribution of preferences, and are therefore more likely to be used.

Effects of supranational influence

The supranational institutions' enforcement activities are associated with certain costs. These costs of supervision are likely to prohibit the complete eradication of state non-compliance, both because of the economic irrationality of investing in enforcement until all non-compliance has been eliminated, but also by the economic reality of budgetary resource constraints. Yet the supranational institutions may gain more enforcement for the same cost by shifting from more to less resource intensive means of supervision. The P–S–A model generates the expectation that the Commission and the ECJ are likely to favor less over more resource-demanding forms of enforcement, in view of their general sensitivity to the relative resource efficiency of alternative forms of supervision. In the EU, resource intensive "police-patrol" enforcement coexists with forms of "fire-alarm" supervision, where the costs are borne primarily by individuals and national courts. If the supranational institutions launch private campaigns to strengthen EU enforcement, they are likely to favor decentralized "fire-alarm" enforcement, over centralized "police-patrol" enforcement.

Conclusion

In this chapter, I have suggested that the strategic relationship between member states and supranational institutions in EU enforcement is best understood as one between principals, supervisors, and agents. To picture the Commission and the ECJ as supervisors in a P–S–A relationship yields a number of important implications. It suggests that the Commission and the ECJ will perform their enforcement functions with an eye to their own interests, that is, promoting "more Europe." To the extent that existing enforcement means are insufficient to secure satisfactory compliance with EU rules, the supranational institutions will work to reinforce these instruments, if necessary by independent action in conflict with government preferences. The mechanisms by which the institutions can induce higher compliance are monitoring and sanctions. Most importantly, however, conceptualizing the Commission and the ECJ as supervisors suggests that their capacity to move EU enforcement beyond governments' explicit wishes is constrained by member states' control mechanisms.

3 The European market and state non-compliance

When the Commission and the ECJ embarked on a crusade to strengthen EU enforcement in the early 1990s, they did so for a clear and identifiable reason. This reason was the European internal market and the compliance problems that threatened the realization of this project. In this chapter, I provide the framing necessary for comprehending the supranational institutions' efforts to strengthen EU enforcement, to be analyzed later in Chapters 4–6. Expressed in the terms of the P–S–A model, the process delineated in this chapter can be described as that of member state agents increasingly attempting to cut loose, as the internal market program raised the costs of compliance and the gains of non-compliance.

The chapter is structured in three sections. In the first, I introduce the internal market initiative and describe the essence of the program's three phases: decision-making, legal implementation, and application. The second section describes the forms of barriers that the internal market program sought to remove, and demonstrates how the process of eliminating these barriers imposed palpable adjustment strains on the political, economic, and administrative structures of the member states. In the third and final section, I trace the effects of these strains on member states' capacity and willingness to comply with EU rules in general, and the internal market provisions in particular.

The internal market program

The internal market program as a political vision had firm roots in the Community's history, but the completion of the project required something other than a continuation of past efforts and practices. In this section, I describe first the route from common to internal market, before I outline the three concrete phases of the internal market program itself.

From common market to internal market

The 1985 launch of the internal market program was not the first attempt to establish a unified market in Europe, and can only be understood in its historical context. The aim of creating a single market was first expressed in the European Economic Community (EEC) treaty of 1957, which laid down a clear path to how the member states should establish a customs union and provided for the creation of the common market.

A conceptual tool that is often employed for the purpose of distinguishing between a customs union, a common market, and other forms of economic integration is Bela Balassa's (1961) ladder of economic integration. The ladder is composed of five stages: free trade area, customs union, common market, monetary union, and economic union. The free trade area consists of an arrangement in which the participating states remove all tariffs and quotas on goods exchanged within the area, but are free to unilaterally set the level of tariffs on imports coming from outside the area. In a customs union, the states go one step further and decide on a common external trade regime versus third countries. The third step is the common market, which entails that the free movement of goods within the customs union is supplemented by the free movement of the factors of production, especially capital and labor. The monetary union consists of a common market with a common currency, while the economic union entails that all economic policy – including fiscal – is conducted by a central authority.

The ambition of the EEC treaty was clearly to establish a common market in the terminology of Balassa, and "common market" was the term generally used when referring to this project. Article 3a of the treaty provided for the free movement of goods and called for "the elimination, as between Member States, of customs duties and of quantitative restrictions on the import and export of goods, and of all other measures having equivalent effect." Article 3b laid down the provisions creating a common external tariff and a common commercial policy. Article 3c, finally, required member states to abolish obstacles to the free movement of capital, persons, and services. In a comparative perspective, the arrangement envisaged was extremely far-reaching in terms of economic integration. In view of the economic adjustment pressure expected from the internal abolition of tariffs and quotas, the member states decided to introduce a transition period of twelve years for the establishment of the customs union, rather than let the provisions gain full effect at the entry into force of the treaty on January 1, 1958.

By 1968, all internal duties and quantitative restrictions had been eliminated, and the external tariffs of the participating states had been aligned so as to form a common external tariff. The customs union was thus completed. Yet the intentions of the common market had not been fully realized:

> Although the EC was able to complete its internal tariff disarmament by the middle of 1968, the task of creating a truly unified market in which goods could move freely was not thereby achieved. There still remained other significant non-tariff barriers (NTBs) which could continue to prevent totally, or in some degree to restrict, or in some way to distort, the flow of intra-Community trade.
>
> (Swann 1995: 133)

While certain initiatives had been taken to facilitate the free movement of capital, persons, and services, very substantial restrictions remained, and the ambition of free movement of the factors of production was far from realized.

Rather than pressing ahead for the purpose of completing the common market in the full sense of the term, the Community now entered a period that made a truly unified market seem increasingly remote. Politically, the member states were occupied by a new set of projects. The late 1960s and the 1970s witnessed the enlargement of the Community to the UK, Ireland, and Denmark in 1973, plans or attempts to establish an Economic and Monetary Union (EMU), a European Regional Development Fund (ERDF), a structured relationship with the ex-colonies (Lomé Convention), European Political Cooperation (EPC) in matters of foreign policy, and a European Monetary System (EMS), as well as developments in the fields of fisheries policy, industrial policy, and science and research policy. Economically, the Community and the rest of the industrialized world in the 1970s and early 1980s were plagued by the most severe recession since the 1930s. The breakdown of the Bretton Woods monetary system and the two consecutive oil shocks were among the sources of this deep economic crisis. Compared to North America and Japan, Europe was hit worst by the recession, and the EC's share of world trade in manufactured goods fell from 45 to 36 percent between 1973 and 1985 (Price 1988). Rather than a continued liberalization of European trade, governments' use of various protectionist instruments proliferated in the face of declining exports, stagnating output, and rising unemployment. Taken together, the political and economic developments in Europe did not call for optimism, and instead terms such as "euro-pessimism" and "euro-sclerosis" became fashionable ways of referring to the gloom of the European economies and the lack of faith in the institutions of the EC.

The notion of removing existing internal barriers to trade re-emerged in the early 1980s, in response to Europe's economic problems. The starting point was the European Council summit in Luxembourg in June 1981, where alarm was expressed about what was now referred to as the "internal market." At a number of consecutive summits, the idea of strengthening and developing the internal market was further elaborated. The most concrete step was the creation of a special Internal Market Council within the framework of the Council of Ministers. Yet it was not until a new team of commissioners took office in 1985 that words were transformed into action. The new Commission, under the leadership of Jacques Delors and with Lord Cockfield as internal market commissioner, prepared a detailed program of 300 measures to be taken for the purpose of achieving a truly unified European market. They also set out a timetable for arriving at this goal by December 31, 1992. This program – the famous White Paper on completing the internal market – was presented to, and endorsed by, the European Council at the summit in Milan at the end of June 1985 (European Commission 1985b). The internal market program – or the "1992 initiative" as it would often be referred to – was subsequently provided with a legal basis in the 1986 Single European Act (SEA).[1]

The internal market program sought a *de facto* completion of the common market as once envisaged in the original EEC treaty. As expressed in the SEA, the aim was to create "an area without internal frontiers in which the free movement of goods, persons, services and capital is ensured." In formal terms, this aim did not contain any new ambitions. In concrete terms, however, it constituted "a disjunction, a dramatic new start" (Sandholtz and Zysman 1989: 95), perhaps "the most ambitious instance of multilateral cooperation since the construction of the post-World War II international order" (Garrett 1992: 533). With the benefit of hindsight, we now know today that the launch of the internal market program in 1985 marked the end of the period of euro-pessimism and the beginning of a new period of intensified integration, culminating in the 1992 Maastricht Treaty. As "the centerpiece of European integration in the last decade" (Begg 1996: 525), the internal market has not only brought economic integration between sovereign states to a new dimension, but also stimulated the development and strengthening of flanking policies in areas such as regional policy, social policy, competition policy, environmental policy, and science and technology policy. In addition, the internal market has functioned as a magnet for countries outside the EU, most notably the members of the European Free Trade Association (EFTA) and countries in Central and Eastern Europe, as well as formed the basis on which the EMU is founded.

Three phases in the internal market program

The endorsement of the Commission's White Paper and the subsequent legal basing in the SEA formed the starting point for a still ongoing process of making the internal market work. This process can be divided into three partly overlapping stages: decision-making, legal implementation, and application of internal market rules on the ground.

The first stage of adopting the internal market measures commenced upon the closing of the Milan summit and was in large part completed as planned by the end of 1992.[2] In legal terms, the 300 measures suggested in the White Paper consisted of approximately 220 proposals for directives and 80 proposals for regulations, decisions, and recommendations.[3] Directives constitute the primary instrument for harmonizing European policies and are binding as to the result to be achieved, but leave it up to each member state to choose the form and the method. For directives to enter into effect, they must first be legally implemented in the member states, which requires the adoption of new legislative acts, the amendment of existing law, or the repeal of provisions preventing the accomplishment of a directive's objectives. The other legislative instruments employed in connection with the internal market program – regulations, decisions, and recommendations – do not require national implementing measures.

The original intention behind directives as a legislative instrument had been to grant the member states a certain freedom in the attainment of the desired harmonization. Yet the decades preceding the internal market program had shown that directives tended instead to be formulated in a very detailed way, often laying down comprehensive uniform standards. Experience had also shown that this approach of total harmonization was extremely cumbersome and time-consuming. With the internal market initiative, the Commission broke with the past and launched the "new approach" to harmonization (e.g. European Commission 1985b; CEN 1994). The essence of the new approach was (1) to introduce a new form of directive that laid down only the essential safety requirements to which products must conform, and (2) to delegate the task of drawing up harmonized standards defining technical specifications to a set of standardization bodies. Moreover, harmonization would only be undertaken when necessary, and the ambition of the Community should be to rely on the mutual recognition of goods to the greatest extent possible. The principle of mutual recognition, laid down in the ECJ's 1979 judgment *Cassis de Dijon* (Case 120/78, 1979), stipulated that a product lawfully manufactured and marketed in one state could be sold freely throughout the Community.

The first step of the decision-making stage was for the Commission to draw up and table proposals on the specific measures outlined in the White Paper.[4] After a slow start, the Commission's drafting of proposals picked up speed and, though the aim of having tabled all proposals by the end of 1988 was not reached, this was achieved in the spring of 1990 (European Commission 1986b, 1987a, 1991b; Cockfield 1994: 81–3).

Measured against the objective of having the internal market in place by the end of 1992, the work of the Parliament, and in particular the decision-making of the Council, lagged behind for a number of years (European Commission 1986b, 1987a, 1988a). A prominent reason for the sluggish passing of proposals in the Council during these first years was the requirement of unanimity. Following the so-called Luxembourg compromise of 1966, unanimity had been the dominating principle in the Council, and each state had been able to exercise a veto when it deemed that very important interests were at stake.[5] This principle was an obstacle to the completion of the internal market. As Lord Cockfield emphasized: "If the Internal Market Programme was to succeed it would be essential to move away from unanimity, the source of much of the paralysis in the Community, to majority voting" (1994: 62).

The SEA fulfilled that very purpose. In force as of July 1, 1987, the SEA introduced qualified majority voting (QMV) in the Council for matters pertaining to the establishment and functioning of the internal market. With few exceptions, the proposals submitted by the Commission now required only the support of a qualified majority, and no state was capable of unilaterally blocking a proposal. The introduction of QMV speeded up the passing of legislation in the Council and, as a consequence, the bulk of the Commission's proposals had been adopted by 1991. As 1992 came to a close, about 90 percent of the White Paper proposals had passed through the Community's legislative machinery (European Commission 1992b: 2).[6]

As directives were adopted in the Council, the internal market process shifted to the second stage of legal implementation. Now the member states were obliged to incorporate the internal market directives into national law – to "transpose" them, in EU parlance. The legal means for transposing directives into national law differ between the member states depending on the respective constitutions and legislative procedures. In general, however, the incorporation of EU directives is everything but a simple and straightforward process. The nature of the directive as a legislative instrument grants certain discretion to member states as to the means for achieving the stated goals, which means that legal incorporation of directives in effect involves a choice between alternative legislative arrangements. In addition, this process must be concluded before the deadline set by the Council, generally two years after the adoption of the directive.

The legal transposition of directives into national law is an absolute prerequisite for the later application of EU rules on the ground. This was reflected in the Commission's repeated emphasis on the need for member states to complete the process of legal implementation: "If the single market is to work properly in practice, that legislation has to be integrated into the national legal systems" (1994c: 15). Though a large number of directives had been transposed before that date, 1990 marks the date when the European Council emphasized transposition as the new stage in the process of establishing the single European market. By November 1990, member states were supposed to have transposed 107 measures, by August 1992 this had climbed to 174, and in late 1993 the deadline had passed for transposing all 220 directives within the internal market program (European Commission 1990c: 17, 1992b: app. 7, 1994c: xii).

The final phase in the process of creating the internal market was embarked upon in 1993. As of that year, most of the internal market directives were in force and individuals and companies could take advantage of the single market, to the extent that member states correctly applied the rules. Yet the passing of the 1992 deadline by no means meant that a fully unified and smoothly working European market was in place. As the Commission noted in its first report on the operation of the internal market:

> [T]he establishment of a single market is not simply a question of adopting Community-level legislation. It is a more complex, long-term process of gradually changing legal structures and administrative practice at the national level and of encouraging new attitudes and behaviour from economic operators in the market. The date of 1 January 1993 represents the beginning, rather than the end, of this process.
>
> (European Commission 1994c: ix)

For the member states, the shift to the stage of application entailed an obligation to correctly apply those rules that regulate state behavior, and to enforce those rules that pertain to the actions of private individuals and companies on their territory. For the supranational institutions, the shift to the stage of application added a large amount of legislation to the already existing body of rules supervised by these institutions.

Deep integration and the pressure of adjustment

In its ambition to remove all barriers to a single European market, the internal market program went beyond previous endeavors of European cooperation and existing multilateral trade agreements. As internal market commissioner Mario Monti concluded in 1996, it was "the most ambitious target that the European Community ever set itself" (European Commission 1996h: ix). In this section, I explain what forms of barriers the program sought to remove and how the process of eliminating these barriers imposed palpable adjustment strains on the member states.

The internal market program as deep integration

While more far-reaching than other multilateral trade initiatives, the internal market program testified to a general trend in international economic relations. "As economic integration progresses, issues of 'deeper' integration emerge on the international agenda. These issues concern 'behind-the-border' policies that had previously not been subjected to international scrutiny or negotiation" (Kahler 1995: 2). These obstacles are generally referred to as non-tariff barriers to trade (NTBs). NTBs include all non-tariff restrictions to trade that provide for a differential treatment of imported and domestically produced goods. NTBs consist of a range of measures that may or may not be designed for the purpose of impeding or distorting trade, but have that effect. Examples of NTBs that are explicitly employed in order to restrict trade are quotas, export subsidies, and government procurement. Examples of NTBs that are employed to meet some other policy target but affect trade flows in the process include subsidization of state-owned companies, health and safety regulations, and customs valuation procedures. As opposed to tariffs, NTBs tend to be opaque and non-transparent in nature, making them particularly difficult to identify, categorize, and ultimately eliminate.

Internationally, policy-makers became increasingly aware of the existence of NTBs as tariffs were gradually reduced within the framework of the GATT. Not only did NTBs stand out more prominently as tariffs were dismantled but trade nevertheless remained restricted, but governments in the industrialized countries also had increasing recourse to these instruments as a way of compensating for the reduction in protection. In the 1970s, when the use of NTBs mounted in connection with the economic downturn, these forms of trade barriers were frequently referred to as the "new protectionism" (e.g. Krauss 1979; Greenaway 1983; Bhagwati 1988; Baldwin 1993). The EEC constituted no exception to this general trend:

> Following the completion of the customs union at the end of the 60's, the history of the Common Market is a fascinating story of how ingeniously governments have invented new instruments to protect markets and keep off unwanted competition. . . . State interference did not vanish away. It changed its outer appearance, different instruments were applied, and other actors at different levels became responsible.
>
> (Kohler-Koch 1996: 177–8)

At the international level, the Tokyo Round of the GATT (1974–9) was the first serious attempt to deal with NTBs. In Europe, the internal market program attacked the prevalence of NTBs with more determination and at greater length than any previous free trade initiative.[7] The 300 measures proposed in the White Paper were aimed at eliminating three main obstacles to the achievement of a single market: physical barriers, technical barriers, and fiscal barriers (European Commission 1985b).[8] The three obstacles contained non-tariff impediments to trade in goods, but also to the free movement of capital, persons, and services.

Physical barriers covered such practices as intra-EC border stoppages, customs controls, and associated paperwork. These were viewed as imposing unnecessary costs on industry, flowing from delays, administration, and transport and handling charges. Technical barriers became a label used for a wide range of measures, which were not necessarily just technical in nature. Prominent among these were barriers created by variations in national product regulations and standards, and protectionist public procurement practices. Fiscal barriers referred primarily to variations in the national systems of indirect taxation, including both general VAT rates and excise duties on, for instance, alcohol, tobacco, and petrol. Differences in these systems were regarded as creating distortions in intra-EC trade as the variations in tax level translated into substantial price differentials.

Strains of adjustment

The internal market program struck at the nerve of the state's involvement in the economy. To implement these measures, states had to refashion domestic regulatory regimes, overturn existing practices, and frame new relationships with the economic operators of the market. This was understood by the Commission when launching the program: "We recognise that many of the changes we propose will present considerable difficulties for Member States" (1985b: 7). Slightly simplified, the internal market program resulted in three forms of strain on the economic, political, and administrative structures of the member states.

First, the implementation act itself put strains on the legislative and bureaucratic branches of government. This is a strain that is familiar from the general literature on compliance with international agreements. "[S]tates must possess the political and administrative capacity to make the domestic adjustments necessary for the implementation of international norms, principles, and rules" (Keohane *et al.* 1993: 20).

To implement the internal market program, member states were asked to transpose a very large body of European legislation into national law within a quite limited time period. The pressure of this process on the legislative machinery of the member states was in many cases formidable. Not only did the 220 internal market directives have to be implemented in accordance with their stated intentions, but also before the deadlines set by the Council, which for most member states proved a challenging task. "[T]he normal legislative procedure often takes much more time than provided by a directive's deadline" (Siedentopf and Hauschild 1988: 56). The degree of strain varied with the legislative capacity of each state, mainly the extent to which constitutional arrangements permitted and facilitated a rapid and correct incorporation of the directives into national law (European Commission 1989c: 8; for a cross-national comparison, see Siedentopf and Ziller 1988).

Implementing the internal market program also required substantial changes in bureaucratic practices. This raised two immediate problems for national governments and their bureaucratic branches. The government, responsible for the correct application of Community law, was faced with the task of altering entrenched administrative behavior and practices. To the extent that the bureaucracy was not positively disposed toward these reforms, administrative implementation posed a control problem for the national government (European Commission 1989c: 8–9). Second, even if the bureaucracy was willing to adjust to the new rules, such changes required that it possessed sufficient administrative capacity. But according to a cross-national study of implementation in the EC in the mid-1980s, administrative capacity varied considerably, with Belgium, Greece, Ireland, Italy, and the UK confronting "serious deficiencies in their administrative capacities" (Siedentopf and Hauschild 1988: 62).

The second strain imposed by the internal market program was more general in nature and concerned governments' role in the economy, ability to intervene in the market, and capacity to structure barriers to their own advantage. "The 1992 programme represented a challenge to the *economic sovereignty of the state* as well as to its political power" (Williams 1991: 98). The post-World War era had witnessed the development in Europe of models of capitalism, which to varying degrees combined free enterprise and competition with state regulation and welfare ambitions. This mixed economy had not only been the distinguishing mark of European states as compared to the US, but also the defining characteristic of the "European model of society" actively promoted by the Community. With the internal market program, this traditional role of the state in the economy was up for re-evaluation and redefinition. Loukas Tsoukalis succinctly summarizes the challenge:

> Domestic government intervention is part and parcel of the established political and economic order in each country. The White Paper was presented as a set of technical measures, presumably intended to assuage nationalist fears. However, a more careful reading of the text . . . would lead to a different conclusion. Many of those measures touched at the very heart of national economic sovereignty; and modern politics is very much about welfare issues. Fiscal harmonization, monetary policy and capital movements, state subsidies, and even industrial standards are the basic material of which the economic role of the state consists; and also the instruments through which governments can influence the direction of votes.
>
> (Tsoukalis 1997: 67)

The elimination of physical, technical, and fiscal barriers entailed that governments would lose many of the traditional tools for influencing the allocation of resources within and between countries. Slightly simplified, deregulation and liberalization meant that the power of the state to intervene in the market was rolled back, whereas regulation and harmonization on the European level meant that national governments agreed to collective standards beyond their unilateral control. It is therefore hardly an exaggeration to say that the measures included in the internal market program threatened to lead to "serious depletions in the stock of traditional instruments used to steer the mixed economy at national level" (Hancher 1996: 55).[9]

A third strain imposed by the internal market program confronted the economic operators in the increasingly unified European market. Companies that had previously profited from state protectionism and a segmented European market were now put under growing economic pressure. For companies in a favorable competitive position, trade liberalization is often a promise of better times; for less efficient producers, it may very well be the end.

Economic studies and business surveys conducted by the Commission confirm that market integration resulting from the completion of the internal market unleashed substantial competitive pressure, to the advantage of some firms and the dismay of others. The internal market promoted a broad restructuring of the European economy, and mergers and acquisitions became the primary means through which firms handled the enhanced competition (European Commission 1996i). Comparing the situation in 1997 with that in 1993, business found competition to be greater in both national and European markets. But, whereas some 45 percent of companies reckoned that competition had been positive or very positive for their business, up to 25 percent of all firms perceived the unleashed competition as negative (European Commission 1997q: iii).

These competitive strains caused deliberately by the internal market program did not only have economic effects for economic actors. To the extent that the disadvantaged companies turned to national authorities for help and continued protection, the economic strains quickly became political. In the first half of the 1990s, the Commission noted growing pressure on national governments from domestic industries in dire straits (e.g. European Commission 1996h: 8).

Non-compliance

Non-compliance offered an attractive way for member states to cushion the adjustment required by the massive legislative program. Like EU rules in general, the internal market program challenged both governments' willingness and capacity to comply (Tallberg 2002b). The compliance problems emerging in connection with the internal market program were of two different kinds: non-compliance in the legal implementation of directives and non-compliance in the practical application of EU rules. These two forms of violation conform to general conceptualizations of non-compliance in the literature on international regimes, which distinguishes between "measures that states take to make international accords effective in their domestic law," on the one hand, and "whether countries in fact adhere to the provisions of the accord and the implementing measures they have instituted," on the other (Jacobson and Brown Weiss 1998: 4). Both problems had existed prior to the internal market program; in fact, non-compliance with EU rules had prompted observers to speak of a "paradox of non-compliance" (Krislov *et al.* 1986: 61), to refer to non-compliance as a "systemic phenomenon" (Mendrinou 1996: 11), and to declare that the EU suffered from an "implementation deficit" (From and Stava 1993: 55). The effect of the internal market program was to exacerbate these pre-existing problems. The internal market program also turned attention to a third form of non-compliance, disrespect for ECJ judgments, that was not primarily caused by the legislative program, but could undermine its long-term importance.

Member governments' legal implementation of internal market directives suffered both from delayed and incorrect transposition. The deadlines set up by the Council for the implementation of internal market directives were frequently violated. In a 1989 report on the completion of the internal market, the Commission stressed that "a change of attitude on the part of the Member States is needed to incorporate the decisions taken into their national law and to do away with the delays which are currently evident in the implementation of Community legislation" (1989b: 3). At the time this report was published, for example, only 2 out of 68 measures in force had been implemented in every member state.

When directives were indeed implemented, transposition was sometimes faulty or partial. The discretion granted to national authorities by directives as legislative instruments resulted in national measures for implementation that did not reflect the spirit of the directives and did not have the requisite binding force (European Commission 1994c: 120). The legal uncertainty resulting from such incorrect transposition could even have effects contrary to the objective of EU regulation: "In some cases, over-bureaucratic implementation of Community rules at national level can appear to maintain the barriers that Community legislation was intended to remove" (European Commission 1995c: 4).

Figure 3.1 tracks the evolution of the rate of legal implementation of all directives in the 1990s, internal market directives included. These data point to the general character of the problem of legal transposition. During this decade, member states consistently failed to comply even on paper with 5–10 percent of all EU directives; a situation the Commission repeatedly expressed its concern about (e.g. European Commission 1991c: 1, 1994c: xii). A backlog of 5–10 percent meant that each member state, on average, had 75–100 directives left to implement by the end of each year. This is a non-negligible number in an EU where only 30–70 directives are adopted each year (Golub 1999: 741). A disaggregation of the EU figure reveals a pattern of cross-national variation, where Italy, Portugal, and Greece tended to fall short of the EU average, whereas Denmark, the Netherlands, and the UK were distinguished by particularly high levels of implementation (Börzel 2001: 815).

The legal implementation of the directives in the internal market program was particularly problematic. At the end of 1990, member states had on average transposed less than 70 percent of the White Paper directives for

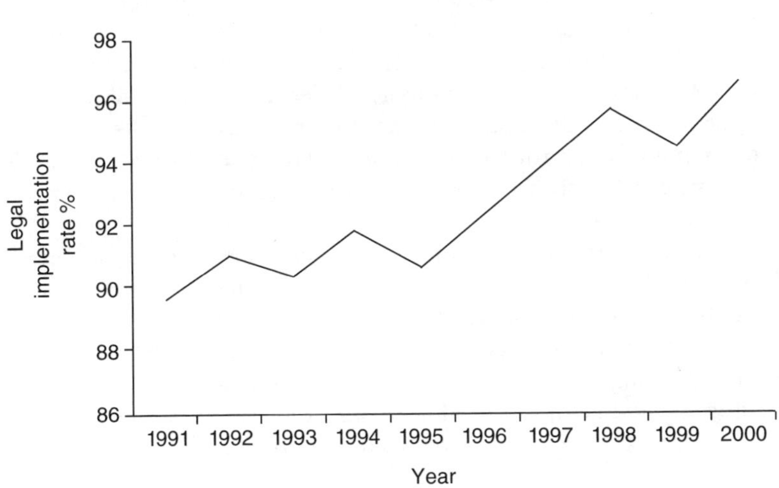

Figure 3.1 Rate of legal implementation (directives), 1991–2000.

Source: European Commission annual monitoring reports.

which the implementation deadline had passed (European Commission 1991b: 5). At the end of 1993, when the internal market had been officially completed for a full year, the rate of legal implementation had improved to about 87 percent (European Commission 1994c: xii). As member states in the mid-1990s increasingly caught up with the backlog, the rate improved to around 93–5 percent, mirroring the general rate of legal implementation in the EU (European Commission 1995c: 11, 1997n: 2). Throughout this period, delays were particularly common in the areas of public procurement, company law, intellectual and industrial property rights, and the insurance sector (e.g. European Commission 1994c: xiii, 1995c: 9, 1996b: 11).

Yet non-compliance was frequent also in states' application of internal market rules on the ground. On the one hand, there were shortfalls in member states' adherence to rules that regulated their own behavior. But equally problematic was uneven national enforcement of rules regulating the actions of private parties, such as companies. Responding to this picture, John Mogg, director-general at the internal market directorate of the Commission, delivered this poignant critique:

> There is no point in having agreed all these rules on the Single Market if they are not respected on the ground. . . . If the Single Market is to work in practice, Member States must apply the rules in practice even if they come under protectionist pressure from narrow interest groups.
>
> (Mogg 1996: 1)

The infringement proceedings initiated by the Commission against member states are an indirect measure of the two forms of non-compliance. The weeding out before formal initiation of cases caused by misunderstanding guarantees that only cases of strongly suspected violations result in proceedings.[10] This measure provides a useful indicator of the compliance problems experienced by the Commission. Yet cross-temporal patterns should be interpreted with care, since factors other than compliance affect these patterns, notably variation in the number of member states, the body of EU law, and the Commission's enforcement practices (for a cautionary note, see Börzel 2001).

Figure 3.2 shows the annual number of proceedings during the period 1978–2000 and distinguishes between the two alternative kinds of non-compliance. It demonstrates that a large majority of infringement proceedings are initiated because of state failure to implement directives correctly and on time. The high frequency of implementation failure as the source of proceedings should be understood in view of the greater ease with which such violations are identified compared to faulty application of rules on the ground.

Figure 3.2 further shows how the number of proceedings has gradually climbed over time, with a sharp increase in the first half of the 1990s, when member states were confronted with the challenge of implementing the

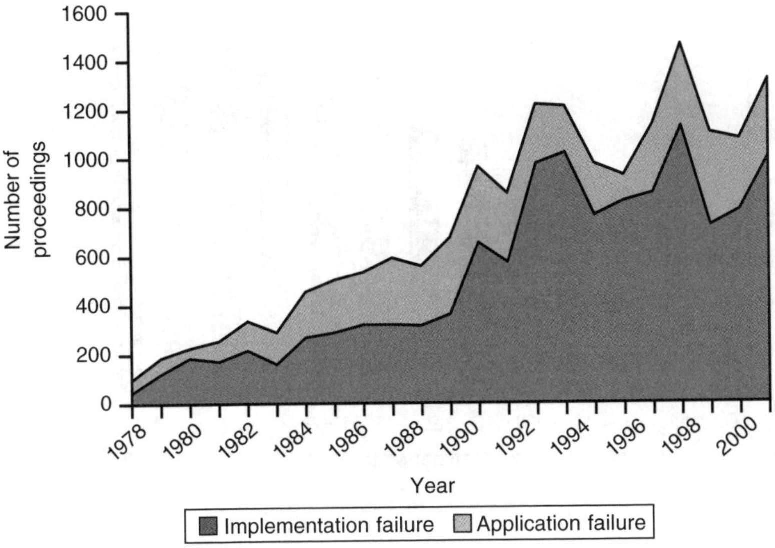

Figure 3.2 Infringement proceedings initiated for non-compliance with EU rules, 1978–2000.

Source: European Commission annual monitoring reports.

internal market program. Whereas the number of proceedings had never reached higher than 600 per year during the 1980s, the early 1990s witnessed a doubling of that figure. If the first jump in the figures around 1990 can be partly explained by the delayed effects of the enlargement to include Portugal and Spain in 1986, the further increase in the number of proceedings to a level of around 1,200 in 1993 and 1994 is more immediately an effect of the bulk of the internal market directives entering into force.

Some member states experienced more serious compliance problems than others. Figure 3.3 shows the average yearly number of infringement proceedings per member state over the period 1978–2000. Member states display clear patterns in non-compliance, with limited variation in the internal ranking over time. The most compliant state during this period was Denmark, followed by the Netherlands, Luxembourg, the UK, Ireland, and Germany. Above the EU average, we find Belgium, Spain, France, Greece, Portugal, and Italy.[11] These cross-national patterns can be directly linked to variation in national rates of compliance, since no evidence exists that the Commission is systematically discriminating between member states in the initiation of infringement proceedings.

A third form of non-compliance that received increasing attention in the late 1980s and early 1990s was state neglect of judgments handed down by the ECJ in infringement cases. In the early 1980s, a total of 30 such cases were registered at the end of each year, but by the end of the 1980s, the

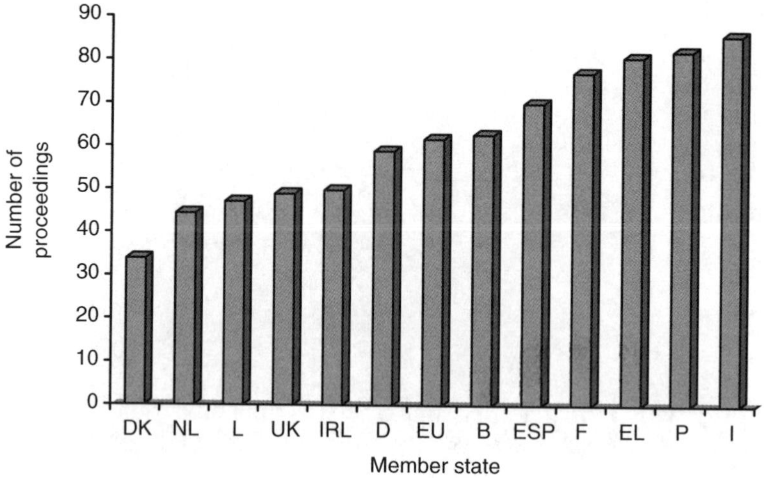

Figure 3.3 Infringement proceedings initiated per member state, yearly average, 1978–2000.

Source: European Commission annual monitoring reports.

Note
DK, Denmark; NL, Netherlands; L, Luxembourg; UK, United Kingdom; IRL, Ireland; D, Germany; EU, European Union; B, Belgium; ESP, Spain; F, France; EL, Greece; P, Portugal; I, Italy.

number had risen to more than 80 (European Commission 1984, 1985a, 1989d, 1990a). These developments were perceived as extremely worrying by the Commission and the ECJ. As the Commission concluded in 1990: "This situation gives cause for concern as it undermines the fundamental principles of a Community based on law" (European Commission 1990a: iii; see also European Commission 1988c: 12, 1989c: 14, 1995b: 1e).

The increase in the number of neglected judgments was not caused by the internal market program *per se*, since the acts of the White Paper simply could not have become the object of ECJ decisions until the mid-1990s. The state of the internal market was nevertheless a prominent concern for the supranational institutions. Since the program was the Community's most extensive legislative exercise ever, increasing disrespect for ECJ decisions was anything but encouraging. Neither were these worries soothed by the fact that the internal market was the policy area most afflicted by member states' disregard of ECJ decisions. The Commission took particular note of this in a 1989 communication:

> A fundamental problem is compliance with ECJ judgments; that the increase in infringement proceedings is reflected not only in a less satisfactory implementation of Community law, but also and more particularly in a growing number of non-enforced judgments, gives real

> cause for concern. . . . The burden of non-implementation of the ECJ decisions is particularly felt in the internal market domain.
>
> (European Commission 1989c: 14)

Conclusion

In its focus on the internal market program and member state non-compliance, this chapter has provided the framing necessary to understand why the Commission and the ECJ in the early 1990s embarked on a mission to reinforce the means of EU enforcement. The launch in 1985 of the initiative to complete the European internal market marked the beginning of a process that would come to entail considerable adjustment pressure on the political, economic, and administrative structures of member states. Non-compliance became a refuge from the most immediate adjustment pressure and a way of softening the blow on domestic structures. In the terminology of P–A theory, the process accounted for in this chapter may be described as that of member state agents increasingly attempting to cut loose, as the internal market program raised the costs of compliance and the gains of non-compliance. Moving to the empirical heartland of the study, the next three chapters explicitly test the hypotheses of the P–S–A model as they trace the Commission's and the ECJ's response to the problem of non-compliance.

4 Centralized enforcement through supranational institutions

The exploitation of existing powers

The perception of growing compliance problems in the late 1980s, and the anticipation of further strains from the internal market program, propelled the Commission and the ECJ into action. As Claus-Dieter Ehlermann, then director-general of the Commission's Legal Service, explained in a speech in 1986:

> Actually, there will be no such area without internal frontiers if Community rules are not applied effectively in all the 12 Member States. Inevitably, therefore, the establishment of the internal market involves . . . the setting up of systems of control to ensure the full compliance of all Member States with Community legislation governing the internal market.
> (Ehlermann 1988: 144–5)

The supranational institutions' efforts to strengthen EU enforcement followed three parallel approaches. This chapter describes the first of these strategies: the Commission's attempts to boost the effectiveness of the supranational institutions' enforcement powers at the centralized EU level. The focus of these efforts was the infringement procedure under the present Article 226 – then Article 169 – which was elevated from the backstage status of a rarely used last resort into a central means for realizing the internal market. As the Commission declared in 1988:

> Article 169 of the EEC Treaty is now an instrument for the achievement of a policy, and not solely an essential legal instrument. The objective . . . to achieve by 1992 an area without internal frontiers, is now the Commission's priority objective and requires a strict application of existing Community law. It is Article 169 which makes it possible to monitor this application and ensures its observance by the Member States.
> (European Commission 1988b: 5)

In this chapter I isolate five measures undertaken by the Commission: internal reforms streamlining the handling of infringement cases, a shift to a firmer enforcement policy, the encouragement of complaints to the Commission, the development of a shaming strategy, and the institutionalization of compliance bargaining. Together, these developments speak of a widening of the Commission's enforcement repertoire, as well as of a shift toward practices that are relatively more resource efficient.

Yet these measures do not qualify as independent supranational influence. The Commission's actions met with approval rather than disapproval from national governments, which were concerned with the functioning of the internal market. To some extent, EU governments were even active participants in the transformation of the infringement procedure. Nothing indicates that the Commission overstepped the boundaries of its powers. In fact, the infringement procedure offered ample room for improvements that did not necessitate a transgression of delegated competences.

The chapter is divided into three sections. In the first, I account for Commission measures that were direct attempts to enhance the capacity of the infringement procedure. In the second section, I describe the Commission's efforts to put the formal procedure to informal use, by introducing shaming and bargaining practices. In the third section, I analyze these five measures in terms of supranational influence.

Enhancing the capacity of the infringement procedure

Three measures undertaken by the Commission were aimed at enhancing the infringement procedure's capacity as a means of enforcement. Streamlining the handling of infringement cases improved the processing capacity, shifting from a careful to a firm enforcement policy reduced the vulnerability to political pressure, and encouraging complaints to the Commission boosted the monitoring capacity of the procedure. Each measure also entailed a shift toward more resource efficient ways of exercising the enforcement powers of the infringement procedure.

Streamlining the infringement procedure

The first measure consisted of attempts to streamline the infringement procedure through internal Commission reforms. The infringement procedure is composed of four distinct phases. In the first phase, the Commission engages in *informal communication* with member governments once it has detected a case of potential non-compliance. If the case is not settled in this first phase, the infringement procedure continues by way of formal means. In the second phase, the Commission sends a *letter of formal notice* to the member state, whereby the Commission informs the state of its grounds for complaint and invites it to submit its views. The third phase consists of the Commission giving a *reasoned opinion*, which elaborates on the legal arguments of the case. If the member state does not comply with the Commission's guidelines and fails to adjust its behavior, the infringement proceeding enters into the fourth and final stage of *referral to the ECJ*.

In its construction, the infringement procedure is thus anything but swift and expeditious. At each of the four stages, the Commission must have sufficient time to scrutinize member state actions and arguments, form a position internally, and express this position to the member state with all the attendant evidence and legal backing. Similarly, the procedure must at all stages permit the member state to react to the Commission's allegations, to conduct its own investigations into the case, and to undertake the administrative or legislative changes necessary to correct the situation.

Already in 1975, Donald Puchala noted: "Article 169 favors national governments because it forces the Commission into procedures which involve almost interminable delays" (1975: 513). The Commission's ambition has been not to let more than 12 months pass between the actual detection of a case of potential non-compliance and the decision on whether or not to initiate a formal infringement proceeding (European Commission 1984: 3, 1993b: 10, 1997d: 9). In practice, however, "this has proved impossible in many cases because of the complexity of the dossier" (European Commission 1993b: 9). The stages of formal notice and reasoned opinion have been quite protracted as well. In the early 1980s, the average time elapsing from the formal letter to the reasoned opinion was 12–16 months, though certain cases could be pending for years. Similarly, the average time between the reasoned opinion and a final reference to the ECJ was 8–11 months. Adding an average of 12–14 months from referral to judgment, we can conclude that it often took 4 to 5 years for a normal case to move from detection to final judgment (Audretsch 1986: 377).

This inefficiency was an obvious obstacle to the completion of the internal market. If the infringement procedure were to function as an effective enforcement tool, nudging member states toward full implementation, then it would have to be more time and resource efficient. Since little could be done unilaterally to compress the structure of the procedure, as the three formal steps were specified in the treaty, the Commission's efforts were aimed at the delaying factor it could most easily affect: its own working methods.

In the second half of the 1980s and the first half of the 1990s, the Commission undertook consecutive sets of changes in the internal handling of infringement cases. Reports indicate that concrete modifications were conducted in the mid-1980s, in 1990, and in 1993 (European Commission 1987b: 4, 1991b: 5, 1997d: 8). These reforms sought to tighten internal rules for the handling of complaints, focus resources on prioritized policy areas, promote the use of an expedited procedure for closing cases, and reduce the interval between Commission meetings at which infringement decisions were taken.

Yet these modifications proved insufficient, even if they helped moderate the pressure from the enormous amount of infringement cases in the first half of the 1990s. In 1996, therefore, the Commission initiated the most far-reaching reforms thus far of its internal handling of infringement cases. In the Commission's own terms, the 1996 reforms were motivated by "[l]engthening timespans, cumbersome and sometimes inappropriate internal procedures, a degree of confidentiality that is perceived as excessive and repeated requests from Parliament for greater speed and transparency" (1997d: 8). These changes carried one overarching theme: greater efficiency, and thus effectiveness, through quicker processing of cases (European Commission 1997d: 8–10; Mogg 1998: 1; interviews, Commission officials, December 15, 1997 and February 3, 1998).

These reform measures can be grouped into three categories. First, the Commission confirmed its priorities in the processing of complaints, stressing the need to proceed quickly with those infringements causing the greatest harm to the EU legal order, that is, non-transposition of directives. Second, the Commission reformed internal procedural deadlines. Most notably, it sought to (1) compress the structure of the infringement procedure by taking decisions on the formal initiation of proceedings at what had previously been the informal stage, (2) facilitate quick decisions on the sending of formal notices and reasoned opinions by increasing the number of Commission meetings, and (3) reduce the time between the decision to issue a reasoned opinion and its actual issuance. Third and finally, the Commission declared its intention to make greater use of a simplified procedure for the closing of cases where complaints were found to be clearly unfounded or the requisite evidence was lacking. The 1996 reforms were the most ambitious attempt thus far to improve the time and resource efficiency of the infringement procedure, and developments since 1996 point to clear and identifiable effects on the time-spans of the procedure (e.g. European Commission 1997c, 1998c: ii, 1999a: iii–iv).

Completing the policy of firm enforcement

The second measure undertaken by the Commission was to continue the shift toward a firm enforcement policy. The Commission thereby confirmed the establishment of an enforcement approach it had first embarked upon in the late 1970s. Prior to 1977, the Commission's enforcement policy had been extremely cautious and sensitive to the potential political repercussions that could result from challenging member states with non-compliance. Rather than making full use of the infringement procedure, the Commission trod lightly and followed the path of least political resistance. H. A. H. Audretsch summarizes the core features of this pre-1977 enforcement policy:

> Recourse to the formal infringement procedure and initiating proceedings before the Court against a Member State was to be avoided as much as possible. Indeed, already the act of sending a warning letter was considered an (unfriendly) political act, and even more so was the issue of a reasoned opinion or decision, and, ultimately, recourse to the Court. Only after it had been proved that all informal efforts remained without effect was a formal step to be taken. That step, as such, was considered

> an *ultima ratio*. For that reason, every formal step was decided upon separately, since it was considered as a political act, having political consequences. . . . As the general political atmosphere deteriorated (owing to internal and external crises) the Commission thought it advisable to follow a safe and selective policy, reducing the risks of a confrontation to a minimum.
>
> (Audretsch 1986: 279)

When the new Commission came to power in 1977, under the presidency of Roy Jenkins, both the philosophy and practice of the Commission's enforcement policy underwent a radical reorientation. Recourse to formal means was to be considered a natural step, whenever there was reason to believe that infringements had occurred. If this first step was not effective in bringing about compliance, there should be no hesitation in proceeding to the subsequent stages in the procedure, even if this might prove unpopular with the member state in question.

Dissecting this new enforcement approach, launched under Jenkins (1977–80), continued under Gaston Thorne (1981–4), and reinforced under Jacques Delors (1985–94), we find five distinct elements (European Commission 1984; Audretsch 1986: 283–9; Dashwood and White 1989: 399–400; Ludlow 1991: 104–5). First, the Commission attempted to strip the infringement procedure of its highly political stigma and to weaken the taboo of bringing member states before the ECJ. Second, challenging the notion that each case carried individual political weight, the Commission introduced a comprehensive approach, according to which decisions were taken on all cases of a similar nature at the same time. Third, the new enforcement approach entailed more systematic monitoring of member state incorporation and application of EU law. Fourth, the Commission introduced a higher degree of strictness into the procedure, as proceedings were now to be initiated almost automatically, whenever a case was detected. Fifth and finally, the Commission embarked on a policy of improving the information to citizens and political actors about member state infringements and its own enforcement actions.

With the launch of the internal market project and the associated pressure on the Commission to contain non-compliance, this shift to a firm enforcement policy was further buttressed (Ludlow 1991: 105; Mendrinou 1996: 16). The primary target of these efforts was member states' transposition of directives into national law. On the one hand, the Commission developed its practices for monitoring compliance by, for instance, instituting means for systematic vetting of national implementation acts and close tracking of transposition deadlines (European Commission 1995c: 9, 1996b: 9). On the other hand, the Commission strengthened the automatic element of its enforcement approach, routinely initiating infringement proceedings whenever member states had failed to notify implementation measures in time (European Commission 1994c: xiii).

Encouraging complaints to the Commission

The third way in which the Commission worked to enhance the potential of the infringement procedure was to further encourage complaints from citizens and companies. Private complaints to the Commission had always been its primary source of information on member states' application of Community law. As one Commission official expressed it: "The best ally of the Commission is the economic operator" (interview, September 27, 1996). By actively facilitating complaints, the Commission attempted to improve the enforcement capacity of the procedure by way of boosting its monitoring machinery.

Since the early 1960s, the Commission had operated an informal procedure through which it recorded and examined complaints from citizens, companies, associations, and national administrations about member state infringements. Consisting of nothing more than a written or oral complaint to the Commission in Brussels or to any of its offices in the member states, the complaint procedure was simple and straightforward, making it "the most direct and effective instrument available to the citizen to ensure the application of Community law, leaving aside of course proceedings before a national court" (European Commission 1988b: 5). For the Commission, the complaint procedure offered a form of monitoring that was far more resource efficient than systematic in-house inquiries (interview, Commission official, September 24, 1996). It also provided access to information about state compliance on the ground, which the Commission itself was unable to gather (European Commission 1996d: 6).

Figure 4.1 depicts the development of complaints and the Commission's own inquiries as sources of cases identified as suspected infringements of EU rules. The figure testifies to the management of centralized monitoring through a system that is largely complaint-based. The factors behind the growing gap are twofold: the aggravation of compliance problems from the mid-1980s, and the steps taken by the Commission to boost complaints as a means of monitoring.

These efforts were aimed at making the infringement procedure more known and accessible to potential complainants. Reporting on its activities in 1992, the Commission communicated the core of this strategy: "The Commission has tried to make people in the Member States more aware of the procedure and to encourage its use with the aim of improving the application of Community law" (1993b: 8).

Whereas the earliest declarations stem from the mid-1980s, the most concrete steps to encourage complaint-based monitoring are more recent in origin. In 1989, the Commission rendered the lodging of complaints simpler and more effective by preparing a one-page standard complaint form to be used by citizens and companies, today accessible via the Internet (European Commission 1989a). As the internal market program shifted to the stage of enforcement, these efforts were reinforced. In the 1993 Strategic

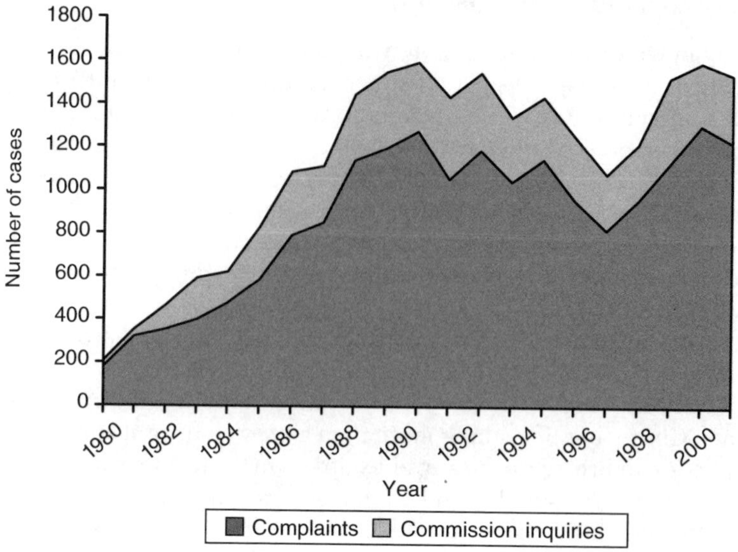

Figure 4.1 Origin of cases of suspected infringements, 1980–2000.

Source: European Commission annual monitoring reports.

Note: In 1990, the Commission started reporting petitions to, and questions asked by, the European Parliament as a separate source of suspected infringements. These petitions and questions are included in the category "Commission inquiries," since this is where the Commission itself chooses to place them in the later part of this period. In 1995, the Commission introduced yet another category: failure to report measures taken to implement EU directives. Since the Commission does not indicate whether this is a new source of information, or whether it has always acted on this information without reporting it as a source, this category is not included in the figure, but reported as follows: 459 (1995), 1079 (1996), 760 (1997), 610 (1998), 677 (1999), 896 (2000).

Programme on the internal market, the Commission stressed the importance of complaints and expressed its intention to further promote this means of monitoring:

> In those areas of the Internal Market legislation in which the Commission relies heavily on *complaints* as a means of detecting problems, steps will be taken to make economic operators and the relevant networks more aware of the methods for drawing attention to difficulties they may encounter, if necessary by means of formal complaints.
>
> (European Commission 1993c: 12)

Following the declaration in the Strategic Programme, the period 1994–8 witnessed a large number of concrete measures. In 1994, the Commission enhanced its information-gathering activities by arranging "internal market weeks" in the member states involving among other things, conferences, public hearings, telephone hot-lines, and radio phone-ins chaired by Commission officials (European Commission 1995c: 3). The strategy of informing citizens of their rights under EU law, and thereby indirectly improving their capacity to function as active complainants, was further developed in association with the information campaign "Citizens First" (for an in-depth treatment, see Chapter 6). Finally, in 1997, the Commission's internal market directorate established a help desk for complaints. When announcing the new help desk in its newsletter to interested citizens and companies, the Commission was clear on the purpose:

> The objective of the Help Desk is to inform people about the role that DG XV can play if they would like the support of the Commission to safeguard their rights in the Single Market. Information is available on complaints procedures, the information needed to support such a procedure and the prospects and time frame of such procedures.
>
> (European Commission 1997 m: 25)

Putting the formal procedure to informal use

Next to its capacity-enhancing measures, the Commission developed practices that sought to exploit the potential for informal pressure and solutions within the formal framework of the infringement procedure. This took two forms: the development of a shaming strategy and the intensification and institutionalization of compliance bargaining. Both encouraged a more efficient use of the Commission's enforcement resources, as shaming generated a self-propelling social and political pressure to comply and compliance bargaining permitted proceedings to be closed through informal, amicable solutions.

Developing a shaming strategy

The first move was to politicize non-compliance and develop an explicit shaming strategy. The Commission made it its strategy from the late 1980s onwards to embarrass laggards into action by publishing regular reports on compliance, issue press releases on infringement decisions, and review compliance records at Council meetings.

This shaming strategy differed substantially from previous Commission practices. Prior to the 1977 reorientation of its enforcement policy, the Commission had been extremely sensitive to political concerns in the execution of its enforcement functions, and had resolutely refrained from exploiting the political potential inherent in these powers (Audretsch 1986: 277). As the Commission's more resolute enforcement policy was gradually implemented in the late 1970s and early 1980s, the merits of political pressure and transparency were increasingly recognized. With the more systematic and less cautious approach to enforcement came a number of concrete changes, which all involved an element of politicization.

In 1984, the Commission began to publish a yearly report on member states' application of Community law, the purpose being "to bring about greater transparency" (European Commission 1984: 4). A second step was to increasingly attempt to exert direct political pressure at the higher political levels in the member states, not least in cases of non-compliance with ECJ judgments (European Commission 1985a: 3, 1986a: 5). Third, the Commission put its trust in the persuasive power of public opinion in the member states; if only the public and national parliamentarians were informed of state non-compliance, then government bureaucrats would find this a less attractive option (European Commission 1986a: 7).

When the internal market program reached the stages of implementation and application in the beginning of the 1990s, these rather disparate steps were transformed into a more coherent strategy. The comprehensiveness of the internal market White Paper and the growing problems of non-compliance motivated the shaping of a political approach alongside judicial activity:

> [T]he challenge of 1992, the comprehensiveness and balance of the White Paper programme and the speeding up of decision making all justify the steps taken to politicize monitoring of the transposition process based on complete transparency of the situation in each Member State.
> (European Commission 1991b: 5)

During the 1990s, this strategy of shaming took on a more concrete form, and with the appointment of the Italian Mario Monti as internal market commissioner in 1995, it gained a firm supporter willing to enter the role as supreme whip (interview, Commission official, March 22, 1996). The measures taken to politicize compliance may be summarized under three headings.

First, the Commission took steps to further enhance the transparency of member states' implementation of the internal market provisions. Transparency was presented as a key area where renewed efforts would have to be made, and the Commission emphasized that it was of manifest importance "in order to put pressure on the laggard Member States . . ., that national incorporation measures should be entirely transparent" (1990a: 1). In practical terms, this took two forms: regular reports and databases (European Commission 1991c: 1, 1994b: 10). The general report on member states' application of EU law was extended on consecutive occasions to provide a more encompassing picture of state compliance. In addition, special internal market reports were issued that analyzed in detail the progress (or lack thereof) in all internal market sectors (e.g. European Commission 1992b, 1994c, 1995c, 1996b). Besides these reports, the Commission organized databases on internal market legislation and national implementation measures – Celex and Info 92 –"whose users can keep a running check on the progress of single market legislation and the transposing of Community law" (European Commission 1991c: 1).

Second, the Commission put in place and gradually extended the practice of issuing press releases when taking decisions on infringement cases. The expressed purpose was to name and shame non-complying member states, not only in Commission reports, but also in the national press. In the late 1980s, the Commission began issuing press releases in the two areas prioritized in terms of compliance, the internal market and the environment (European Commission 1988b: 6). In the early 1990s, this practice was extended to infringement decisions in all policy areas, though the internal market and environment remained dominant (European Commission 1993b: 10).[1] In 1995 and 1996, the practice of issuing press releases was further intensified and extended, motivated not least by the desire to fully complete the internal market (European Commission 1996d: 10, 1997d: 1). Declared the Commission in 1997: "Publicity is now the general rule for decisions to issue reasoned opinions and referrals to the Court of Justice" (1997d: 10).

Third, the Commission encouraged peer pressure at Council meetings by presenting increasingly detailed reports on member states' implementation and application of internal market legislation. For each meeting of the Internal Market Council, the Commission prepared reports where it indicated the state of play, especially as regards the transposition of directives (European Commission 1994c: xiii, 1995c: 9). In 1996, this practice was stepped up when the Commission moved toward a more comprehensive report (interview, Commission official, September 25, 1996). The rationale was clear:

> The purpose is to put greater pressure on states by way of transparency, which is one of the keys to getting member states to implement directives. It means that a member state not only sees its own position, but also that of other member states, and obviously member states do not like to see themselves at the bottom of the list.
>
> (Interview, Commission official, September 25, 1996)

In 1997, this strategy of peer pressure and shaming was further reinforced when the Commission introduced the biannual internal market scoreboard, which in great detail compares the member states in terms of implementation, compliance, and infringement proceedings (see, e.g., European Commission 1997j, 1999b, 2001a). Emphasized Commissioner Monti: "I . . . intend to publicise any discrepancies between the Member States' political statements of support for the Single Market and their actual record on respecting the rules in reality" (Monti 1997). More than any other Commission measure, the scoreboard – or "scareboard," as it has also been called – epitomized the new shaming strategy of the Commission.

Extending the use of compliance bargaining

The other way in which the Commission put its formal enforcement powers to informal use was by way of compliance bargaining (Jönsson and Tallberg

1998; Tallberg and Jönsson 2001). Whereas the infringement procedure, with its consecutive steps for resolving conflicts, had always formed an invitation to bargaining, it was not until the late 1980s that these practices became institutionalized. What made bargaining solutions to compliance problems possible, despite the seemingly formal and inflexible framework of the infringement procedure and the Commission's lack of authority to compromise with EU law, was the coexistence of three elements: discretion for the Commission, mutual and conflicting interests, and a multiple-step sanctioning ladder.

First, when deciding about infringement proceedings, the Commission enjoyed a degree of discretion that granted it room for maneuver and bargaining within the framework of the infringement procedure (Audretsch 1986: 36; Dashwood and White 1989: 399). At a most basic level, the Commission's infringement decisions were the consequence of its own view of the situation at hand.[2] In addition, the confidentiality of its handling of infringement cases made it difficult for other parties to judge the validity of these decisions. This discretion provided a setting in which the Commission could arrive at "compromise solutions in a flexible way through negotiations, conciliatory measures, and mutual concessions" (Audretsch 1986: 440).

Second, the infringement procedure offered both cooperative and conflictual elements – a prerequisite for bargaining. On the one hand, the parties disagreed as to what actions were in breach of Community law. Simultaneously, however, both parties shared a common interest by preferring amicable solutions to continued proceedings. As one Commission official put it: "Legal proceedings are not good for anyone" (interview, September 24, 1996). For the Commission, with its limited workforce and heavy workload, the option of informal solutions was very attractive in comparison to the highly resource intensive alternative of full, formal proceedings. For the member states, infringement proceedings in general, and ECJ judgments against them in particular, were highly uncomfortable and tarnished their reputation as cooperative partners.

Third, the four stages of the infringement procedure functioned as a sanctioning ladder that progressively raised the pressure and the costs of non-compliance, thereby inviting bargaining between the parties. Exploiting its unilateral power to decide on infringement cases, the Commission attempted to persuade member states to comply by communicating the threat that the case may be brought to the next step in the procedure. Since 1995, the communication of these threats or warnings has included the reminder that economic sanctions may be imposed on the state in question if it fails to comply with ECJ judgments (European Commission 1995b: 1e; interview, Swedish government official, December 6, 1996). "When the State appears to persist in the violation, an attempt will be made to raise the cost of violation or to lower its profit" (Audretsch 1986: 410). The shaming strategy was an integral part of this sanctioning ladder. By exposing member states' wrongdoings, the Commission exploited their concern with reputation and the fact that "no member state wants to have infringement proceedings in front of the Court of Justice against it" (interview, Commission official, September 24, 1996).

In the late 1980s, important changes occurred in the nature of this compliance bargaining between the Commission and the member states. Whereas previous interaction had predominantly consisted of bargaining in the broad sense, what now emerged was pure negotiation in the narrow sense. Instead of expressing threats, promises, and compromise alternatives in the formal exchange of views inherent in the procedure, the Commission introduced a practice of actually meeting in person with responsible government officials. The introduction of such meetings, so-called package meetings, led one observer to conclude that what we had witnessed was "a significant change since the mid-1980s in the dominant mode of settling infringement disputes" (Snyder 1993: 30).

The term package meeting stems from the nature of these encounters, as each meeting deals with a badge or package of cases rather than singular files. Package meetings are held with one member state at a time and cover all cases currently under review by the Commission in a particular area. "These meetings ensure that the situation is kept constantly under joint review and allow the Commission to bring extra pressure to bear on the competent national departments" (European Commission 1992a: 2).

The practice of holding package meetings was first introduced in the internal market domain in the late 1980s, but spread later to other areas of EU regulation, most notably environment (European Commission 1989c: 5, 1990a: v, 1994b: 6, 1995b: 1e, 1997d: 16). Encouraged by the perceived success of this practice, which led to the closing of a large number of infringement cases, package meetings became an explicit component in the Commission's approach for dealing with compliance problems after 1992 (European Commission 1992a: 11, 1993b: 17). As the Commission declared in the Strategic Programme:

> In view of the considerable success of *package meetings*, an instrument of partnership between the Commission and the Member States which is designed to arrive at non-contentious solutions to existing litigation concerning national compliance with Community law, the Commission will, as appropriate, extend them to all Member States and increase their frequency.
>
> (European Commission 1993c: 13)

Today, package meetings are a prominent aspect of the Commission's handling of infringement cases. Compliance negotiations are seen as a cooperative approach on top of the otherwise conflictual approach of the infringement procedure (interview, Commission official, September 25, 1996). Francis Snyder eloquently captures this complementarity:

> We usually think of negotiation and adjudication as alternative forms of dispute settlement. It may be suggested, however, that in the daily practice and working ideology of the Commission, the two are not alternatives but instead are complementary. The main form of dispute settlement used by the Commission is negotiation, and litigation is simply a part, sometimes inevitable but nevertheless generally a minor part, of this process.
>
> (Snyder 1993: 30)

Compliance bargaining contributes to a sharp reduction in violations from one step in the infringement procedure to the next, as Table 4.1 demonstrates. Of the total number of infringement proceedings initiated between 1978 and 2000, only 38 percent reached the stage of reasoned opinions, and only 11 percent were referred to the ECJ. All member states display the same preference for backing down or finding amicable solutions at the early stages of the infringement procedure. Yet some states, such as Denmark, the UK, the Netherlands, and Spain, go to great lengths to settle cases as early as possible; others, such as Italy, Belgium, Greece, and France, tend to persist in their violations and end up having a higher share of cases referred to the ECJ.

Table 4.2 provides a snapshot of the closure of cases at various stages of the infringement and sanctioning procedures in one given year (1999). Of 1,900 cases closed, as many as 95 percent were solved before referral to the ECJ. The table demonstrates further how the closure of cases continues even after referral. Member states back down before judgment, after a court decision, when charged with the non-implementation of a judgment, or, ultimately, when confronted with the threat of sanctions. Informal compliance bargaining is a key source behind this effectiveness of the formal infringement procedure in combating detected violations.

Table 4.1 Infringement cases per member state by stage, 1978–2000

State	*Formal notice*	*Reasoned opinion (%)*		*ECJ referral (%)*	
Belgium	1,443	652	45.2	236	16.4
Denmark	779	103	13.2	22	2.8
Germany	1,352	517	38.2	136	10.1
Greece	1,611	659	40.9	198	12.3
France	1,772	721	40.7	234	13.2
Ireland	1,143	405	35.4	121	10.6
Italy	1,970	1,010	51.4	396	20.1
Luxembourg	1,083	409	37.8	130	12.0
Netherlands	1,021	288	28.2	72	7.1
Portugal	1,230	483	39.3	63	5.1
Spain	1,048	349	33.3	74	7.1
UK	1,125	304	27.0	50	4.4
EU 12	15,577	5,900	37.9	1,737	11.2

Source: European Commission annual monitoring reports.

Table 4.2 Infringement cases closed in 1999 by stage in the procedures

Stage	*Number*	*Percentage*
Before formal notice	763	40.2
Before reasoned opinion	593	31.2
Before ECJ referral	435	22.9
Before ECJ judgment	40	2.1
Before second formal notice	46	2.4
Before second reasoned opinion	12	0.6
Before second ECJ referral	10	0.5
Before ECJ sanctioning judgment	1	0.1
Total	1,900	100.0

Source: European Commission 2000a.

Centralized enforcement and supranational influence

The preceding sections have demonstrated two important points. First, that compliance problems related to the internal market induced the Commission to strengthen its enforcement operations and widen its enforcement repertoire. Second, that the Commission consistently introduced or reinforced practices which were relatively more resource efficient and thus yielded more enforcement for a given amount of resources. Taken together, these conclusions encourage an additional observation – that the Commission, in the exercise of its supervisory role, evidently enjoyed sufficient room for maneuver to shape centralized enforcement. This observation raises the fundamental question of whether or not the Commission exerted independent influence when transforming the use of the infringement procedure. In this section, I conclude in favor of an alternative explanation, namely, that the Commission enjoyed the explicit or implicit support of member governments, which favored an infringement procedure that was sufficiently efficient and effective to secure mutual commitments and the realization of the internal market.

The absence of overt conflict

Did the Commission employ its delegated enforcement means in ways that conflicted with the intentions of member governments, or did it act in conformance with the interests and expectations of member states? To adjudicate this question, it is essential to consider member governments' response to the Commission's actions. If national governments countered these reforms with allegations of competence transgression and either threatened or imposed sanctions, the Commission was not sensitive to government preferences. If, on the contrary, the Commission's upgrading of its enforcement practices met with explicit or implicit approval, it is less likely that these actions were in conflict with the interests of EU governments.

The empirical record sends a clear message. In no instance did the Commission's actions result in open conflicts with member states. Neither the improvements in the infringement procedure's enforcement capacity, nor the informal practices developed in connection with this procedure, drove member governments to challenge the Commission's execution of its enforcement function. National governments had three opportunities during this period to effectively demonstrate that they did not support the way the Commission exercised its enforcement powers: the 1986, 1991, and 1996–7 IGCs. On neither occasion, however, was the question of a *reduction* in the powers of the infringement procedure on the agenda.

Quite to the contrary, all three IGCs witnessed proposals for *extensions* of the Commission's direct enforcement powers, and in two of the three cases these suggestions even resulted in treaty revisions reinforcing the Commission's arsenal (see Chapter 5 for an in-depth analysis of the 1991 and 1996–7 IGCs). First, at the 1986 IGC, member states decided to introduce, by derogation from Article 169, an accelerated procedure for bringing a state directly before the ECJ in certain internal market matters (Article 100a, as revised by the SEA). Second, at the 1991 IGC, national governments supplemented Article 169 with a new Article 171 in which they conferred on the Commission and the ECJ the power to financially sanction member states that refuse to comply with compliance judgments. And third, at the 1996–7 IGC, certain governments, inspired by a Commission proposal, suggested that Articles 100a, 169, and 171 be revised, so as to confer special enforcement powers on the Commission in the internal market domain.

These proposals for extensions of the Commission's competences in centralized EU enforcement motivate an obvious counterfactual and rhetorical question: is it likely that member governments would have proposed and united to delegate more far-reaching enforcement instruments to the Commission had they considered the Commission's exercise of its existing powers unacceptable and in conflict with their interests? The answer, of course, is no.

The absence of information asymmetry

Yet it cannot be concluded from the absence of overt conflict alone that the Commission's actions did not constitute an exercise in supranational influence. As suggested by the notion of information asymmetry, government principals may not always register and fully understand the implications of supranational behavior, thereby permitting undesired actions to go unpunished. Does any part of the empirical evidence suggest that the Commission exercised its powers in ways other than governments desired or originally intended, and that governments lacked the information to identify these actions?

In none of the five reform measures did the Commission transgress its formal mandate or the legal structure of the infringement procedure.[3] The reforms to streamline the internal handling of infringement cases, the shift to a firmer enforcement policy, the encouragement of complaints, the politicization of infringements, and the introduction of package meetings, all conform to the formal enforcement powers laid down in the treaty – the ultimate expression of member states' collective will.

That said, it is doubtful whether governments in the 1950s anticipated the extent to which the infringement procedure would be transformed within its given legal boundaries. The Spaak report, which served as the basis for the treaties of Rome, testifies that national governments were well aware of the fact that they were granting the Commission exceptional enforcement competences compared to international secretariats in general (Audretsch 1986: 18–19). But, partly because it was such a rare feature in the world of international organization at the time, it is reasonable to assume that member states did not envisage that up to 1,200 new proceedings would come to be initiated each year, and that the procedure would function as everyday enforcement instrument, rather than as an extraordinary means for settling the occasional case of treaty violation.

Nothing suggests, however, that governments in the 1980s and 1990s were unaware of the Commission's efforts to reform the infringement procedure, and that information asymmetry prevented governments from intervening. The five reform measures ranged from transparent to very transparent. While least open to government oversight, the Commission's internal reforms were described in official Commission reports presented to EU governments. The gradual turn from a careful to a firm enforcement policy was concretely felt by member states, as the Commission became far less hesitant about initiating infringement proceedings. Nor was it a secret that complaints had been an important source of information on state infringements ever since the early 1960s, and that the Commission undertook efforts to further facilitate complaints. Shaming and compliance bargaining were exceedingly transparent strategies; the very point of shaming was for governments to take notice as performance rates were officially compared, and compliance bargaining even involved member governments' active cooperation as one party to the package meetings.

Collective self-commitment

European Union governments' lack of opposition to the Commission's transformation of the infringement procedure is best explained by the logic of self-commitment. Existing evidence suggests that member governments in fact welcomed the Commission's attempts to improve the capacity of the infringement procedure. Expressed in terms of the P–S–A model, government principals appreciated the need to exploit the procedure's full potential, if it were to effectively function as a means for collective self-commitment, capable of ensuring the realization of the internal market.

Member states' IGC suggestions for extensions of the Commission's enforcement powers demonstrate that governments were aware of the problems the Commission sought to combat. First, the fact that member governments at the 1986 IGC decided unanimously to introduce an accelerated infringement procedure shows that they shared the Commission's concerns about the normal procedure being slow and cumbersome. Second, the fact that EU governments agreed at the 1991 IGC to supplement Article 169 with a provision for financial sanctions in a revised Article 171 proves that they recognized the limits of the infringement procedure as a means of deterrence. And third, the fact that all proposals for a strengthening of the Commission's enforcement powers were specifically focused on the internal market domain, suggests that member states appreciated the problem of non-compliance with internal market rules.

Existing documentation lends further support to the notion of member state approval. Next to compliance bargaining, which would not take place unless member states found it to be in their interest as well, the best example is the strategy of shaming. From the perspective of member states, few things are as embarrassing and uncomfortable as the public announcement of their failures to meet well-known obligations. Nevertheless, national governments chose to endorse the internal market scoreboard, a core feature of the strategy of shaming. At the informal meeting of internal market ministers at Echternach, Luxembourg, in October 1997, where Commissioner Monti first presented the planned contents of the scoreboard, there was wide support for the aim of the exercise and its coverage of compliance, but hesitation about plans for a business survey (internal Commission memo, October 10, 1997).

As the second and third scoreboards were presented during 1998, governments grew increasingly enthusiastic. As *European Voice* reported the week before the presentation of the third scoreboard in September 1998: "Some ministers are also expected to push for the scoreboard to be published four times a year rather than twice to 'name and shame' countries who fail to stick to timetables" (September 17–23, 1998: 2). Rather than expressing strong dislike for the new measure or sanctioning the Commission for creative use of its supervisory means, member governments thus welcomed this instrument for keeping a check on each other and embarrassing laggards into action.

Conclusion

In this chapter, I have described the reforms undertaken by the Commission in the second half of the 1980s and the first half of the 1990s for the purpose of strengthening the infringement procedure at the centralized EU level. These measures were fivefold: internal reforms streamlining the handling of infringement cases, a continuation of the shift to a firm enforcement policy, the encouragement of complaints to the Commission, the development of a shaming strategy, and the intensification of compliance bargaining.

Together, these developments testify to a strengthening of the Commission's enforcement operations, a widening of its enforcement repertoire, and a sensitivity to the resource intensity of alternative means of enforcement. Yet, as much as these five measures reinforced the enforcement potential of the infringement procedure, neither qualifies as independent supranational influence. Recognizing the negative implications of non-compliance for the internal market as a collective endeavor, member governments endorsed rather than sanctioned the Commission's development of the infringement procedure into a more efficient and effective enforcement tool.

5 Delegation of enforcement powers

The supranational quest for sanctioning authority

The Commission's measures to improve the effectiveness of the centralized infringement procedure could not compensate for what the institutions experienced as a serious omission in their supervisory competences – the absence of sanctions against non-complying states. In this second chapter on the supranational institutions' efforts to strengthen EU enforcement, I trace their attempts to induce the delegation of sanctioning powers. The focus of the chapter, which covers largely empirical developments not previously accounted for, are the negotiations on sanctions at the 1991 and 1996–7 IGCs.

As points in time when the basic contract between government principals is renegotiated, IGCs provide an opportunity for the supranational supervisors to exert independent influence in EU enforcement. Through the placing of proposals on the IGC agenda, the Commission and the ECJ may succeed in inducing member state principals to delegate new enforcement powers they would never have considered or consented to in the absence of supranational maneuvering. Though by definition IGCs are intergovernmental affairs between national delegates, the supranational institutions – the Commission in particular – are involved in the IGC process. All the supranational institutions contribute to IGC agenda setting by presenting reports on the functioning of the treaties prior to a conference. Only the Commission, however, is part of the entire process, including the key negotiating stage. "[P]resent but not quite a full participant" (Dinan 1997: 250), the Commission monitors the negotiations, advances proposals, builds coalitions, and brokers agreements for the furthering of its own and the EU's interests.

In this chapter, I advance one argument about each of the three sets of hypotheses generated by the P–S–A model. First, at both IGCs, the conditions typically inducing independent supranational action were present and acted upon. The inadequacy of existing enforcement powers spurred the Commission to push for new powers. Second, on both occasions, the Commission failed in engineering sufficient support for the suggestions it advanced. The main reasons were the proposals' implications for national sovereignty and the ease with which governments could identify these consequences due to their privileged position vis-à-vis control of the agenda in IGC negotiations.

Third, the proposals either presented or planted by the Commission confirm the notion that the supranational institutions are sensitive to the resource efficiency of various means of enforcement.

The chapter is divided into three substantive sections. The first accounts for the omission of sanctions in the EEC treaty and early supranational calls for sanctions to be added to their enforcement arsenal. The second section covers the 1991 IGC and the introduction of sanctions under a revised Article 171 championed by the UK, while the third deals with the 1996–7 IGC and the forced adaptation to government preferences of the Commission's proposal to upgrade Articles 169 and 171.

Wanted: sanctions against non-complying states

In P–A theory as well as IR literature, enforcement is generally taken to mean the existence of both monitoring and sanctions. Prior to 1991, however, neither centralized "police-patrol" enforcement through infringement proceedings nor decentralized "fire-alarm" enforcement through national courts could be backed up with a general threat of financial sanctions if member states refused to comply. This absence of sanctions seriously handicapped EU enforcement and challenged the supranational institutions' ability to fulfill effectively their role as supervisors securing member state compliance. On repeated occasions, the supranational institutions called on government principals to also delegate the power to impose sanctions of some form or other on member states in breach of Community law.

The absence of sanctions in the EEC treaty

The 1957 EEC treaty did not provide for any form of sanction against member states in breach of their obligations. Article 169, which "was not designed as a punitive measure" (Steiner and Woods 1996: 410), only laid down the steps leading to an ECJ judgment, and Article 171, which obliged member states to comply with these judgments, amounted to little more than a proclamation: "If the Court of Justice finds that a Member State has failed to fulfil an obligation under this Treaty, the State shall be required to take the necessary measures to comply with the judgment of the Court of Justice" (Article 171 EEC). In effect, the ECJ's judgment in infringement proceedings under Article 169 was nothing but declaratory. To the extent that member states refused to comply with decisions handed down by the ECJ, the only measure available was renewed infringement proceedings under Article 171.

The absence of sanctions in the EEC treaty was no coincidence; it was the result of an active decision to safeguard national sovereignty (Cahier 1967: 159; Everling 1984: 228; Steiner 1993: 3). While in line with practices common in international relations at the time, the lack of sanctions in the treaty broke with the rules governing existing European cooperation in the European Coal and Steel Community (ECSC). As Karen Alter notes: "Negotiators of the Treaty of Rome . . . actually weakened its enforcement mechanisms compared to what they were in the European Coal and Steel Community (ECSC) Treaty in order to protect national sovereignty, stripping the sanctioning power from European institutions" (1998a: 127). The enforcement provisions in the ECSC treaty differed in two essential ways from weaker counterparts in the later EEC treaty. First, under the ECSC treaty, the Commission itself could find a member state in breach, subject to review by the ECJ, whereas, under the EEC treaty, it was the ECJ that determined whether a violation had occurred.[1] Second, and more importantly, the ECSC treaty provided for sanctions against the non-complying state if it chose to ignore the Commission's decision or the ECJ's judgment. Subject to the assent of a two-thirds majority in the Council, the Commission could suspend payments eligible to the state and authorize countermeasures to correct the effects of the infringement.

For the supranational institutions, the absence of sanctions in the EEC treaty constituted an omission with potentially severe consequences for compliance. This was a view shared by certain legal observers: "This omission posed a real threat to the uniform application of Community law, indeed to the Community's very existence. Without solidarity, the full compliance with Community law by all Member States, the Community would be unlikely to survive" (Steiner 1993: 3).

Early supranational calls for sanctions

The absence of sanctions in the EEC treaty was not interpreted by the supranational institutions as the final word in this matter. On a number of occasions during the 1970s and 1980s, the institutions called on government principals to delegate the authority to impose sanctions of some form on member states in violation of Community law. In none of the cases did national governments respond by conferring sanctioning powers through treaty revision. The proposals put forward included both suggestions to give the ECJ and the Commission the right to inflict financial penalties on member states, and suggestions that some kind of state liability principle should be developed to the effect that individuals could claim compensation from non-complying states.

Already in 1975 the ECJ publicly developed its position on the question of sanctions in a report motivated by the vision of constructing a European Union (European Court of Justice 1975). Addressing the Community's legal structure, the ECJ stressed that a genuine rule of law in a future Union would be impossible if legal certainty could not be guaranteed, and true legal certainty required the capacity to sanction non-compliance:

> [L]egal certainty entails the filling of a legal gap in the Treaty of Rome in that it does not in terms provide for any effective sanction against a state

which fails to temper its obligations, to the detriment of states which do. It is therefore desirable firstly that, in its judgement against a defaulting state, the Court should be able to specify those steps which that state is invited to take, secondly that the execution of the judgment should be subject to an appropriate systematic control and finally that any advantages sought by the state concerned would be conditional upon its rectification of the failure.

(European Court of Justice 1975: 17)

In the mind of the ECJ, the lack of sanctions in the treaty constituted an omission that ought to be corrected through amendment, and the suggestions it presented bore apparent similarity to the sanctioning powers under the ECSC treaty (Audretsch 1986: 141). In the same document, the ECJ also signaled that it was not alien to the notion of some form of damages against non-complying member states. Addressing the question of how individuals' rights under Community law could be better protected, the ECJ suggested that one improvement would be to create a remedy, through which citizens could claim damages from states violating the preliminary ruling procedure under Article 177 (European Court of Justice 1975: 18).

In 1983, the European Parliament publicly sided with the ECJ in the so-called Sieglerschmidt report, which made explicit reference to the ECJ's 1975 suggestions (European Parliament 1983a). Drawn up in response to signs of an increase in infringements, the report and the subsequent EP resolution presented suggestions on how to remedy this situation. Most far-reaching was the proposal to introduce sanctions against member states:

[The EP:] Is aware of the problem that the existing Treaties do not permit any enforcement action against the Member States and regrets, with the Court of Justice, that only the ECSC Treaty permits flanking measures in favour of Member States which have complied with the Treaty or against Member States which have acted in breach thereof; Calls upon the Member States to adopt an amendment to the EEC Treaty, as suggested by the European Court of Justice, to provide effective sanctions against a Member State in default of a judgement.

(European Parliament 1983b: 33)

Also the EP recognized that an alternative way of introducing sanctions would be to make it more possible for individuals to claim compensation from member states in breach of the treaty rules:

Although under the Treaties presently in force no penalties may be imposed on the Member States, Member States which have infringed the Treaty should at least be obliged to compensate for all losses of property which have occurred as a result of the infringement.

(European Parliament 1983a: 24)

Although the Commission had not formally presented any concrete proposals, such as those of the ECJ and the EP, it had informally advocated the introduction of some system of sanctions. In a 1986 speech, for example, Claus-Dieter Ehlermann, then director-general of the Commission's Legal Service, suggested that one of the ways in which the Community could come to terms with disrespect for ECJ judgments would be the creation of "a penalty system on the lines of the one provided for in Article 88 ECSC" (1988: 147). As the IGC scheduled to begin in December 1990 approached, the Commission confirmed, in an opinion targeting the IGC, its interest in the establishment of a sanctioning mechanism. Again, the rationale was the effectiveness of the institutions and non-compliance with ECJ judgments: "One disturbing fact remains: in the absence of sanctions, the Court of Justice rulings are not always implemented. The Commission may consider proposing a system of sanctions to deal with this type of situation" (European Commission 1990b: 14).

In view of member governments' disregard of these supranational propositions, H. A. H. Audretsch was in 1986 highly pessimistic about the chances of ever seeing sanctions incorporated into the treaty: "[I]t may be questioned whether proposals for sanctions will not remain purely academic, at any rate for many years to come" (1986: 141). Audretsch's prophecy could not have been more off-target.

The 1991 IGC and the introduction of sanctions

With the perception of mounting compliance problems in the second half of the 1980s and the imminent arrival of the 1992 deadline for the completion of the internal market, the question of sanctions was put in a different light. The supranational supervisors renewed their calls for sanctioning provisions, and for the first time ever member state principals perceived non-compliance as sufficiently serious to motivate compromises with national sovereignty. At the 1991 IGC, resulting in the Treaty on European Union (TEU), member governments agreed to introduce financial penalties against states refusing to comply with ECJ judgments. The sanctioning arrangements advocated by the Commission were consistently discarded because of their far-reaching consequences for national sovereignty, as EU governments settled for a less consequential alternative proposed by the UK.

Non-compliance incites British sanction proposal

The shift in governments' position on sanctions can only be understood against the backdrop of two interrelated developments in the late 1980s and early 1990s: the perceived deterioration in compliance and the putting in place of internal market provisions. For a number of years, there had been a steady rise in infringement proceedings, conveying the impression that Community rules were increasingly disrespected. Whereas the internal market program in itself was one source behind this development, it was also clear that continued violations of this magnitude would seriously challenge the vision of a unified European market.

For member governments, sanctions were a question that had to be considered if non-compliance were not to erode previous and future achievements, the internal market in particular. For the supranational institutions, the emergence of sanctions on the agenda of the 1991 IGC was a moment long waited for and an opportunity to maneuver governments into reinforcing the supervisory arsenal.

Somewhat surprisingly, given the UK's traditional preference for solutions safeguarding national sovereignty over those leading the way toward a federal Europe, it was London that put sanctions on the agenda of the IGC. As the *Financial Times* pointed out at the time: "[It is somewhat ironic that] a sovereignty-conscious UK should come up with one of the most supranational proposals since the 1952 European Coal and Steel Treaty provided for the unused power to suspend budget payments to a recalcitrant government" (February 6, 1991: 20).

However, to the UK government, it made perfect sense. A continuation or worsening of existing compliance problems would have risked undermining the internal market, embraced by the UK as the most important deregulatory exercise ever (Shackleton 1991: 596; Mendrinou 1996: 14). Britain relished the idea of a frontier-free Europe and was "an enthusiastic supporter of liberalization, which accorded with long-standing demands of British industry, the competitiveness of British service providers, and Thatcherite ideology" (Moravcsik 1998: 319). National barriers sustained through non-compliance would have left the UK with the worst possible outcome: restricted access to the European market combined with the "federalist" political reforms already agreed in the SEA, most notably the introduction of qualified majority voting. Moreover, the UK had traditionally been one of the most compliant member states in the Community. Sanctions would thus not be a measure that primarily threatened to afflict them. Rather, financial penalties would be a way of correcting existing asymmetries in member states' compliance records. By the same token, it was thought that "[s]anctions could have the effect of constraining the approach to the development of various other policies of states that, viewed from the British perspective, appeared to be over-enthusiastic in agreeing ways forward but less impressive in implementing them" (Mendrinou 1996: 14).

Prepared to compromise with national sovereignty, given the promise of a level and open playing field in Europe, the British government answered the supranational institutions' calls for sanctions. The UK proposal targeted disrespect for ECJ judgments, though it was thought that this *ultima ratio* option would also have a deterrent effect on non-compliance in general. The essence of the proposal was a revision of the existing Article 171 that would add teeth to this declaratory article. Under this proposal, the Commission and the ECJ would have the option of imposing financial penalties on a member state once non-compliance with a first judgment had been established in a second decision, following a repeated infringement proceeding.

The UK proposal was favorably received by the other member governments. In view of previous reluctance to consider sanctions, this degree of support may seem puzzling. Three factors explain the endorsement. To start with, the other governments, too, found the compliance problems worrying. Whereas not every government fully shared the UK's enthusiasm for the deregulatory aspects of the internal market exercise, and some had supported it for its reregulatory and integration-driving elements, all found widespread non-compliance threatening to the realization of the project. This was evidenced not least by a declaration on the implementation of Community law that was attached by the member governments to the TEU at Maastricht.[2]

Second, it bears repeating that the UK constituted the most sovereignty-conscious member state of all. If the British government supported this reinforcement of the supranational institutions' powers, then it would have been surprising indeed, if the others had found the consequences for national sovereignty prohibitive. The member states that should have found the trade-off between compliance and sovereignty least attractive were those with the most to lose from the introduction of sanctions. However, the states with the worst compliance records concerning ECJ judgments were Italy and Belgium – two staunchly federalist countries and ardent supporters of the supranational institutions.

The third and final factor explaining the widespread approval of the UK proposal was the proposal itself. For a treaty revision introducing sanctions, the amendment of Article 171 could hardly have been less consequential in terms of national sovereignty. The design of the sanctioning mechanism, with the requirement of two judgments and two full rounds of the infringement procedure, guaranteed that only very few cases could become subject to the imposition of sanctions, and that this would not be a means for everyday enforcement of EU rules.

The Commission widens the range of possible sanctions

The Commission's immediate response to the British proposal was not one of overwhelming enthusiasm. Stephen Weatherill and Paul Beaumont describe the Commission's response as "lukewarm" (1995: 210). Yet this response must be seen in the tactical context of the IGC. When the UK put the question of sanctions on the IGC agenda, this provided a window of opportunity for the Commission. Not since the founding fathers had decided against the inclusion of sanctioning provisions in the EEC treaty, had sanctions been on the table of intergovernmental negotiations in the Community. In addition, the reaction of other member governments was one of support for the UK's initiative. In this context, it would have been unwise of the Commission to enthusiastically endorse an option regarded as secondary to other alternative sanctioning mechanisms. Instead, the Commission chose to distribute a paper at the IGC that evaluated a wide set of possible arrangements, the UK proposal and its own prioritized options included (European Commission 1991a). This contribution is given an in-depth treatment here as it unveiled the Commission's thinking on sanctions, constituted an attempt to induce governments into endorsing the sanctioning arrangements most favored by the Commission, and set forth proposals that the supranational institutions would later act on independently in spite of member governments' dismissal at the IGC.

The document sketched four alternative ways of introducing penalties for failure to comply with European rules. The first possibility, immediately dismissed by the Commission, was a sanctioning provision such as the one in the ECSC treaty. Given earlier Commission statements in favor of this form of sanctioning arrangement, the dismissal was somewhat surprising. Two explanations were forwarded. First, the provisions in the ECSC treaty had never actually been used, and there was a suspicion that the same misfortune would afflict corresponding means in the EEC treaty. Second, and more importantly, the sanction of countermeasures, though conceivable in a limited policy domain such as coal and steel, ran the risk of actually dismantling the internal market by introducing new barriers as member states retaliated against non-compliance.

The second possible arrangement was the British proposal. The approach was, as noted above, one of careful and constructive criticism. The Commission considered this form of mechanism doable and suggested that one alternative would be to give the ECJ the power to decide, or to authorize the Commission to decide, to suspend payments to the offending state or to impose a financial penalty. As for the downside of the proposal, the Commission stressed practical as well as political difficulties. Practically, it would be difficult to set the penalty at such a level that it would be both effective and balanced, given the divergences in member states' financial situation. Politically, it was essential that an independent institution – either the ECJ alone or the Commission acting with the ECJ's authorization – set the amount and imposed the sanction, and that the Council was left out of the matter: "If the Council were to be involved, the spirit of mutual understanding between the Member States, or indeed their complicity (if several of them were guilty of an infringement), could make the sanction ineffectual in practice" (European Commission 1991a: 130).

Having dismissed ECSC sanctions and presented its reservations regarding the UK proposal, the Commission turned to the two options it preferred. Both pertained to decentralized enforcement through national courts, both involved the sanction of state liability, and both were relatively less resource demanding for the supranational institutions. The third alternative sanctioning mechanism was an amplification of Article 5 of the EEC treaty. In its existing version, Article 5 conferred a general duty on the member states to take all appropriate measures to ensure the fulfillment of their obligations under Community law. One of the requirements imposed by this article and the ECJ's jurisprudence in the matter was the adequate provision in national legal systems of remedies for individuals suffering from state non-compliance with Community rules. Uneven and sometimes inadequate provision of such remedies rendered the situation far from satisfactory, however, spurring the Commission to suggest that these requirements be spelled out explicitly in the treaty. Among the requirements the Commission wished to see specified were judicial remedies for citizens, financial liability of public authorities toward the victims, and the possibility of interim measures. The Commission concluded by stating that the EU institutions could be endowed with the power to harmonize or coordinate the rules in national legal systems on this point.

The fourth sanctioning arrangement considered by the Commission was a suggestion to extend the jurisdiction of the ECJ in cases concerning state non-compliance with treaty obligations. Here, the Commission canvassed a number of possible extensions, among them, the power to annul or declare national law incompatible with Community law, and the power to specify what measures a member state had to take to end an infringement. Most favored was the proposal for granting the ECJ the power to explicitly declare in judgments that infringements render offending member states financially liable toward those individuals whose EC rights had been violated. Comparing state liability to the British proposal for a sanctioning mechanism, the Commission found the first to be superior: "A real possibility of having this liability duly established would have a much greater deterrent effect on Member States than the possibility of being ordered to make fixed or periodic penalty payments" (1991a: 133).

The outcome: a revised Article 171

The Commission did not succeed in garnering government support for its preferred solutions. Article 5 had already been criticized by member governments as being a tool too frequently used by the ECJ to expand the European judicial order (Caranta 1995: 704). Furthermore, the specification by an intergovernmental treaty of the procedural rules of internal legal systems would have infringed the institutional autonomy of national courts, as would also the Commission's audacious bid for powers to harmonize remedy provisions in national legal orders. The proposals to endow the ECJ with the power to specify the consequences of its compliance judgments – measures to be taken and financial compensation to victims – challenged entrenched government positions on the ECJ's competence. In the case of financial liability for public authorities, the realization of the proposal would have introduced a principle that did not even exist in all national legal systems for violations of national law. While, indeed, the dismissal of these suggestions spoke for itself, EU governments also took the opportunity to respond in point, in the declaration 19 attached to the TEU: "[I]t must be for each Member State to determine how the provisions of Community law can best be enforced in light of its own particular institutions, legal system and other circumstances."

Member governments settled instead for a less consequential and more sovereignty-friendly alternative. The UK proposal had been presented in the early stages of the IGC and the Commission's paper was distributed later in the spring of 1991. When the Luxembourg Presidency summed up the negotiations thus far in its draft treaty in June 1991, the British suggestion for amendment of Article 171 was included (Weatherill and Beaumont 1995: 210). Little suggests that the question was up for re-evaluation, as the Luxembourg draft proposals remained in place in the final version of Article 171, agreed at Maastricht in December 1991.

In their revision of Article 171, member governments followed the recommendations of the supranational institutions that the Commission should propose the amount of the penalty, while the ECJ should take the final decision to impose the penalty on the faulting member state. At the same time, however, governments opted for a more restricted choice of financial penalties, when excluding the possibility of suspending EU payments to offending member states. The revised Article 171 specified that the Commission, at the end of a second infringement proceeding, could propose a lump sum or penalty payment to be approved by the ECJ, if it found that the member state had failed to comply with its earlier judgment.[3]

The 1991 IGC and supranational influence

The process through which Article 171 was equipped with sanctions motivates a number of important theoretical observations.

First, both supranational supervisors and government principals were spurred into action by a growing awareness that existing enforcement means were insufficient to prevent non-compliance from undermining the internal market. Only by amending the treaty and adding sanctions to the enforcement arsenal could disrespect for Community rules be contained, argued the supranational institutions. That governments also came to support a move in this direction can only be understood in view of the threat posed by non-compliance to the completion of the Community's most ambitious project so far.

Second, the Commission sought to affect governments' choice of sanctioning mechanism by introducing alternative proposals, preferred from a supranational perspective. These proposals were consistently more resource efficient from the point of view of the supranational institutions, and were aimed at decentralized rather than centralized enforcement. However, the Commission's suggestions were also more threatening to national sovereignty.

Third, enjoying a privileged position vis-à-vis control of the agenda, national governments had little difficulty unveiling the consequences of the supranational proposals and blocking unwanted initiatives. By balancing the distribution of information and offering governments an extreme form of participation-based monitoring, the format of the IGC made supranational maneuvering exceedingly difficult. On the one hand, the IGC format, as opposed to everyday policy-making in the EU, entailed that governments were free to present their own proposals for sanctioning mechanisms without involving the Commission. Stripped of its monopoly on initiative, the Commission could not ensure that all possible agreements would have to be built around its own proposal. On the other hand, the IGC format permitted governments to fully peruse the Commission's suggestions for alternative sanctioning arrangements and to identify their implications. Well aware of the competing proposals' consequences for national sovereignty, EU governments chose a restrictive reinforcement of centralized enforcement over the more far-reaching alternative of formally recognizing and extending the decentralized enforcement system.

The 1996–7 IGC and the failure to boost sanctions

Though highly effective when used, the construction of the new sanctioning mechanism prevented it from functioning as an everyday enforcement weapon. In view of this limit, the Commission proposed at the 1996–7 IGC that Articles 169 and 171 be upgraded, so as to further boost the supranational supervisors' enforcement means. This time, member state principals were reluctant to confer new powers. Despite clever maneuvering on the part of the Commission, member governments had few difficulties identifying the implications of its proposals. The Commission was forced to dilute its suggestions until it could finally gain unanimous support for an extremely weakened intervention mechanism in the post-IGC period.

The new Article 171: effective when used, but seldom employed

The TEU entered into force on November 1, 1993 and in June 1994 the Commission informed member states that it was planning to make full use of its new enforcement instrument (European Commission 1995b: 1e). In formal terms, the new Article 171 granted additional competence primarily to the ECJ. Yet, in practical terms, it was the Commission that would be the real manager of this sanctioning power. It was up to the Commission to set sufficiently deterrent penalty levels and to decide when cases should be referred to the ECJ for a decision. In mid-1996, the Commission implemented the new sanctioning provisions by laying down criteria for the setting of penalty levels. The criteria were communicated to member states in the form of two memoranda that fulfilled the twin function of deterrence as well as information (European Commission 1996e, 1997b).

The Commission stated that it would employ penalty payments rather than lump sums, in view of the former measure's superior deterrence capacity. The level of the penalty payments would be based on the seriousness of the infringement, its duration, and the need to ensure that the penalty was sufficient to deter future infringements. To secure a sufficiently deterrent effect, the Commission would take into consideration the member states' ability to pay, as well as their weight in the Council. No member state – whether rich or poor, powerful or powerless – should have the capacity to lightly ignore the ECJ's judgments.

The Commission made use of the new sanctioning power for the first time in January 1997, when proposing penalties on Germany and Italy in five cases. Reflecting the criteria laid down by the Commission, the amounts suggested were highly deterrent, ranging from 26,400 to 264,000 euros per day. Commenting on the decision, Commissioner Ritt Bjerregaard stated:

> It is the first time that the Commission makes use of its powers according to article 171 in the Treaty. It is also high time. The public and the European Parliament are waiting impatiently as they rightly see article 171 as a needed means to improve implementation in general and in the environment and internal market in particular.
>
> (European Commission 1997a)

Table 5.1 summarizes all the cases where the Commission requested penalties between 1997 and 2001. The unequivocal picture is one of a highly deterrent mechanism. The table illustrates that member states have been quick to back down when penalties have been proposed. In only one case have the Commission and the ECJ been forced to actually impose the proposed penalties (Greek waste-dumping in Crete). In most cases, member states complied once the Commission had taken its decision, and before their cases were referred to the ECJ for the second time. The domains with the greatest number of cases have been environmental policy, internal market policy, and social policy; while Greece, Germany, France, and Italy are the member states that have been subject to the greatest number of penalty decisions.

Notwithstanding this effectiveness in bringing about compliance, the revised Article 171 has been a mixed success. The provisions have only been employed in a limited number of cases, and the mechanism certainly has not demonstrated any capacity to function as a general means of enforcement. The sanctioning procedure has suffered from weaknesses similar to those of the infringement procedure, which is not surprising, since it consists of two such proceedings with the threat of sanctions tagged on at the end. The two rounds of informal consultations, letters of formal notice, reasoned opinions, referrals to the ECJ, and court judgments have made the procedure extremely heavy (interview, Commission official, December 15, 1997). In addition, governments effectively circumscribed the compliance problems that could be addressed by this enforcement weapon, when only permitting sanctions to be applied in response to non-compliance with ECJ judgments.

Reflecting on the Commission's enforcement instruments as upgraded by

Table 5.1 Commission requests for penalty payments under Article 228 (ex. Art. 171), 1997–2001

Member state	*Policy area*	*Date of first judgment*	*Date COM decision*	*Penalty euro/day*	*Status*
Italy	Environment	09.06.1993	29.01.1997	159,300	Closed before penalty
Italy	Environment	13.12.1991	29.01.1997	123,900	Closed before penalty
Germany	Environment	17.10.1991	29.01.1997	158,400	Closed before penalty
Germany	Environment	03.07.1990	29.01.1997	26,400	Closed before penalty
Germany	Environment	28.01.1991	29.01.1997	264,000	Closed before penalty
Greece	Environment	07.04.1992	26.06.1997	24,600	Closed after penalty
Belgium	Environment	08.07.1987	10.12.1997	7,750	Closed before penalty
Greece	Internal market	15.03.1988	10.12.1997	61,500	Closed before penalty
Greece	Internal market	23.03.1995	10.12.1997	41,000	Closed before penalty
France	Internal market	13.01.1993	31.03.1998	158,250	Closed before penalty
France	Environment	27.04.1988	24.06.1998	105,500	Closed before penalty
Greece	Internal market	02.05.1996	24.06.1998	39,975	Closed before penalty
Italy	Environment	12.12.1996	02.12.1998	185,850	Closed before penalty
Luxembourg	Social policy	02.07.1996	02.12.1998	14,000	Closed before penalty
France	Social policy	13.03.1997	21.04.1999	142,425	Withdrawn
Greece	Internal market	02.07.1996	01.07.1999	57,400	Closed before penalty
Belgium	Internal market	03.05.1993	22.12.1999	43,400	Closed before penalty
Luxembourg	Social policy	29.10.1998	22.12.1999	6,000	Closed before penalty
Italy	Transport	11.11.1999	21.12.2000	88,500	Closed before penalty
Germany	Environment	22.10.1998	21.12.2000	237,600	Withdrawn
UK	Environment	14.07.1993	21.12.2000	106,800	Withdrawn
Spain	Environment	12.02.1998	23.05.2001	45,600	In process
France	Fishing	11.06.1991	20.12.2001	316,500	In process
Luxembourg	Transport	16.12.1999	20.12.2001	9,000	In process

Source: European Commission 2002a: 15–18.

the revised Article 171, a centrally placed Commission official concluded in 1996: "It could be argued that the Commission's enforcement powers against member states ultimately are not all that strong, and it may be something that ought to be looked at in the context of the IGC" (interview, March 22, 1996). The Commission would later launch intense efforts to place this issue on the agenda of the 1996–7 IGC, and to engineer government support for revisions to its infringement and sanctioning procedures.

Calls for further sanctioning powers meet with state opposition

The decision to convene a new IGC in 1996 had already been taken by EU governments at the preceding IGC and had been subsequently inscribed in the TEU. Following a decision by the European Council at its Corfu summit in June 1994, a "Reflection Group" was set up and charged with the task of preparing the work of the IGC. The Reflection Group – composed of representatives of the member states, the Commission, and the Parliament – began its work in early June 1995 and presented its final report at the European Council summit in Madrid in December 1995. The IGC was opened in Turin on March 29, 1996.

Neither of the supranational institutions touched upon the new sanctioning provisions in their 1995 reports to the Reflection Group. The Commission's Legal Service held the position that no assessment could be conducted, since no case commenced under the new regime had yet reached the sanctioning stage (internal Commission memo, February 22, 1995). On this note, the Commission shied away from suggesting further revisions, and instead repeated its intention of making use of this new power when given due reason and opportunity (European Commission 1995e: 33). Echoing the Commission, the ECJ declined to comment on the amended Article 171, as it had still not been asked to apply the new provisions (European Court of Justice 1995: 3, 5).

The question of sanctions was nevertheless raised in the work of the Reflection Group. In an oral presentation to the Group, the Belgian member, law professor Franklin Dehousse, proposed that Article 171 be removed and its sanctioning provisions inserted into Article 169 (internal Commission memo, November 15, 1995; interview, Commission official, January 7, 1998). The rationale of this proposition was to simplify and shorten the sanctioning procedure. Financial penalties would be already imposed on member states after the first ECJ judgment and the subsequent establishment of continued non-compliance. This suggestion received meager support among the other state representatives, who generally considered it politically unacceptable (interview, Commission official, January 7, 1998). In its final report, the Reflection Group confined itself to noting: "A few have suggested the possibility of enabling the Court to enforce more swiftly the penalties it may impose" (1995: 33).

Despite the negative reception of the Belgian proposal, this was the spark that set the Commission in motion and made the upgrading of supranational enforcement powers a question also for the 1996–7 IGC. No longer was the absence of actual proceedings under the new Article 171 a sufficient reason to refrain from criticizing the weaknesses of this sanctioning arrangement. In truth, it did not take actual experience of the new provisions to understand that the sanctioning procedure would be excessively, perhaps even prohibitively, slow and cumbersome.

In an internal analysis, the Commission's Legal Service found the Belgian proposal an attractive solution to the problem of protracted infringement and sanctioning proceedings (internal Commission memo, November 15, 1995). Yet the proposed solution suffered from a number of deficiencies as well.[4] This motivated the Legal Service to suggest that a preferable option would be to maintain Article 171, but to remove its administrative phase, so that the ECJ could be seized immediately.

In late 1995 and early 1996, the Commission services continued discussing ways of shortening the sanctioning procedure (internal Commission memos, December 8, 1995, January 15 and 22, 1996). The suggestion of eliminating the administrative phase of the sanctioning procedure received growing support. In addition, the internal market directorate campaigned for greater enforcement powers within its policy domain. When the Commission presented its opinion on the themes of the IGC in late February 1996, the inclusion of both these elements marked an essential difference compared to the Commission's report to the Reflection Group one year earlier:

> To consolidate the rule of law as the basis of the Union, the proper implementation and enforcement of Community law has to be assured. . . . The Commission therefore believes that: the means available to it to enforce Community law should be made more effective, notably as regards the internal market; there should be a stronger role for the Court of Justice, particularly as regards compliance with its judgments.
>
> (European Commission 1996c: 4)

The Commission's calls fell on deaf ears. Whereas the Commission had mobilized for a campaign on the issue of supranational enforcement powers, member governments had not found any reason to re-evaluate this question. Summarizing the negotiations two months into the IGC, the Italian Presidency flatly concluded that a strengthening of existing enforcement powers was a non-issue: "[I]t is not thought necessary to amend Article 171 of the TEU" (IGC 1996b: 8).

Commission maneuvering reinstates enforcement on the agenda

Government intransigence did not deter the Commission. The supranational supervisor was intent on providing member state principals with additional opportunities and reasons to delegate the enforcement means necessary to effectively combat non-compliance. Instead of taking no for an answer, the Commission reformulated its original proposals and sought intergovernmental channels for reinstating them on the IGC agenda.

In the spring of 1997, with only a few months left to the closing of the IGC, the Commission's internal market directorate prepared a proposal with concrete suggestions on how to improve the speed and efficiency of the infringement and sanctioning procedures (internal Commission memo, April 3 , 1997). Two propositions were presented that combined in a solution not previously considered. First, it was suggested that reasoned opinions should be replaced by reasoned decisions, in effect granting the Commission the competence to adjudicate compliance cases. Second, it was suggested that the sanctioning provisions of Article 171 be attached to Article 169 instead, thereby reducing the time it takes to get to the stage of sanctions. If a member state decided not to comply with the Commission's reasoned decision, then the case together with a penalty request could be referred to the ECJ for approval.

One way for the Commission to plant issues on the agenda of an ongoing IGC is to convince receptive governments to present its proposals as their own. As a Commission official in the task force monitoring the IGC put it: "You can always lobby a member state or the Presidency to present a Commission proposal under their own name" (interview, January 26, 1998). This was the strategy chosen to put the new proposal on the agenda. In early May 1997, the Italian government submitted a proposal to the IGC that was, as one Commission official modestly expressed it, "Commission inspired" (IGC 1997b; interview, February 3, 1998). Save for two, admittedly important, modifications, it was exactly the same document. Both alterations weakened the Commission's original proposal. First, the Italian government suggested limiting the upgrading of Article 169 to the field of the internal market by inserting instead a new paragraph in Article 100a. Second, rather than removing Article 171 and attaching the sanctioning provisions to Article 169, it was proposed that the administrative stage of the sanctioning procedure be eliminated.

This proposal, which had not been part of Italy's original position on the themes of the IGC, did not fly with the majority of the other member governments (IGC 1996a). However, it inspired the Spanish government to present a slightly revised version in early June, following domestic turbulence in Spain that pointed to the need for rapid means to safeguard the internal market. The Spanish proposal did not differ in any major way from the Italian one, and was granted the same reception by governments (internal Commission memo, June 9, 1997). When the IGC came to a close with the European Council summit in Amsterdam, June 16–17, 1997, the treaty agreed upon did not contain any new provisions that strengthened the enforcement weapons of the supranational institutions.

Analyzing the failure, the Commission suggests two primary reasons why the Commission-inspired Italian and Spanish proposals did not gain the support of the other governments. The first explanation points to the late arrival of the issue on the agenda (interview, Commission official, December 15, 1997). With only a few weeks to go and an immensely crowded IGC agenda – most of the important decisions had been put off until the end – new, controversial issues were less than welcome, and stood a very limited chance of being worked out in time to be included in the new treaty. The second explanation stresses the consequences for national sovereignty of the proposed measures. These proposals included variants of suggestions that governments had discarded at the 1991 IGC and at earlier stages of the 1996–7 IGC. On every occasion, a corresponding strengthening of the supranational institutions' enforcement powers had been perceived as highly threatening to national sovereignty. As one Commission official involved in the drafting of the original proposal acknowledged: "No matter when introduced [during the IGC], the proposal would have been too contentious" (interview, February 3, 1998).

But why did governments oppose more effective sanctions in 1997 when they had been in favor of introducing sanctions in 1991? A brief comparison between 1991 and 1996–7 suggests that governments' compliance concerns had evolved in a direction that made them less willing to pay the price in national sovereignty for the gain in improved compliance. Whereas member state principals in 1991 had been receptive to the idea of stronger enforcement powers because of mounting compliance problems and the approaching 1992 deadline, the situation in 1996–7 did not produce similar concerns. The internal market was up and running (albeit with certain childhood diseases), the primary focus had shifted to the process of enlarging the EU to Central and Eastern Europe, and non-compliance with ECJ judgments had actually declined since the early 1990s.

The post-IGC game: stripping the proposal of contentious elements

Though unmistakably a failure, the conclusion of the IGC still left hope for the future. At Amsterdam, the Commission had managed to get a "hook" into the European Council conclusions, which opened the door to future supranational proposals in this area:

> The European Council underlines the crucial importance of timely and correct transposition of all agreed legislation into national law, the need fully to inform citizens and business about the Single Market, and the necessity of active enforcement of Community law in the Member States and the introduction of more rapid and effective procedures for problem-solving including deliberations at Council level in cases of recurring problems. The European Council requests the Commission to examine ways and means of guaranteeing in an effective manner the free movement of goods. It requests the Commission to submit relevant proposals before its next meeting in December 1997.
>
> (European Council 1997: 11–12)

This hook provided the Commission with an opportunity to revise its proposal and present it anew to member governments in a format more likely to be accepted (interviews, Commission officials, December 15, 1997 and February 3, 1998). The practice of using summit conclusions as a launching pad for Commission proposals was nothing original, but a common Commission tactic. As one senior Commission official, cited by John Peterson, has asserted: "[Summit declarations] give you a knock out blow in negotiations. If you can cite a European Council conclusion in a debate you're away" (Peterson 1995: 72). In this case, it permitted the Commission to develop a proposal for a regulation during the fall of 1997.

When the Internal Market Council met for an informal meeting in Echternach, Luxembourg, at the beginning of October 1997, Commissioner Mario Monti recalled the Amsterdam mandate and declared his intention to present a legislative proposal for means to rapidly correct internal market violations (internal Commission memo, October 10, 1997). At the meeting, the governments of Italy, Spain, and Portugal were, not surprisingly, quick to support this initiative. On November 18, the full Commission adopted the proposal for a Council regulation (European Commission 1997f; see also 1997g, 1998c: iv; *European Voice* November 6–12, 1997: 1). The regulation would endow the Commission with special powers in cases involving serious obstacles to the free movement of goods. The Commission would be permitted to request, through a binding decision, member states to remove such obstacles within a particular time period, after which it could rapidly seize the ECJ through an accelerated infringement procedure. While still an appeal for new substantive enforcement powers, the proposal was nevertheless a shadow of its former self. Drafted on the philosophy that "a limited proposal is more likely to be accepted by the member states" (interview, Commission official, February 3, 1998), this version excluded the most contentious elements of the Commission-inspired Italian and Spanish proposals presented at the IGC.

The reception of the proposal was mixed. When member governments were given the opportunity to react at the Internal Market Council in late November, their general response was positive, though with certain legal and institutional objections (internal Commission memo, December 1, 1997). When the issue was next considered at the informal meeting of the Internal Market Council in Cambridge in mid-February 1998, governments repeated their support for the idea in principle, but also "expressed doubts about the proposal, questioning the legal basis for Internal Market Commissioner Mario Monti's attempts to speed up procedures to punish governments which fail to dismantle serious obstacles" (*European Voice* February 19–25, 1998: 31). The positive element should be understood against the backdrop of the Commission's now more sovereignty-friendly proposal, as well as the French lorry drivers' strike in late 1997, which illustrated graphically that the Commission lacked the powers necessary to secure the free movement of goods in Europe (*European Voice* February 5–11, 1998: 5, February 19–25, 1998: 31). The negative element should be understood in view of the still far-reaching strengthening of the Commission's powers that such a regulation would entail and the fear that it would have implications for the democratic right to strike, laid down in the national law of the member states (European Commission 1998e; *European Voice* February 5–11, 1998: 5, February 19–25, 1998: 31).

Though weaker than previous proposals, the draft regulation was still not uncontroversial and certainly did not enjoy the support of all governments, which was necessary given the requirement of unanimity in the Council. On the contrary, the Commission testifies that almost all governments opposed the proposal as it stood: "[L]a quasi-unanimité des Etats membres s'est opposée au mécanisme d'intervention tel que proposé par la Commission car, selon eux, il conférait un pouvoir de décision à la Commission qui allait rompre l'équilibre institutionnel voulu par le Traité" (European Commission 1998h: 11). It was clear that the Commission would have to agree to a further dilution of the proposal if it wanted anything to come out of its efforts.

Following the failure of Commissioner Monti to secure support for the proposal at the Internal Market Council in late March 1998, the British Presidency engaged the other governments in attempts to find a solution which would be acceptable to all parties. The late spring of 1998 witnessed the welding of such a compromise, and at the Internal Market Council on May 18, member governments reached a unanimous political agreement on the establishment of a rapid intervention mechanism (*European Voice* May 20–7, 1998: 31). In substance, the agreement entailed a significant weakening of the Commission's November proposal. Instead of special powers, the Commission was only granted the right to notify states of the existence of barriers to the free movement of goods, and in a non-legally binding resolution, member states confirmed their commitment to this principle.

Through consecutive steps of adaptation to the preferences of EU governments, the Commission proposal, envisaging a significant upgrading of Articles 169 and 171, had been watered down to an unrecognizable regulation, laying down an impotent intervention mechanism.[5]

The 1996–7 IGC and supranational influence

The negotiations in association with the 1996–7 IGC bring home three points of particular relevance to the P–S–A model.

First, the Commission responded to the incapacity of existing means to secure compliance with requests that member state principals delegate more far-reaching powers, and with attempts to maneuver governments into accepting supranational proposals. The impetus behind this activity was not actual experience of the new Article 171 as much as the realization that the construction of the sanctioning mechanism limited its capacity to effectively contain non-compliance. All the Commission's suggestions were targeted at ways in which the infringement and sanctioning procedures could be made more efficient, and thereby more effective and deterrent.

Second, from beginning to end, this process illustrates the Commission's limited capacity to engineer agreement for proposals that would have brought an increase in the supranational institutions' enforcement powers. Because of government principals' control over the agenda at the IGC, and the relative symmetry of information on the consequences of treaty article revisions, it was exceedingly difficult for the Commission to gain approval for planted proposals, even when these were dressed up as government initiatives. At no stage did the consequences of the Commission's enforcement-enhancing suggestions escape member governments. These results accord with general assessments of the IGC. Mark Pollack notes that the 1996–7 IGC constituted an "an information-rich context relatively unconducive to entrepreneurial agenda-setting" (1999: 13) and Andrew Moravcsik and Kalypso Nicolaïdis (1999) attribute the general lack of supranational influence to clear and stable member state preferences and a balanced distribution of information.

Third, member states' greater reluctance to strengthen EU enforcement in 1996–7, as compared to 1991, is best explained by shifts in the trade-off between national sovereignty and compliance. The proposals presented at the 1996–7 IGC would have entailed a more profound reinforcement of supranational enforcement powers. But, in addition, compliance concerns figured less prominently, with the internal market in place and the compliance with ECJ judgments improving.

Conclusion

Intergovernmental conferences offer an opportunity for the EU's supranational institutions to exert independent influence by planting and engineering accord for proposals that governments otherwise would not agree to. This chapter has shown, however, that the format of the IGC facilitates member state control and effectively reduces the capacity of the institutions to push enforcement beyond governments' wishes. The inadequacy of existing enforcement means moved the supranational supervisors to request more far-reaching powers at both the 1991 and 1996–97 IGCs. Balancing the distribution of information, governments' control of the agenda and the transparency of the supranational proposals enabled state principals to easily identify the implications for national sovereignty. Member governments' decision in 1991 to introduce sanctions into the treaty, while refraining from a further reinforcement of this power in 1997, is best explained by their unprecedented concern with non-compliance in the early 1990s.

6 Decentralized enforcement through national courts

The supranational creation of new powers

The third and final strategy in the supranational institutions' efforts to boost EU enforcement consisted of the independent creation of new means of supervision. Perceiving centralized "police-patrol" enforcement as limited in its capacity to secure adequate compliance, and decentralized "fire-alarm" enforcement as holding the promise of more efficient and effective supervision, the supranational supervisors independently initiated a gradual shift toward the latter in the late 1980s. Through a string of important decisions, the ECJ laid down principles and requirements, strengthening the hand of individuals wishing to enforce their EU rights in national courts. In parallel, the Commission launched policy initiatives aimed at ameliorating weaknesses in the existing structure of decentralized enforcement.

These efforts qualify as attempts to move the EU's enforcement system beyond the wishes of national governments, which explicitly had decided not to strengthen decentralized enforcement at the 1991 IGC. Reflecting the variance in the monitoring mechanisms of member state principals, the Commission was markedly more constrained in its actions than the ECJ, whose judicial independence greatly facilitated the introduction of enforcement measures unwelcome in the capitals of Europe. Member states responded through two parallel attempts to sanction the ECJ: the campaign by some member governments to clip the wings of the ECJ at the 1996–7 IGC, and the recalcitrant reception of the new jurisprudence by some national governments and courts. While the sanction of treaty revision failed as a result of the high institutional barriers involved, the sanction of inaction succeeded in limiting, at least partially and temporarily, the effects of the ECJ's activism in the area of enforcement. Yet the net result of this process is a clear supranational imprint on the system of enforcement in the EU.

This chapter is divided into four sections. In the first, I account for the motives behind the shift toward greater reliance on decentralized enforcement, as well as introduce the gist of the Commission's and the ECJ's steps. The second section analyzes the ECJ's establishment of the principle of state liability, while the third section deals with the Commission's Citizens First and Robert Schuman programs. The fourth and final section examines the two forms of sanctions launched against the ECJ.

Toward effective decentralized enforcement

The supranational supervisors' motives for shifting the center of gravity in EU enforcement rested both with the limits of centralized supervision and the merits of decentralized supervision. Yet decentralized supervision, too, suffered from certain deficiencies. The supranational institutions' efforts to boost enforcement through national courts were directed at these identified weaknesses.

The promise of effective decentralized enforcement

It became increasingly clear in the late 1980s that centralized enforcement alone would not be sufficient to secure compliance with European rules in general and internal market rules in particular. As the influential director-general of the Commission's Legal Service, Claus-Dieter Ehlermann, stated at the time: "After almost ten years of energetic policy regarding infringements, practical and legal limits of this centralized control mechanism have now become clearly apparent" (1988: 146; see also Ehlermann 1992: 225; Steiner 1993: 6–7). As described in Chapters 4 and 5, the next decade would bring a set of efficiency-enhancing reforms as well as the delegation of certain sanctioning powers. These improvements notwithstanding, centralized enforcement suffered from inherent and permanent weaknesses, limiting its ability to secure adequate compliance.

The infringement and sanctioning procedures were by design exceedingly slow, or as the Commission itself put it, "by definition time-consuming" (1997d: 8). While the Commission's internal reforms succeeded in reducing the time required for handling infringement cases within the institution, they were not capable of changing the structure of these procedures. Lamented one Commission official: "No matter how much we speed it up, it is always going to be a slow procedure" (interview, February 2, 1998). In addition, the management of centralized enforcement was extremely resource demanding. Given the Commission's limited resources, further reliance solely on this form of supervision would have resulted in a declining quality of enforcement.[1] With the shift from legal implementation to concrete application of the internal market rules, the need for effective monitoring would reach an "unprecedented scale" (European Commission, 1989c: 4), in view of which the Commission perceived its existing resources as "clearly insufficient" (ibid. 1993c: 11).[2] The limits of the means of centralized enforcement obliged the supranational institutions to consider and search for alternative forms of supervision. Concluded Ehlermann: "[C]entralized control alone will never ensure that Community law is observed in all Member States, whatever effort is made to strengthen this control" (1988: 147).

A boosting of decentralized enforcement became the supranational supervisors' solution to the problem of inadequate enforcement means at the centralized level. This idea had been brewing in Brussels and Luxembourg for quite a few years. As shown in the previous chapter, early supranational calls for the delegation of sanctioning powers had included the option of some form of principle of state liability permitting individuals to sue and obtain compensation from non-compliant states in national courts. In the mid- to late 1980s, early thinking crystallized into a concrete alternative for the enforcement of Community rules. Again, Ehlermann expressed most clearly the Commission's reasoning at the time:

> I would like to present you with the following principle: instead of concentrating only on the functioning of centralized control, the Commission, the European Parliament and the Council should focus as much, if not more, attention on strengthening decentralized control of the implementation of Community law. . . . In a Community of 12 Member States, with some 320 million inhabitants, we think it more important also to be able to count on the decentralized control mechanisms, triggered by private individuals and enterprises obtaining redress before national courts.
>
> (Ehlermann 1988: 147–8)

Sharing this vision of how EC supervision should develop, Giuseppe Ciavarini Azzi, director in charge of enforcement coordination at the Commission's Secretariat General, submitted that "the future lies with the 'decentralized control' of the application of Community law" (1988: 200). The ECJ's consent to this assertion is most evident in the string of judgments that it began to hand down in the mid- to late 1980s, and the EP, too, encouraged a development in this direction (European Parliament 1988: 10). These public announcements indicating a new line of thinking on enforcement prompted a legal observer to conclude in 1989: "The advantages of decentralized supervision on the enforcement of Community law, through national courts and other bodies, are beginning to find wider recognition" (Bronckers 1989: 529).[3]

From the perspective of the supranational institutions, decentralized enforcement carried two primary advantages, mirroring the general merits of "fire-alarm" supervision, in comparison to "police-patrol" oversight (McCubbins and Schwartz 1984). First, decentralized enforcement would not be constrained by the Commission's limited resources. Instead, it would shift the costs of supervision to individuals, enterprises, and national courts, and thereby alleviate some of the burden of enforcement placed on the Commission and the ECJ. This was particularly important in view of the internal market program:

> National courts must be in a position to resolve a larger proportion of cases concerning the conformity of rules or behaviour with Community law – the number of which can be expected to increase substantially in the context of the Single Market – if the Commission and the Court of Justice are not to be inundated.
>
> (European Commission 1993c: 17; see also 1996f: 23)

Furthermore, a move to decentralized enforcement would permit monitoring of state compliance on the ground, which centralized supervision was unable to perform.

Second, decentralized enforcement would allow individuals to secure their rights under Community law more directly and more quickly (European Commission 1993b: 11). Whereas the centralized enforcement procedures did not allow any direct access for citizens and companies, national procedures would grant individuals judicial standing and permit them to pursue directly cases against non-complying member states. Enforcement through national courts also held the promise of a quicker processing of cases, and thus of a more rapid correction of member state infringements. In a wider perspective, this advantage of decentralized enforcement tied into the more general wish to involve citizens more closely in European affairs.

> Whatever the reaction of any government, a 'grass roots' construction certainly responds better to the aspirations of the 320 million Europeans living in the Community than the prospect of an insatiable superstructure which in the last resort is unable to ensure compliance by national administrations with the Community legal system.
>
> (Ehlermann 1988: 150)

The weaknesses of existing decentralized enforcement

The basic building blocks of the decentralized enforcement structure had been laid down already in the 1960s with the ECJ's establishment of the principles of direct effect and the supremacy of EU law. Through these doctrines, the ECJ turned the preliminary ruling system under Article 177 from a mechanism that allowed individuals to challenge EC law in national courts into a means for challenging national law and enforcing EC law in national courts (Stein 1981; Rasmussen 1986; Weiler 1991). The principle of direct effect, laid down in the 1963 judgment *Van Gend & Loos* (Case 26/62, 1963), posited that EC law created legally enforceable rights for individuals, allowing them to invoke Community provisions directly before national courts. The principle of the supremacy of EC law, first established in the 1964 decision *Costa* v. *ENEL* (Case 6/64, 1964), stipulated that EC law "trumps" national law when in conflict. Together, these doctrines turned the preliminary ruling procedure on its head, as the combined effect was to make national courts legally compelled to ignore conflicting national law and to enforce individuals' rights under EC law.

When the supranational institutions took steps to boost decentralized enforcement in the late 1980s and early 1990s, this form of "fire-alarm" supervision had already been in operation for more than two decades. After some initial opposition among many national courts, these had accepted the obligation to enforce the EC rights of citizens and companies, and to refer cases to the ECJ when interpretative uncertainty so demanded.[4] National courts had become the linchpins of the European legal system and had entered into a symbiotic relationship with the ECJ. A functional division was established, where the ECJ interpreted Community law, while national courts referred cases to the ECJ and later applied its interpretation to the facts of these cases. From a very limited number of references yearly in the 1960s, these increased to around 50 in the mid-1970s, slightly over 100 in the early 1980s, and close to 200 around 1990 (Stone Sweet and Brunell 1998: 74).

While revolutionary in its creation of a new tier of enforcement, this transformation of the preliminary ruling system was not sufficient to turn national courts, individuals, and enterprises into effective enforcers of Community law. As Josephine Steiner notes: "Although the fundamental principles of direct effect and supremacy of Community law were laid down in the 1960s and developed in the 1970s they did not prove adequate in themselves to protect individuals' Community rights or to deter member states from breaching Community law" (1995: 171). A number of problems plagued this decentralized enforcement structure, as it stood in the mid-1980s, rendering it insufficient both in terms of protecting Community rights and as a complement to centralized enforcement.

The first and primary weakness was the substantial differences between national legal systems in terms of procedural and substantive rules, making it exceedingly difficult to achieve an even and effective level of enforcement of Community law across all member states. Whereas all were obliged to enforce EC law, national courts were part of national legal systems, formed by different legal traditions and cultures. While stating in its early case law that it was not for the ECJ to harmonize or create new procedures and remedies, it nevertheless tried to achieve some degree of uniformity by laying down three basic principles to be followed by national courts: national treatment, non-discrimination, and effectiveness. The classic formula, containing all principles, was first introduced in the 1976 judgment *Rewe-Zentralfinanz* (Case 33/76, 1976). According to the ECJ, it was for the domestic system of each member state to designate the courts having jurisdiction and the procedural rules governing the protection of EC rights, as long as these conditions were not less favorable than those relating to similar domestic actions and did not make it impossible in practice to secure Community rights.

Notwithstanding these attempts by the ECJ to lay down principles ensuring an even and uniform enforcement of EC rules, there were substantial divergences in practice. Francis Jacobs, advocate-general at the ECJ, expresses the accepted truth among legal observers: "The inevitable consequence of relying on national remedies and procedures for the enforcement of Community law is that the latter is not applied with complete uniformity throughout the Community" (1997: 26). This was widely interpreted as a major weakness in the system of decentralized enforcement, not least in view of the entry into force of the internal market provisions in the early 1990s (e.g. European Commission 1992c: 38–51, 1993c: 16, 1996f: 18; Van Gerven 1995, 1996). Noted the Commission with concern:

> If businesses and individuals are to operate confidently in the single market, they need to know that there are adequate means of redress available to them should they run into problems. In a single Community market covering different national jurisdictions, this cannot be taken for granted.
>
> (European Commission 1995c: 15)

Jacobs went as far as to state: "The need for uniformity has often been stressed but the explanation is quite simply that, in the absence of uniformity, there would be no Community law" (cited in Van Gerven 1996: 514fn).

A second and related weakness emerged from the ECJ's attempts over the years to lay down conditions, criteria, and principles ensuring an effective and deterrent judicial protection of EC rights in national courts. Established one by one in a patchwork fashion, these rules and requirements brought near harmonization to certain aspects of national legal procedures and to the protection of certain EC rights, but not to others. One of the areas where the ECJ had taken few steps prior to the mid-1980s was remedies in national courts. Remedies are, slightly simplified, legal means or procedures that aggrieved parties may seek, and include, for example, the right to restitution of money paid contrary to applicable rules, the right to interim relief pending judgment, the right to damages for losses suffered as a result of infringements, and the right to judicial review. In the mid-1980s, it was highly unclear what forms of remedies were available for breaches of EC law, and where existing case law provided clues, the conclusion was not necessarily advantageous to the effective protection of EC rights (Steiner 1987; Szyszczak 1992: 691; Prechal 1997: 4). Most important in this chapter, it was recognized that no such thing as a general principle of state liability existed.

The third weakness of the decentralized structure of enforcement was informational. Enforcement through citizens and enterprises, safeguarding their European rights in national courts, can only be effective if individuals are aware of these rights and lawyers and judges are capable of identifying the Community dimension of the cases before them. In the late 1980s and early 1990s, however, the Commission found the awareness of EC rights and law wanting in both these key groups, which clearly impeded the effectiveness of decentralized enforcement (European Commission 1989c: 14, 1992c: 27–8, 38, 45, 1993c: 16). Not only did this lack of awareness entail a lower than optimal level of enforcement generally, but it also contributed to unfortunate variations in the application of EC law throughout the Community.

Boosting decentralized enforcement

As the ECJ and the Commission moved to boost decentralized enforcement, their efforts were directed at these identified weaknesses.[5] Like many times before, the supranational institutions worked in tandem for the attainment of a common goal (e.g. Stein 1981; Mancini 1991: 179; Burley and Mattli 1993: 71; Schmidt 2000). In this process, the ECJ laid down legal principles and requirements that the institutions had advocated for quite some time. These would ensure both a more uniform protection of EU rights and a more deterrent weapon against state non-compliance. The Commission, for its part, launched policy programs aimed at strengthening decentralized enforcement, which drew support and power from the principles and requirements laid down by the ECJ.

The ECJ's campaign to boost national courts as enforcers of EC rules began in the mid-1980s and stretched over more than a decade. Noted Steiner in 1995: "[T]he last decade has seen a determined effort on the part of the Court of Justice to increase the effective enforcement of Community law by extending the scope for its enforcement by individuals before their national courts" (1995: 171). The heart of this campaign coincided with, and was an expression of, what is widely acknowledged as a period of activism in the ECJ's jurisprudence, before a period of consolidation began in the early 1990s (Tridimas 1996: 200; Dehousse 1998: ch. 6). The focus of these efforts was the remedies available in national courts. As one observer concluded in 1992: "The recent case law of the Court reveals an intention to develop a coherent system of legal remedies" (Bebr 1992: 564).

In a string of groundbreaking decisions, the ECJ laid down principles and requirements for the remedies and procedures that citizens and companies should have access to in national courts when wishing to safeguard rights granted by EU rules. Marking the initiation of the ECJ's crusade, the judgment in *Von Colson* (Case 14/83, 1984) expanded the principle of effectiveness and required that national legal remedies be both sufficiently effective to protect individuals' EU rights and function as a deterrent against future non-compliance. In *Factortame I* (Case C-213/89, 1990) and *Zuckerfabrik* (Joined Cases C-143/88 and C-92/89, 1991), the ECJ substantially enhanced individuals' right to interim relief and established that this form of remedy would have to be provided, even where no such provisions existed in national law. In *Emmott* (Case C-208/90, 1991), the ECJ limited member states' ability to apply national limitation periods to cases brought against them and thereby to bar individuals from securing their rights in national courts. In *Marshall II* (Case C-271/91, 1993), the ECJ expanded individuals' rights to obtain damages from member states directly violating effective directives, stating that compensation must be adequate in relation to the damage. The culmination of the ECJ's attempts to ensure effective remedies in national courts was, however, its judgment in *Francovich* (Joined Cases C-6 and 9/90, 1991), where a completely new damages remedy was created – state liability – granting individuals and companies the right to financial compensation from non-complying member states.

Taken by themselves, these steps might seem disparate. But, as Francis Snyder emphasizes, when considered together with existing enforcement means in national courts and at the centralized Community level, "these elements can be seen to be interconnected, interdependent, forming a coherent whole and, in this sense, systematic" (1993: 40). Some legal observers describe this judicial campaign as the third stage in achieving a decentralized enforcement system, after the initial development of the doctrines of direct and indirect effect and EC law supremacy, while others compare it to the third pillar in an enforcement edifice (Steiner 1995: ch. 2; Goebel 1997; Dehousse 1998: 46–56). As Renaud Dehousse explains:

> [T]he ECJ has been able to construct a remarkable enforcement system, which is without precedent on the international plane. The whole edifice rests on three main pillars: an interpretation of the EC Treaty as a source of rights which may be invoked by private parties before courts, a procedural avenue for the dialogue between national courts and the ECJ (Article 177 preliminary rulings) and, more recently, a system of state liability for violations of Community law.
>
> (Dehousse 1998: 46)

Parallel to the ECJ's case law development, the Commission attempted to perfect the functioning of decentralized enforcement by launching a number of policy initiatives within the general framework of managing the internal market. The origin of these initiatives was a report presented in 1992 by the so-called High Level Group on the Operation of the Internal Market, chaired by former commissioner Peter Sutherland. The High Level Group had been requested by the Commission to identify potential problems and suggest a strategy as to how the full benefits of the internal market could be secured post-1992 (European Commission 1992c). On enforcement, the message was clear and unequivocal: centralized supervision must be increasingly supplemented by decentralized enforcement through national courts. Concrete recommendations stressed the need to raise the awareness of internal market rules among citizens and business, to improve the knowledge of EU law in the legal professions, to promote an approximation of sanctions against non-complying private parties, to inform individuals about the possibilities offered by the principle of state liability, and to generally work toward a uniform and effective enforcement of EU rules in national courts.

Most of the suggestions on enforcement outlined in the Sutherland report were subsequently included in the Commission's 1993 Strategic Programme on how to make the most of the internal market (European Commission 1993c; interview, Commission official, September 25, 1996). The Strategic Programme firmly endorsed the measures proposed and stressed the need to ensure that "the capacity of national courts to apply Community law is optimised" (European Commission 1993c: 16). Drawing on this general philosophy and the more specific proposals, the Commission developed, from about 1993 onward, a set of concrete policy initiatives aimed at boosting decentralized enforcement. The Citizens First initiative answered the calls for an information policy, making individuals aware of their rights in the internal market and how they should go about securing these. The Robert Schuman project sought to improve the knowledge of EU law in the legal professions. A Commission communication was issued, stressing member states' obligation to ensure that penalties in national courts against private parties infringing internal market rules were effective, proportionate, and dissuasive (European Commission 1995a). In another communication, the Commission proposed a Council act on improved judicial cooperation between the member states, in particular, a reinforcement of the mutual recognition of judgments (European Commission 1997i).

In the next two sections, I provide a detailed analysis of, first, the ECJ's development of the principle of state liability, and second, the Commission's launching of the Citizens First and Robert Schuman programs.

The ECJ and the principle of state liability

With the establishment of the principle of state liability, the ECJ created new, decentralized sanctions against member states who fail to comply with EU law. The fact that government principals had explicitly decided against fiercer sanctions than Article 171, as well as discarded the alternative of a state liability principle, did not discourage the supranational supervisor. The ease with which the ECJ could introduce measures colliding head on with the positions of EU governments is best attributed to member states' lack of capacity to intervene in ECJ decision-making through participation-based monitoring.

The ECJ establishes and expands the principle of state liability

The establishment of the principle of state liability is a cornerstone in the reinforcement of decentralized enforcement and one of the most significant developments in EU law in the 1990s.[6] Before this principle was introduced, national courts could only under very limited circumstances award damages to individuals who had suffered from member state non-compliance. The principle of direct effect only provided a remedy in the individual case, where Community acts clearly conferred directly enforceable rights. However, many directives did not fulfill the requirements of direct effect (e.g. directives pertaining to employee and consumer protection). To the extent that member states failed to implement such directives correctly or in time, individuals were deprived of the rights granted by these rules as well as incapable of claiming compensation in national courts. Neither did the principle of indirect effect offer a solution in this very common situation. As it stood in 1990, the decentralized enforcement system therefore provided neither adequate protection of individuals' EC rights, nor effective sanctions to deter member states from non-compliance.

The case of *Francovich* provided the perfect opportunity for the ECJ to close these dual gaps. The case arose as a result of the Italian government's failure to implement a directive regulating protection of employees in the event of an employer's insolvency. The directive required member states to operate guarantee institutions that would ensure the payment of outstanding salaries in cases of bankruptcy. The directive was supposed to have been implemented already in 1983, but despite this lengthy time period and an infringement judgment against the Italian state in 1989, no implementing measures had been taken when the *Francovich* case came before the ECJ in 1990 and was decided in 1991. The direct reason for the referral of the case to the ECJ was a suit in an Italian court against the Italian state by an employee, Mr Francovich, who had suffered from the non-implementation of this directive.

Recognizing that existing legal remedies did not offer any right to financial compensation in cases like this, the ECJ introduced a completely new remedy – state liability – that previously had not been acknowledged by the ECJ or recognized by legal observers as inherent in Community law (see, e.g. Simon and Barav 1987; Barav 1988). The ECJ established that the new principle was general in nature, and thus not dependent on direct effect. Relying on purposive and teleological reasoning, the ECJ argued that the full effectiveness of Community law would be called into question and that the protection of individuals' rights under it would be weakened, if compensation could not be obtained in cases where member states had violated EC law. The ECJ concluded by stating that this principle, given previous case law and the aims of the treaty, was in fact inherent in this judicial order:

> It follows that the principle whereby a State must be liable for loss and damage caused to individuals as a result of breaches of Community law for which the State can be held responsible is inherent in the system of the Treaty.
>
> (*Francovich*, para. 35)

In more specific terms, the ECJ determined that an individual can claim compensation, given that three conditions are satisfied:

1 that the directive confers rights on individuals;
2 that the contents of those rights are apparent from the directive; and
3 that there is a causal link between the state's failure to implement the directive and the loss suffered by the persons affected.

By introducing a new, general principle of state liability, the ECJ circumvented the weaknesses of existing remedies, improved individuals' possibility of obtaining compensation when their rights have been infringed, and provided a powerful incentive for member states to comply with EU rules (Steiner 1993: 11; Jarvis 1996: 235). As Paul Craig concluded:

> [I]t is clear that the rationale for the existence of state damages liability for breach of EC law is in part deterrence, in the sense of providing an incentive for Member States to comply with Community law; and in part the desire to ensure the effective protection of Community rights through the provision of compensation when those rights have been infringed.
>
> (Craig 1997: 85)

The price for this new principle was a challenge against the institutional and procedural autonomy of national courts. While the ECJ had previously asserted that the treaty "was not intended to create new remedies in the national courts to ensure the observance of Community law" (*Rewe-Zentralfinanz*, para. 5), this was exactly what it did with the principle of state liability. "[T]he time has come to accept that the ECJ has created a new, *sui generis*, tort" (Steiner and Woods 1996: 380). *Francovich* thereby marked the definitive departure from the traditional approach, where the ECJ's part had been confined to the definition of rights and duties, while the procedures and remedies of decentralized enforcement depended entirely on the legal systems of the member states (e.g. Caranta 1993: 282; Ross 1993; Gardner 1996: 280–2).

Most national legal systems did not provide a liability remedy against the state in matters of *national* law, making it all the more difficult to offer one for actions brought under *Community* law. National governments and courts would therefore have to create or designate new legal procedures to allow for claims brought on the basis of the principle of state liability. Concludes Snyder:

> While thus recognising that Community rights are to be enforced primarily in national courts, the Court's jurisprudence has none the less impinged increasingly on national legal remedies. . . . The Court of Justice is beginning to contribute to the restructuring of national procedural systems.
>
> (Snyder 1993: 45–6)[7]

But *Francovich* raised as many questions as it closed. For example, did the principle of state liability apply to all kinds of Community acts, treaty articles as well as other kinds of provisions; to all kinds of breaches either lacking or having only late and incorrect implementation; to breaches by all branches of government, administrative as well as legislative and judicial? Familiar with the ECJ's custom of gradually expanding established principles, legal observers expected a progressive continuation. Malcolm Ross noted: "The elasticity of the key passages in the Court's judgment in

Francovich provides ample ammunition for an expansive approach to the future development of individual protection" (1993: 57). Steiner concluded: "A principle of State liability is a powerful instrument in the enforcement of Community law; it is likely that the Court of Justice will seek to maximise its use" (1993: 11).

In 1996, these expectations were fulfilled when the ECJ answered the outstanding questions in a long line of cases that elucidated and specified the principle. In the linked cases *Brasserie du Pêcheur* and *Factortame III* (Joined Cases C-46 and 48/93, 1996), the ECJ expanded the principle when establishing that it applies to *all* breaches of *all* Community law, that is, regardless of whether the infringed rule is a treaty article, directive, or regulation, and regardless of whether the infringement results from actions of the legislative, executive, or judicial branches of government. The ECJ had thereby confirmed the general applicability of the principle of state liability. Aligning the principle with the conditions governing liability of the EU institutions under Article 215, the ECJ differentiated, however, between situations where the member state in its actions enjoyed little discretion (e.g. implementation of directive) and wide discretion (e.g. legislation involving choice between alternative arrangements). In the latter situation, state liability would only arise if the infringement fulfilled the additional condition of having been "sufficiently serious."

In the remaining three formative judgments that followed during 1996 – *British Telecommunications* (Case C-392/93, 1996), *Hedley Lomas* (Case C-5/94, 1996), and *Dillenkofer* (Joined Cases C-178, 179, 188, 189, and 190/94, 1996) – the ECJ addressed what had become the key remaining question: the definition of a sufficiently serious breach of Community law. In *Brasserie du Pêcheur* and *Factortame III*, the ECJ had already specified that a breach was sufficiently serious when a member state had manifestly and gravely disregarded the limits of its discretion, which it clearly had if the breach continued despite a relevant ruling from the ECJ or settled case law. In addition, the ECJ had suggested a number of other factors that might have to be considered.

Elaborating on these conditions, the ECJ held in *British Telecommunications* that a breach was not sufficiently serious if the directive was imprecisely worded and capable of bearing the meaning given to it by a government acting in good faith. In *Hedley Lomas*, the ECJ strengthened the principle of state liability by stating that the mere infringement of EU law could be enough to establish the existence of a sufficiently serious breach, given that the member state at the time had little or no discretion. Finally, in *Dillenkofer*, the ECJ clearly stated that all instances where member states have not implemented a directive in time constitute *per se* serious breaches of EU law, thus giving individuals the right to financial compensation. As 1996 came to a close, the ECJ had achieved what it, and for that matter the Commission, desired. Concluded a councilor with the Commission's Legal Service: "Everything is now set. Today we cannot think of any action of a member state that could not give rise to state liability" (interview, February 18, 1998).

The cases handed down in 1996 reinforced the impression that the price for this potent enforcement weapon was a challenge to the functional division between the ECJ and national courts. Whereas the establishment of state liability in 1991 impinged on the institutional and procedural autonomy of national legal systems, the subsequent elaboration in 1996 challenged the notion that the ECJ interprets and national courts apply EU law. The highly detailed conditions and specifications laid down by the ECJ left little to be settled at the national level, as Craig observes with respect to *Brasserie du Pêcheur* and *Factortame III*: "This 'guidance' from the ECJ effectively resolved the crucial factual issues in the two cases" (1997: 86; see also Emiliou 1996: 410–11).[8] This dual challenge led one legal scholar to conclude that the principle of state liability had brought a clear shift in the relationship between the ECJ and national courts:

> The logic is not consociational, but one of control. It entails the construction by the Court of Justice of positive legal institutions in a more detailed and extensive manner than previously, with a corresponding loss of autonomy for national courts whose role would be reduced to that of fact-finding agencies and administrators of the Court's judgments.
>
> (Chalmers 1997: 191)

In the period 1998–2000, the ECJ delivered another six judgments on state liability: *Norbrook* (Case C-127/95, 1998), *Brinkmann* (Case C-319/96, 1998), *Konle* (Case C-302/97, 1999), *Andersson* (Case C-321/97, 1999), *Rechberger* (Case C-140/97, 1999), and *Haim II* (Case C-424/97, 2000). These cases contained no innovations in relation to *Francovich* and the 1996 judgments (for an analysis, see Tridimas 2001). Instead, the ECJ concentrated on refining the principle of state liability, focusing, in particular, on the condition of causation. Today, the principle of state liability is a well-established part of EU law.

ECJ maneuvering and supranational influence

The establishment of the principle of state liability constituted an essential step in the ECJ's efforts to reinforce decentralized, "fire-alarm" enforcement. By conferring on individuals the right to obtain compensation from non-complying member states, the ECJ greatly expanded the role of citizens and companies in the enforcement of EU law, and equipped decentralized supervision with a highly deterrent sanction. Were these actions in line with governments' wishes, or did the ECJ move beyond state preferences when introducing the principle of state liability?

All existing evidence firmly indicates that the ECJ exploited its privileged position of interpretation to introduce a means of enforcement that collided head on with government preferences at the time, and with their original intention when delegating supervisory powers to the European court. The ECJ's judgment in *Francovich* was delivered on November 19, 1991, just a few weeks before the closing of the Intergovernmental Conference (IGC), at a time when it was clear that member governments at that very conference had discarded the alternative of introducing state liability sanctions, and instead had chosen to revise Article 171. Not surprisingly, therefore, the decision provoked loud cries about judge-made law and judicial activism in European capitals.

European Union governments had expressed their positions on state liability directly to the ECJ before the passing of the judgment. Member states' preferences with respect to a particular case or principle are best revealed through the legal briefs, "observations," they may submit to the ECJ on all actions before it. These observations are also the primary instrument through which they can actively signal their positions to the ECJ and attempt to influence jurisprudence (Everling 1984: 228; Stone Sweet and Caporaso 1998: 115). As a consequence, the ECJ is always well informed of governments' preferences regarding a particular case.

Besides the Italian government, the defendant, three other governments submitted written or oral observations in the *Francovich* case. All rejected the argument that anything like a principle of state liability was inherent in the treaty, and all emphasized the need to preserve the institutional and procedural autonomy of national legal systems (*Francovich*, paras. 15–17). The UK stated that there was no basis in Community law for the proposition that an individual has the right to obtain compensation from a member state that has failed to fulfill its obligations. On the contrary, the ECJ's case law showed that the treaty was not intended to create new remedies in national courts. The Dutch government submitted that there was no Community law on the question of state liability, and that, consequently, possible liability could only be determined on the basis of national liability rules. In addition, the Dutch government stressed the institutional autonomy of national courts, stating that it was for national legal systems to lay down the applicable substantive and procedural rules. The German government, finally, contended that the liability of member states did not fall within the competence of the Community.

When the question of state liability returned in 1996 with *Brasserie du Pêcheur* and *Factortame III*, there were still governments insisting that state liability was a question of national law and that no basis for such a principle could be found in the treaty (*Brasserie du Pêcheur* and *Factortame III*, paras. 30–46). This time, governments opposed to the principle – the German, the Irish, and the Dutch – also made a point of firmly emphasizing that the 1991 IGC had decided not to lay down any general rules governing state liability and instead had chosen to revise Article 171. In its extremely forceful observation, the German government even went as far as to openly accuse the ECJ of judicial activism and of violating the institutional balance in the EU:

> The *German Government* considers that it was not the intention of the Community legislature to establish any general liability on the part of Member States for infringements of Community law. It points out that during the negotiations concerning the Maastricht Treaty the Member States did not adopt any rules in that regard. The new version of Article 171 of the EC Treaty merely provides for the imposition of penalties on Member States which do not comply with the Court's judgments. The German Government further states that an extension of Community law by judge-made law going beyond the bounds of the legitimate closure of lacunae would be incompatible with the division of competence between the Community institutions and the Member States laid down by the Treaty, and with the principle of the maintenance of institutional balance. The institutions having legislative competence, in particular the Council and the Parliament, cannot be excluded from the establishment of a general right to compensation, which requires democratic legitimation. Furthermore, such a principle requires an alteration of the Treaty entailing financial implications which also necessitate the consent of national parliaments.
>
> (*Brasserie du Pêcheur* and *Factortame III*, para. 32)

The case of state liability passes the demanding counterfactual test recommended by intergovernmentalist scholars whenever suspected instances of supranational influence are identified. It is extremely unlikely that EU governments would have stepped in to introduce this decentralized sanction had not the ECJ done so. The form of open conflict exposed in this case precludes the inference that what appears as a supranational institution acting with substantial autonomy in fact is a perfectly controlled agent/supervisor. Rather than pre-empting negative reactions by avoiding undesired actions, the ECJ charged ahead with a principle that challenged explicit government preferences and later would induce some governments to launch the first formal attack ever on the ECJ.

From this perspective, it is interesting that Geoffrey Garrett, Daniel Kelemen, and Heiner Schulz (1998) use the principle of state liability as a case confirming the explanatory power of their intergovernmental theory of legal politics in the EU. The core of Garrett, Kelemen, and Schulz's legal politics argument is the assertion that the ECJ is sensitive to, and acts on, government preferences. Applying this proposition to the development of state liability, they argue that the string of judgments delivered in 1996 illustrate how the ECJ limited the principle in ways desired by powerful national governments. "These cases suggest that the ECJ is willing to tailor its state liability rulings in ways that the core member governments, especially France and Germany, wish" (Garrett *et al.* 1998: 173).

This conclusion does not hold when confronted with the empirical evidence presented here, and indeed seems to have been based more on theoretical assumption than on a detailed examination of this doctrinal development. The argument is subject to both empirical and logical limits, of which four are particularly notable. First, and most importantly, the 1996 judgments cannot be interpreted as a retreat in the face of member state opposition. Whereas, correctly, the sufficiently serious condition added in *Brasserie du Pêcheur* and *Factortame III* constituted a clarification of the criteria that must be fulfilled for states to be liable, this was combined with the *extension* of state liability to *all* breaches of *all* Community law. Rather than a limitation of the principle, these two judgments are therefore generally interpreted in the legal community as a broadening of the state liability doctrine (e.g. Wooldridge and D'Sa 1996: 167; Craig 1997: 77; Quitzow 1997: 693; Dehousse 1998: 55; interview, Commission official, February 19, 1998). Moreover, in both *Hedley Lomas* and *Dillenkofer*, the ECJ further strengthened the principle by chipping away at the sufficiently serious condition. Second, even a cursory reading of the German observation submitted on *Brasserie du Pêcheur* and *Factortame III* suffices to rule out the conclusion that the ECJ should have tailored its ruling to the preferences of the German government. Third, if indeed we were to accept their argument, then we would expect the ECJ to accommodate governments in some other way than by introducing a condition (sufficiently serious breach) that required such detailed instructions to national courts as to seriously challenge their autonomy in applying EU law. Finally, it is logically flawed to assume that the ECJ suddenly became sensitive to government preferences *after* the principle had been established in *Francovich*. The observations submitted by EU governments, as well as the positions taken at the 1991 IGC, had fully revealed member states' sharp opposition to a principle of state liability, and the strong reaction therefore came as no surprise. An ECJ rationally adapting its judgments to government preferences would never have proceeded with the introduction of state liability in the first place.

Judicial independence and the absence of intrusive monitoring

How can we explain this degree of autonomy for the ECJ? The P–S–A model posits that the capacity of member state principals to prevent unwelcome supranational initiatives rests with the monitoring mechanisms they can furnish, while maneuvering that has already occurred may be undone only at a second stage through sanctioning. Whereas member states' attempts to sanction the ECJ will be treated at length in a later section of this chapter, I explain here why they lacked the monitoring means to forestall the ECJ's actions.

The case of state liability well illustrates the analytical value of the distinction between participation- and observation-based monitoring. The notable ease with which the ECJ could introduce the principle of state liability is best explained by member states' absence of means for interfering through participation-based monitoring. As reflected in the observations submitted in *Francovich*, governments were fully aware of the potential implications of a general state liability principle. Still, they were unable to prevent the ECJ from proceeding with the establishment of the principle.

This autonomy from intrusive monitoring is an expression of the ECJ's judicial independence, which indeed constitutes a prerequisite for the ECJ to function as a court in the first place. Member states' forced recourse to observation-based monitoring makes it uniquely easy for the ECJ to introduce measures, such as state liability, that go beyond many governments' interests. Whereas member states can often limit or stop unwanted Commission actions through active monitoring of an ongoing process, the only means they have at their disposal with respect to the ECJ are *ex post* sanctions. Inability to prevent the ECJ from taking unwanted action is the price that national governments pay for the existence of a neutral and hierarchical judicial system within the EU.

Yet member governments' lack of means to intervene in the ECJ's decision-making process should not be taken as evidence that the ECJ is free to lay down whatever doctrine it wishes. "The absence of formal external constraints implied by judicial independence does not . . . entail that judicial power is exercised free from political or social constraints" (Chalmers 1997: 171). If judicial independence is a prerequisite for a court to function as a court, so is judicial legitimacy. Without legal legitimacy and authority, courts are unable to command compliance with the judgments they deliver, and ensure respect for the interpretations they present. The legitimacy of a court is dependent on its legal reasoning, which must be consistent with existing doctrine and with the methodological requirements of legal deduction. Given that legal reasoning is perceived as consistent with these conditions, and only to the extent that it is, legal legitimacy may be exploited to advance political goals. Submit Anne-Marie Burley and Walter Mattli:

> [L]aw functions both as mask and shield. It hides and protects the promotion of one particular set of political objectives against contending objectives in the purely political sphere. In specifying this dual relationship between law and politics, we uncover a striking paradox. Law can only perform this dual political function to the extent that it is accepted as law. A 'legal' decision that is transparently 'political,' in the sense that it departs too far from the principles and methods of the law, will invite direct political attack. It will thus fail both as mask and shield. . . . In short, a court's political legitimacy, and hence its ability to advance its own political agenda, rests on its legal legitimacy.
>
> (Burley and Mattli 1993: 72–3)

Jurisprudence that clearly challenges or violates the requirements of sound legal reasoning risks ruining the judicial legitimacy and authority of a court.

This, rather than the political implications of pro-Community campaigns, has been the main reason why certain legal scholars have criticized the activism of the ECJ. Notes Hjalte Rasmussen, a chief proponent of this view: "If Court-curbing or Court-destroying initiatives were to be launched by some countervailing power(s), an irreparable harm would be inflicted on the Court's authority and legitimacy. Although slower, a day-to-day erosion may cause equally detrimental effects" (1986: 9).

In the case of state liability, law failed miserably both as mask and shield; the apolitical language of the ECJ neither masked the political content of its decisions nor shielded judges from political criticism. The extent to which this activism also caused permanent damage to the legitimacy of the ECJ will be illuminated in the later section on member state sanctions against the European court.

The Commission and decentralized enforcement

Parallel to the ECJ's enforcement-enhancing judgments, the Commission launched initiatives that supplemented these actions. I will provide an indepth analysis of the two most important programs: the Citizens First initiative and the Robert Schuman project. In their aim to enhance the awareness of EU law and legislation, these programs served to reduce informational barriers in decentralized enforcement. The formulation and implementation of both programs testify to the more extensive control mechanisms member states possess as regards the Commission, which undertook adjustments both in anticipation of governments' reactions and in response to actual criticism. Counterfactual reasoning suggests, however, that the Commission succeeded in exerting limited independent influence by employing drafting techniques that shielded these programs from government rejection.

The Citizens First initiative

In the overall scheme of decentralized enforcement, the Citizens First initiative served to encourage citizens and companies to turn to national courts, when their EU rights are infringed upon. In 1994 the Commission recognized: "The adoption and implementation of legislation must be accompanied by an active information policy in order that citizens and companies are aware of their rights and obligations and can act quickly whenever they are infringed" (1994c: xvi). Citizens First, launched in 1996 as the most ambitious information initiative ever undertaken by the Commission, put such an active policy in practice (European Commission 1997l: 3).

In the actual formulation of the Citizens First initiative, the objective of encouraging individuals to secure their rights in national courts was fitted to the broader objective of raising people's awareness of their rights in the EU. Ever since the backlash in public opinion in connection with the TEU, the

Commission had been concerned about Euro-skepticism. One of the sources of this skepticism, it reasoned, was the fact that European citizens knew very little about the rights and opportunities they enjoyed under EU law, especially with respect to the internal market (interview, Commission official, February 16, 1998). With an information campaign like Citizens First, the Commission would consequently meet two objectives: (1) increase citizens' awareness of their rights and opportunities in the EU, and (2) improve the necessary conditions for decentralized enforcement, as "enforcement through citizens is a non-starter if citizens are not aware of their rights" (interview, Commission official, February 16, 1998).

The first phase of the initiative, covering the rights of EU citizens to live, work, and study in another EU country, started in November 1996, and the second, focusing on traveling, equal opportunities, and goods and services, began in November 1997.[9] The campaign used a formula of layered information: general information through free phone-numbers, an Internet site, and brochures on the various themes; detailed information through specialized fact sheets; and expert advice through a signpost service. To advertise the launch of the initiative, a media campaign was conducted in all the member states but the UK.

The reach of the campaign was considerable. The Commission reports that during the first year 75 million people became aware of the initiative and over one million contacted Citizens First to obtain brochures and fact sheets (1997h: 1). In the second year, the response to the campaign remained high, and a tremendous increase was identified in Internet-based requests for information (European Commission 1998g: 4–5). Within the Commission, Citizens First was perceived as a clear success, which raised the question of whether this initiative should be placed on a permanent footing. Commission analysis of citizens' inquires showed that most problems encountered resulted from lack of information, suggesting the need for a continuous program (European Commission 1997k, 1998a, 1998b). At the Amsterdam summit in June 1997, a proposal for such a permanent program – "Dialogue with Citizens and Business" – was adopted as part of the Commission's Action Plan on the internal market. The new program was launched in June 1998, primarily oriented toward citizens, with an extension to business in January 1999 (European Commission 1998f: 4–5, 1998i: 2–3). In 2001 the Commission went one step further when launching the Interactive Policy Making (IPM) initiative, which aims to improve governance by using the Internet for collecting and analyzing reactions in the marketplace for use in the EU's policy-making process (European Commission 2001b, 2001d).

While aimed primarily at improving individuals' knowledge of their internal market rights, all aspects of Citizens First also contained an enforcement dimension. Most concretely, all information brochures contained a page on "How to get your rights recognized and enforced," which informed citizens of the legal routes they could follow if they encountered problems in exercising their rights. The Commission's explicit recommendation was to turn to national courts, and it tempted victims of state infringements with the prospect of financial compensation under the newly established principle of state liability:

> You should start by following national procedures, because you have a variety of possibilities open to you and you may be awarded compensation. National courts must ensure that rights based on Community law are respected and, where necessary, set aside any measure which infringes it.
>
> (European Commission 1996j: 14; see also 1996h: 9–10, 1996k: 1)

Should national procedures prove inadequate or inconvenient, the brochures also informed citizens of alternative enforcement routes, such as a complaint to the Commission, which might open infringement proceedings, or a complaint to a Member of the European Parliament (MEP), who in turn could put questions to the Commission and the Council. Also the factsheets and the signpost service served enforcement purposes. The factsheets clearly laid out relevant EU law in the area in question and indicated how citizens could go about enforcing these rights, while the signpost service provided important feedback to the Commission on problematic areas – information that could be used both to improve internal market rules and to launch infringement proceedings (interview, Commission official, February 16, 1998).

In May 2000, the Commission supplemented the enforcement information of the issue-specific brochures with a detailed guide called "Enforcing your rights in the Single European Market" (European Commission 2000b). The guide provides comprehensive information on what action can be taken at local, national, and European level if citizens and businesses have problems exercising their EU rights. The guide is in turn backed up by country-specific factsheets that explain step-by-step how to use national systems of redress, both administrative and legal.

Formally, member states' consent was not required for the launching of Citizens First, which was a Commission program only subject to the budgetary limits set by the EP. In practice, however, the campaign could not be undertaken without their cooperation (interview, Commission official, February 16, 1998). The active participation of national governments was required not least for the distribution of brochures and factsheets, and for the drafting of detailed instructions on how EU rights were best asserted in that particular country. Consequently, national governments already became involved at the formulation stage of the program. The initiative was discussed in the Internal Market Council, in an advisory group, and in bilateral visits the Commission made to all the member states (interviews, Commission officials, February 16, 1998).

The formulation and implementation of Citizens First caused three primary points of contention between the Commission and member governments (interviews, Commission officials, February 16, 1998). First, "member states did not trust the Commission one inch" in terms of being able to provide straightforward, factual information (interview, Commission official, February 16, 1998). To meet this concern, the Commission agreed to show all drafts of the information material to member governments, but kept editorial control. Second, "member states were afraid that the Commission would use the information to encourage citizens to complain about the national administration, which would make them look bad" (interview, Commission official, February 16, 1998). To overcome this suspicion, the Commission introduced the concept of a signpost service, which would not only be a complaint service but also a constructive way of solving problems. Still, there were many difficult discussions with national governments, of which the most skeptical were the UK, Germany, France, the Netherlands, and Denmark. The third area of contention was the actual implementation of the campaign, where certain national governments had very strong ideas. The UK under the Major administration was against publicizing the initiative and caused major problems in 1996 by not participating in the first phase of Citizens First.[10] Likewise, the Danish government was very skeptical and only agreed to a low-profile campaign initially. In a second group, the Netherlands and Portugal thought it politically unacceptable to have a European phone line, and in both countries the campaign ended up using national information services.

The fact that member states to such a degree still accepted the initiative, despite the attendant risk of being exposed for non-compliance and being taken to court, is best attributed to the realization among national governments that *their* citizens, safeguarding their rights in the internal market, would primarily put pressure on *other* governments. "That was the trick," asserts a senior Commission fonctionnaire – an impression that is confirmed by other officials with insight into the process (interviews, February 3 and 16, 1998). Other important factors were adjustments to the campaign made by the Commission in response to government reactions, and the obvious problem for national governments in finding legitimate arguments against informing citizens about their rights and opportunities.

The Robert Schuman project

In the general structure of decentralized supervision, the Robert Schuman project served to reduce the second important informational barrier: insufficient knowledge of EU law in the legal professions. The idea behind the program can be traced to 1992–3, when the pivotal role of national judges, prosecutors, and lawyers in making the internal market work was first emphasized by the Commission (1992c: 45, 1993c: 16). Unless national judges and lawyers could be assumed to have a sufficiently developed "EU reflex," leading them automatically and systematically to check whether European solutions apply to the cases they handle, they would be unable to secure individuals' internal market rights and to facilitate decentralized enforcement. Surveys indicated, however, that severe gaps existed in the awareness of EU law among legal practitioners. In 1995, two out of three lawyers considered their knowledge of EU law inadequate or very inadequate, and only 25 percent of those who practiced EU law were satisfied with their knowledge (EOS Gallup Europe 1995: 12).

In view of this situation, the objective of the Robert Schuman project was to raise the awareness of EU law among judges, prosecutors, and lawyers. Explained Commissioner Monti:

> The effective and uniform application of common rules throughout the internal market now constitutes the main political priority for the Commission. The Robert Schuman Project would enable us to target direct judges and lawyers, the key players in the correct application of internal market rules.
>
> (European Commission 1996k: 1)

It was explicitly recognized that the Robert Schuman project constituted a necessary supplement to the Citizens First initiative (European Commission 1996g: 2).

The Robert Schuman project was designed to financially encourage and support national initiatives that sought to improve the knowledge of EU law in the legal professions. The program would rest on a partnership between national professional associations and the Commission, and would not require member governments' active cooperation to be implemented. The proposal for a program was first submitted to the Council in late 1996, after lengthy internal preparations (European Commission 1996g). Two pilot phases of the project were launched in 1997 and 1998 respectively, involving support to a limited number of pilot initiatives (European Commission 1998j). An amended proposal was submitted by the Commission in late 1997 and, at the Council meeting of November 27, 1997, a deal was finally reached on the action program, which officially entered into force in July 1998 for a period of three years (European Commission 1997e). Over the period 1997 to 2001, the Robert Schuman project supported a total of 180 initiatives, involving approximately 15,000 legal practitioners (European Commission 2002b).

As opposed to the Citizens First initiative, the Robert Schuman project required the formal consent of member states. Given the legal basis of the program, the co-decision procedure applied, which meant that the project required the backing of a qualified majority in the Council. The Commission was aware that the program would be a sensitive issue and therefore took great care drafting the proposal for a decision (interview, Commission official, February 3, 1998). This partly explains the considerable time that passed from the first formulation of the ideas in 1992–3 to the presentation of the proposal in late 1996. During this time, the Commission also distributed a working document among governments to elicit a first reaction. Despite these careful preparations, the proposal encountered tough negotiations in the Council (interviews, Commission officials, February 3 and 26, 1998).

The UK under the Tories was very much against the entire project, and even if the British became more positive after the change in government in May 1997, they remained adamant on key points of contention. Also the Netherlands, Sweden, and Germany were less enthusiastic. France and Luxembourg were supportive of the proposal, while small states like Portugal, Greece, Finland, Ireland, and Austria were positive in general, but not active. The points of dissatisfaction varied in nature. Apart from a number of objections concerning minor substantive issues – many of which were solved in the Council negotiations – some member governments questioned the entire legitimacy of the project on the basis of the principle of subsidiarity. Was it really the Commission's and the EU's task to sponsor the training of national lawyers and judges? From the perspective of the Commission, the project was fully in line with the principle of subsidiarity: "The Robert Schuman Project shall support and complement training and information work on Community law undertaken by the Member States while not encroaching on their responsibility for defining course content and organising vocational training" (1997e: 8).

The most contentious area was the legal basis of the proposal.[11] The Commission argued that the proposal should be based on Article 100a of the treaty (today Article 95), since it served the purpose of securing the establishment and functioning of the internal market. Stated the Commission:

> The effective and uniform application of Community law with a view to approximating national legislation is a condition for the smooth functioning of the Internal Market. The Robert Schuman Project has intentionally been integrated into overall arrangements which . . . are designed to ensure the optional functioning of the Internal Market. It complements these arrangements by conveying the idea that, in addition to infringement proceedings instituted by the Commission . . . or the imposition of penalties, the effective and homogenous application of Community law depends on raising the awareness of national legal professionals whose task it is to apply that law on a decentralized basis.
>
> (European Commission 1996g: 5)

By contrast, certain member states advocated Articles 126 and 127 (today Articles 149 and 150) – cooperation in education and vocational training – as the legal basis for the proposal. The decision rule was not the reason for the controversy, since qualified majority voting would apply in both cases. What mattered was the orientation of the program and its continuation after the first three years. If the Council took the decision based on Articles 126 and 127, there was no reason why the project, at a second stage, could not be extended or redirected to professions completely unrelated to the original purpose of the initiative. The Commission obviously wanted to secure the program against any such dilution. Member governments, for their part, feared that a decision based on the general Article 100a would set a precedent, leading to an increase in the Commission's powers, whereas a decision based on Articles 126 and 127 would close the door on such future claims.

In the intergovernmental discussions in Coreper and the Council, a coalition sufficient to block the proposal – the UK, the Netherlands, Sweden, and Germany – had taken a tough stance against Article 100a and advocated Articles 126 and 127 as the legal basis. As the negotiations moved to a vote in the Council after a heated discussion, the UK decided to support the Commission's proposal, which consequently passed.

In its analysis of the negotiations, the Commission points to three reasons why member governments actually accepted the proposal, even if this meant facilitating decentralized enforcement through individuals suing non-compliant states in national courts (interview, Commission official, February 26, 1998). First, compared to Citizens First, this program was much more indirect in its influence; improving the knowledge of the legal professions is not the same thing as advising people to take member states to court. Second, just as in the case of Citizens First, national governments were concerned with the possibilities for *their* citizens to enforce their rights in *other* member states' courts. Third, it may be less embarrassing for a government to have a national court declare that it has not fully implemented a directive, than to be exposed in infringement proceedings at the central EU level.

Member state control constrains the Commission

The Citizens First initiative and the Robert Schuman project demonstrate how the Commission worked in tandem with the ECJ in the boosting of decentralized, "fire-alarm" enforcement. Both programs sought to mend holes that had previously weakened the power and effectiveness of enforcement through national courts. Notwithstanding the differences between these two programs, they paint a similar picture of the Commission's capacity to promote decentralized supervision beyond governments' preferences. Member state control restricted the Commission's enforcement-enhancing projects, but did not prevent them from being carried through.

Member governments largely endorsed the two programs. An important reason was the *de facto* control that followed from the prerequisite of member state approval. Citizens First and Robert Schuman illustrate how member states' control mechanisms are far more intrusive with respect to the Commission than is the case with the ECJ. National governments followed carefully the Commission's moves, intervened in the policy formulation, and forced it to adapt its proposals. Sanctions were an integral part of this process, as illustrated by the UK's opting out of Citizens First. In both cases, the Commission consulted governments and took their reactions into consideration, yet only the Robert Schuman project required the formal consent of member states. To the extent that Commission initiatives require member states' active cooperation at the implementation stage, it is of less importance whether their consent is formally required or not, since the Commission nonetheless has to seek approval. Both projects also give evidence of how the Commission attempted to anticipate contentious issues at the drafting stage. Conforming to the picture of a perfectly controlled agent, the Commission sought to improve the chances of approval by avoiding or eliminating features thought challenging to government preferences.

Yet we must be careful not to equate member state approval with lack of supranational influence. Empirical evidence and counterfactual reasoning suggest that member governments were unsuccessful in ridding the programs of all unpopular elements, and that the Commission succeeded in shielding the programs from rejection through a set of strategic drafting techniques. The two programs remained surprisingly intact, given intrusive monitoring by governments and the objective of strengthening decentralized enforcement. In the case of Citizens First, government interference affected slightly the means employed and reduced the initial participation of the UK and Denmark, but in no way threatened the overall objective and implementation of the campaign. With respect to Robert Schuman, both the Commission's authority to launch this measure and the legal basis on which this was done were questioned, but the project escaped this battle unharmed.

Counterfactual reasoning suggests that the programs introduced measures member states would preferably have avoided. The likelihood that EU governments, in the absence of the Commission's initiatives, would have stepped in to undertake the same measures must be regarded as limited. The Citizens First initiative and the Robert Schuman project made it more likely that citizens and companies would sue member states in court, possibly for damages, and would do so with competent legal help trained to detect and prosecute infringements. Both programs thereby reinforced a structure of enforcement that governments had actively refrained from strengthening at the 1991 IGC, and would actually challenge at the 1996–7 IGC.

The enforcement objectives of the Citizens First and Robert Schuman programs indicate that government consent may not necessarily reflect a lack of influence. The source of this supranational influence is the strategic shaping of the two programs. The Commission made use of what I will refer to as the techniques of "packaging," "framing," and "co-optive justification" (Tallberg 2000a; for related concepts, see Ross 1995: 39; Cram 1997: 162).

Packaging entails that the Commission manipulates the cost–benefit calculations of national governments by linking unpopular measures to popular ones, or by presenting a number of proposals that appeal to different member states. In the Citizens First initiative, the Commission linked the unpopular measure of encouraging individuals to sue governments in national courts to the broader and less contentious aim of informing citizens about their rights and opportunities in the EU. Similarly, in the Robert Schuman project, the Commission linked the objective of promoting even and effective enforcement in national courts to means that contributed to the funding of education and training in the member states. In addition, the Commission exploited the presence of a collective-action problem, since national governments were led to endorse the two programs because this would make it easier for *their* citizens to enforce their rights in *other* member states' courts, when collectively, this meant turning the gun on themselves.

Framing rests on the exploitation of information asymmetries, and refers to the notion that the Commission may succeed in getting approval for a controversial proposal by presenting it in a way that appeals to governments, while withholding consequences that are likely to be interpreted as negative. In contrast to the Robert Schuman project, where the potentially threatening objective of decentralized enforcement was openly stated, the Commission in the formulation of the Citizens First initiative actively played down the knock-on effect of encouraging individuals to turn to national courts. Typically, the enforcement objective of Citizens First is absent from all publications presenting the program and its purpose.

Co-optive justification implies that the Commission, by appealing to principles and beliefs heralded by member states, justifies decisions or policy proposals in a way that renders them more difficult for governments to reject. A variant of this technique is the justification of decisions through reference to a European Council conclusion or other collective statements by EU governments. In Citizens First, the Commission publicly justified the information campaign by referring to the need to "bring citizens closer to Europe and Europe closer to the citizens," which was welcomed rather than feared by member states in the wake of growing Euro-skepticism (interview, Commission official, February 16, 1998). The overall aim of the initiative was presented as being "to improve the understanding which people have of their rights and opportunities in the European Union and its Single Market" – an objective national governments obviously had problems challenging with legitimate arguments (European Commission 1997k: 1). In the proposal for the Robert Schuman project, the Commission appealed to the generally embraced principle of "the rule of law," the concept of "a Community of law," and the smooth functioning of the internal market, "the apex of Community construction" (1996g: 1). The ensuing difficulty of rejecting the project can partially explain why critical member governments chose instead to challenge the legal basis of the proposal. In search of additional springboards, the program proposal also made explicit reference to, and derived legitimacy from, member states' declaration on the implementation of Community law, attached to the TEU.

In sum, the two Commission programs demonstrate the extent to which the Commission, as opposed to the ECJ, was restricted by member state control in its enforcement-enhancing efforts. Yet the Commission's practice of packaging, framing, and co-optive justification helped shield the programs from wholesale rejection.

State principals sanction supranational maneuvering

In the preceding sections, I have shown how the ECJ and the Commission in the late 1980s and 1990s shifted the balance in EU supervision toward a form of enforcement that member states perceived as more threatening to national sovereignty, and therefore had chosen not to reinforce through intergovernmental decisions. Yet this is not the end of the story. The P–A literature suggests that principals will respond to unwanted actions by sanctioning the agent/supervisor, improving control mechanisms, or attempting to undo the effects of the agent's/supervisor's actions.

Principal–agent analysis in the study of European integration identifies four kinds of sanctions against unwanted supranational initiatives. The first sanction – cutting the budget and refusing to appoint personnel – is seldom effective in the EU context, and would not have been so in this case either. Its bluntness would have handicapped the ECJ's capacity to perform functions supported by member governments. In addition, it would have been insufficient to correct the effects of the ECJ's enforcement-enhancing measures. The second sanction of rewriting the ECJ's judgments through new legislation was not available, since only decisions based on secondary legislation can be rewritten by statute, and not judgments based on the treaty, such as *Francovich*. The two sanctions that remained open to member states were treaty revision and non-compliance, and they pursued varieties of both.

The sanction of treaty revision

Just because the ECJ's competences were enshrined in the treaty and had not previously been formally challenged, this did not mean that member governments would forever refrain from attempting to clip its wings. The early 1990s witnessed growing signs that national governments had become increasingly uncomfortable with the way the ECJ expanded Community law into domains previously thought off limits. The two most vocal critics were the German government under Chancellor Helmut Kohl and the British Tory government headed by Prime Minister John Major.

In October 1992, Kohl went as far as to openly accuse the ECJ of judicial activism:

> If one takes the Court of Justice . . . it does not only exert its competencies in legal matters, but goes far further. We have an example of something that was not wanted in the beginning. This should be discussed so that the necessary measures may be taken later.
>
> (*Agence Europe* October 14, 1992)

That same year in December, at the Edinburgh summit, Germany attempted to table a proposal that suggested curtailing the power of national courts to refer cases to the ECJ under the preliminary ruling procedure, limiting this right to the highest courts only (Weiler 1993: 444; interview, Commission official, February 18, 1998). Allegedly, the reason was the need to reduce the work load of the highly strained ECJ, but most observers agree that the German government's true intention was to eliminate the source of most of the ECJ's doctrinal developments: referrals from lower national courts (e.g. Weiler 1993: 444; Alter 1998a: 140; Dehousse 1998: 167).

The other member state that showed signs of desiring a re-evaluation of the supranational institutions' competences, and the ECJ's in particular, was the UK. British Euro-skeptics had reacted strongly against ECJ judgments delivered in the late 1980s and early 1990s (e.g. Neill 1995). Most notably, *Factortame I* had been viewed as challenging the closely heralded British doctrine of parliamentary sovereignty, and *Francovich* as introducing a completely new principle, not previously recognized and with far-reaching consequences for national judicial orders. British discontent with the ECJ made its mark outside legal circles. Surveying the trend of growing criticism against the ECJ, *The Economist* recognized that "by far the most vociferous recent critics have been the British, who think of the court as an unguarded back door through which national sovereignty is being carted away" (May 17, 1997: 35).

The IGC scheduled for 1996 provided the perfect opportunity to voice this discontent and turn these threats into action. The ECJ knew what was coming. In its contribution to the upcoming IGC, the ECJ took an explicitly defensive position and responded to the threat of treaty revision: "The Court considers it indispensable, if the essential features of the Community legal order are to be maintained, that the functions and prerogatives of its judicial organs be safeguarded in the forthcoming process of revision" (1995b: 2). In particular, the ECJ defended the preliminary ruling procedure under Article 177. Targeting directly the informal German suggestion that references be limited to the highest courts, the ECJ strongly advised against any such revision: "To limit access to the Court would have the effect of jeopardizing the uniform application and interpretation of Community law throughout the Union, and could deprive individuals of effective judicial protection and undermine the unity of the case-law" (1995b: 6). The ECJ further rejected the idea that the competence to give preliminary rulings be split, so as to let the Court of First Instance take on certain categories of cases.

Member states bent on challenging the ECJ were undeterred by its defense. In September 1995, David Davis, the UK representative to the Reflection Group, circulated a paper, which contended that certain ECJ judgments, *Francovich* and *Emmott* in particular, "have led to significant unforeseen consequences for member states, have been disproportionate in their effect and have created severe practical problems" (Davis 1995: 1). To correct this situation, the UK proposed that the IGC should decide on three measures. First, to limit member state liability for breaches of EU law to cases of grave and manifest disregard of a European obligation. Second, to state explicitly the ECJ's power to limit the retrospective effect of judgments, since the ECJ only had used this option in exceptional cases. And third, to extend governments' capacity to apply national time limits to cases based on EU law, and restrict exceptions to cases of grave and manifest disregard. In addition, the British government offered a number of suggestions for improvements of a more "practical" and "procedural" nature: to create an ECJ appeals procedure, to facilitate the rapid amendment of EU legislation in cases where the Council believes that the ECJ has interpreted a provision in a way not originally intended, and to introduce an accelerated procedure for time-sensitive cases.

The first three proposals were an explicit attempt to meddle in the ECJ's domain *par excellence* – its case law. Rather than recognizing the ECJ's discretion to lay down, define, and develop principles and conditions governing state liability, retrospective effect, and national time limits, the British sought to bring these under government control by fixing them in the treaty. There was nothing in the existing order that denied the ECJ the authority to limit state liability and retrospective effect of judgments, or to allow national time limits to be applied. The British hoped, however, that having them enshrined in the treaty would encourage the ECJ to use them and provide a basis for challenging judgments in the proposed appeals procedure (Alter 1998a: 141).

Nor were the "practical" and "procedural" suggestions as innocent as they were portrayed. Most notably, the suggestion of an appeals procedure sought to give the ECJ a second chance to reflect on its judgments in light of political reactions, while the proposal for a rapid amendment procedure manifestly challenged the division between the legislature and the judiciary in the EU, and questioned the Commission's monopoly on initiation. As the Commission's Legal Service remarked, the ECJ's power to interpret EU law and impose its interpretations on governments, citizens, and economic operators alike, is the foundation of the rule of law (internal Commission memo, October 19, 1995). While some of these suggestions thus sought to limit the effects of particular judgments, and others constituted direct sanctions against the ECJ itself, all challenged the existing judicial system of the EU. As one legal observer concluded: "The implementation of many of these proposals might grossly impede the work of the ECJ" (Wooldridge 1996: 284).

A majority of the members in the Reflection Group were not prepared to back the UK proposals, though the French and German representatives indicated a certain level of approval (internal Commission memo, October 27, 1995). Other members of the group sympathized with the one or the other of the suggestions, but no single proposal ever gathered the support of a majority, never mind the unanimity required for treaty revision. The small states, Belgium in particular, remained faithful to the ECJ (internal Commission memo, October 27, 1995; interview, Commission official, January 7, 1998). In its concluding report of December 1995, the Reflection Group took notice of the UK proposals, but also indicated that no other member government had formally joined the British in their quest (1995, p. 33).

Notwithstanding this setback in the Reflection Group, the UK persisted in its campaign against the ECJ. The IGC opened in March 1996, and in July the UK delegation distributed a refined and elaborated version of the proposals previously presented in the Reflection Group (IGC 1996c; for an analysis of this memo, see Wooldridge 1996). While dressed up in a more legal garb, the suggestions were essentially the same. Again, the main emphasis was on the perceived need to limit the effects of the judgments strengthening decentralized enforcement:

> The risk of excessively large and unpredictable financial liabilities, particularly for national exchequers, has been substantially increased by: (a) the Court's recognition in *Francovich* that there is a Community law principle in accordance with which a Member State is liable to pay damages to persons whose rights have been adversely affected by its breach of Community law; and (b) the inability of a Member State, following the judgment in *Emmott*, to rely on its national time limits for actions brought in cases in which it has in any way failed to implement a directive correctly.
>
> (IGC 1996c: 4)

This time as well, the UK proposals – "infused with distrust of the creative role of the ECJ" – failed to gather sufficient support (Wooldridge 1996: 284). Whereas most member governments rejected the British suggestions outright, some were sympathetic to the idea that the ECJ should be sent a warning. "The UK was marginalized, but not alone" (interview, Commission official, January 7, 1998). In particular, the British enjoyed the moderate support of the German and French governments (internal Commission memo, March 19, 1997).[12] While spending most of the time hiding behind the more extreme British position, these governments came out in the open when it became increasingly clear that the UK proposals would be dismissed by the IGC.

In October 1996, Germany presented a suggestion that collided head on with the declared position of the ECJ, when arguing for the splitting of its competence with respect to preliminary references from national courts, and the transfer of certain domains to the Court of First Instance (IGC 1996d). In March 1997, the French government tabled a proposal with modified versions of the British suggestions concerning the limitation of the retrospective effect of judgments, the power of the Council to amend EU law when the ECJ has interpreted a provision "incorrectly," and the possibility of relying on national time limits (IGC 1997a). Though milder, the French suggestions nevertheless retained the essence of the British proposals. One Commission official monitoring the negotiations denotes all these proposals as "blatant attempts by certain member states to weaken the Court" (interview, January 7, 1998).

In the end, none of the proposals suggesting revisions of the ECJ's existing competences gathered anything close to the support of all member governments, and none found its way into the Amsterdam treaty.[13] The ECJ had escaped the first formal and most serious attempt ever at clipping its wings. But, as Dehousse puts it: "The message to the Court was . . . very clear: stick to your role of ensuring the uniform application of Community law, and do not interfere in policy choices, lest the risk of political overruling" (1998: 168).

The sanction of inaction

Inaction at the national level functioned as a second form of sanction. Recalcitrant reception and implementation of the principle of state liability by some national courts and governments reduced, partially and temporarily, the impact of this supranational measure. In general terms, member states are obliged under Article 10 (ex. Art. 5) to facilitate the achievement of the Community's tasks and to refrain from measures that could jeopardize the attainment of its objectives. In their capacity as EU courts, national courts are charged with the duty to apply EU law, and national governments must enable and allow domestic courts to fulfill this function. When the ECJ introduced the principle of state liability, it was the obligation of national governments and courts to ensure that citizens and companies could actually rely on this remedy.[14] If the substantive and procedural conditions for state liability laid down in national law were sufficient to satisfy the standard of protection set by the ECJ, these were to be relied on. If not, then national legal systems would have to be adjusted – either through governments legislating to the effect that appropriate remedies were created, or through courts recognizing a new cause of action or adjusting existing remedies.

Many national legal systems did not provide a corresponding damages remedy against the state in matters of national law, and where they did, this seldom permitted actions against the legislative and judicial branches of government (Caranta 1993; Jarvis 1996; Van Gerven 1996; Andersson 1997; Craig 1997; SOU 1997; Claes and de Witte 1998). "[I]t is clear that in most, if not all, member states, national law will not be effective (in any sense of the word) to protect individuals' rights under *Francovich*" (Steiner 1995: 52). In the UK, existing procedures did not fully satisfy the necessary conditions, therefore requiring that a new cause of action either be recognized, or existing torts be adapted to fulfill the requirements of EU law. The German legal system did not recognize that the legislature could be held liable, nor did the law of Belgium and Luxembourg. In Sweden, Finland, and Austria, neither the legislature nor the highest courts could be found liable under national law. In Irish law, much stricter conditions had to be satisfied for state liability to arise than those specified by the ECJ, while Italy more or less lacked functioning rules on state liability. By contrast, the French and the Dutch legal systems had few difficulties receiving and accommodating the new European rules on state liability, nor did Danish law raise any obstacles to the application of this principle in national courts. Summarized one legal observer in 1996: "The ECJ has indeed entered deep constitutional waters" (Jarvis 1996: 235).

Francovich and the ensuing string of cases therefore introduced something that was partially or completely new, and which required that new remedies be created through judicial or legislative action. Yet, six years after *Francovich*, no member state had taken legislative action to accommodate the development in EU law. According to a Swedish official report investigating the need to adjust Swedish law in response to the state liability principle, only two member governments – the UK and Sweden – were even in the process of considering legislative modifications (SOU 1997: 104). Based on the information collected for that report in cooperation with the Ministries of Justice in the other member states, the Swedish investigator described the prevailing approach in most governments as the ostrich strategy of burying the head in the sand (interview, SOU investigator, February 18, 1999). Rather than duly initiating the legislative measures required for national law to fully accommodate the EU rules on state liability, national governments confidently refrained from any action and accepted the less-than-optimal fit resulting from the existing order or the modifications national courts might undertake.

The other way in which national legal systems could have been adjusted would have been for national courts to modify existing procedures to meet the specified needs and requirements. These adjustments could have consisted either of the recognition in national case law of how individuals can make use of the state liability remedy, or from a *de facto* practice of accepting such claims, even though national law does not explicitly designate an appropriate procedure. The degree of adjustment in national procedures, *de jure* or *de facto*, is difficult to assess. Yet the fact that this is a question of court discretion raises the problem of procedural and legal incertitude. Italy and the UK provide examples of how individuals have been unable to rely on the principle of state liability because of inadequately modified or designated national procedures (Caranta 1993: 290–1; Chalmers 2000: 99–100).

Patterns in the cases handled by national courts are an indirect indication of the extent to which citizens and companies have been able to rely on the principle of state liability. Available data point to limited, but growing numbers of cases (European Commission 1997d: 475–7, 1998c: 313–5, 2000a: 49–52, 2001c: 52–5; FIDE 1998). As regards cases brought before courts based on incorrect or no transposition of directives, many member states – Belgium, Germany, the UK, Sweden, France, Ireland, Italy, and the Netherlands – had seen only a few cases by early 1998 (FIDE 1998). At the same point in time, an entire group of states – Austria, Denmark, Finland, Greece, Portugal, and Spain – had not witnessed a single state liability case raised on these grounds. While these figures must be interpreted with great care, they do suggest that the practical implications of state liability have been less far-reaching than often predicted.[15]

The picture is mixed as regards the cases decided by national courts (European Commission 1997d: 475–7, 1998c: 313–5, 2000a: 49–52, 2001c: 52–5; interview, Commission official, February 18, 1998; FIDE 1998; Biering 2000: 963–4; Chalmers 2000: 98–9). In relatively few cases have the claimants actually been awarded compensation; often, their claims have been dismissed on procedural or substantive grounds. It is slightly ironic that among the examples we find the cases that established and expanded the principle of state liability: *Francovich* and *Brasserie du Pêcheur*. Mr Francovich's first action failed because he had not employed the proper procedure for pursuing a state liability claim, though the Italian legal system had not clearly designated what procedure to use (Caranta 1993). Similar dismissals of liability claims on procedural grounds have occurred, for instance, in the UK.

Claimants may also be denied compensation on substantive, legal grounds. Known rejections suggest a certain hesitation about awarding compensation on the grounds of state liability. Claims have been dismissed based on the arguments that the causal link between state violation and individual damage suffered was insufficient, that the EU rule breached did not confer rights on individuals, or that the infringement could not be considered sufficiently serious. *Brasserie du Pêcheur* is a case in point. Whereas most legal observers regarded liability as effectively established in *Brasserie du Pêcheur* and *Factortame III* after the ECJ's judgment, and criticized the European court for meddling in the business of national courts, the German Federal High Court very surprisingly ruled against the claimant when the case returned from the ECJ. On the basis of how some national courts in this and other decisions have skillfully exploited legal loop-holes to avoid finding member governments liable, Elspeth Deards concludes: "Despite the dire warnings as to the consequences of the judgment in *Brasserie du Pêcheur/Factortame III*, it is evident that the judgment in fact allows national courts quite easily to avoid awarding damages against a Member State" (1997: 624).[16]

Special and more obvious cases of national court recalcitrance are the instances where higher courts have dismissed liability claims by refuting the supremacy of EU law over national law. Consider the Italian case where two lower courts had taken the view that the Italian state was obliged to pay compensation because of legislative breach, but where the Supreme Court of Appeal – disregarding the legal duty under EU law to create an effective remedy if one does not exist – took the view that the Italian state could not be held liable, since there were no such provisions in Italian law (European Commission 1997d: 476).[17]

Available data suggest that many national courts and governments were hesitant in their reception of the ECJ's state liability case law. Through various forms of inaction – not adjusting national legal systems to the requirements of EU law, not designating appropriate procedures and courts, and not applying the rules to the advantage of claimants – national courts and governments emasculated the principle and, at least temporarily, limited its enforcement-enhancing effect. As a councilor with the Commission's Legal Service concluded: "When it comes to the real possibilities, it remains very difficult to sue a member state in its own courts" (interview, February 18, 1998).

When inaction is more effective than action

The attempt by some member governments to punish the ECJ at the 1996–7 IGC illustrates well the difficulties involved in revising the agent's/supervisor's mandate in the EU. Reforming the core institutional set-up, altering the mandates of the supranational institutions, and reversing ECJ decisions based on the treaty necessitate constitutional amendments agreed upon at an IGC. Given the requirement of unanimity, the ECJ and the Commission will remain unsanctioned, and the result of their actions will survive unscathed, as long as this is preferred by just a single government. In view of, for instance, Belgium's staunch backing of the ECJ, it is unlikely that this institution will see its wings clipped as long as unanimous agreement is required for treaty amendments.

Fritz Scharpf (1988) has captured in formal terms the essential features and likely consequences of the institutional conditions present at IGCs. According to Scharpf, a "joint-decision trap" emerges in the EU whenever the institutional conditions are such that (a) decisions at the central EU level are directly dependent on the agreement of the constituent governments, and (b) the agreement of the constituent governments must be unanimous or nearly unanimous. In situations characterized by these institutional arrangements, the central EU level, in the form of the Council, will be unable to respond to internal and external demands, which in turn will lead to sub-optimal decisional outcomes. The joint-decision trap carries negative implications for governments' capacity to rein in agents by way of treaty revision (Pollack 1997; Alter 1998a).

In the negotiations on the ECJ at the 1996–7 IGC, both the decision rule and the distribution of government preferences pointed in favor of the ECJ.[18] The skepticism of the UK, Germany, France, and Spain was not sufficient to turn around the remaining governments. Since the ECJ's jurisprudence on state liability was based on treaty articles rather than secondary legislation, the judgments could not be reversed with less than the full accord of EU governments. Likewise, unanimity was required for revisions of the ECJ's competences. In one deal, member state principals could have revised the powers delegated to the ECJ, improved control mechanisms, and reduced the effects of supranational maneuvering. Now, a stern warning was the end result of the attack on the ECJ at the 1996–7 IGC.

In comparison with the act of revising the treaty, the sanction of inaction has greater chances of succeeding. This sanction is not subject to barriers at the supranational level, such as decision-making rules and the distribution of preferences among national governments. Moreover, as it consists of political and judicial inaction rather than action, it does not have to pass the hurdles of the domestic decision-making process to be effected. Rather, this sanction is automatically executed, whenever an official member state actor, whose active cooperation is required for supranational decisions to gain practical importance, prefers instead to maintain the status quo. The attitude of national courts is of seminal importance in judicial inaction. In the EU, national courts are the carriers of dual identities, loyalties, and purposes. Rather than being only courts of a member state, or only European courts, national courts are both. Neither the ECJ nor member governments can therefore entirely control national courts or expect their full allegiance.

In the case of state liability, discontented governments were privileged to enjoy the assistance of certain national courts in the attempts to emasculate the principle. A probable explanation for this reluctance is the interference of the principle in national constitutional orders and the challenge against the institutional and procedural autonomy of national courts. As Joseph Weiler observed with regard to *Francovich*, *Emmott*, and *Factortame I*:

> [T]he recent line of cases represents a potential encroachment of Community law and the authority of the European Court into procedural matters which hitherto were within the almost exclusive province of national courts. In the past the European Court was always careful to present itself as *primus inter pares* and to maintain a zone of autonomy of national jurisdiction even at the price of non-uniformity of application of Community law. If the new line of cases represents a nuanced departure from that earlier ethos, the prize may be increased effectiveness, but the cost may be a potential tension in the critical relationship between European and national courts.
>
> (Weiler 1993: 442–3)

It is typical that the most telling examples of reticent national courts, such as the German judgment in *Brasserie du Pêcheur* and the Italian case of disrespect for EU law supremacy, involved the highest courts rather than lower courts. The highest courts in the national legal systems have traditionally been the most reluctant to accept principles introduced by the ECJ, not least the path-breaking introduction of EU law supremacy.

> While EC law supremacy posed a threat to the influence and authority of high courts and implied a significant compromise of national sovereignty, lower courts found few costs and numerous benefits in making their own referrals to the ECJ and in applying EC law.
>
> (Alter 1996: 466)

This logic was at work in the case of state liability as well, where some high courts, intent on policing and preserving national legal systems, found the new principle too offensive to apply in full.

The sanction of inaction forces us to question what actually constitutes successful supranational influence. A focus on legal output and formal sanctions alone would have called for the conclusion that the strengthening of decentralized enforcement was home free once state liability had been established by the ECJ and saved from countermeasures at the IGC. As member states' recourse to evasion and inaction has shown, however, such a conclusion would have overestimated the immediate influence of these supranational actions on European governance. This qualified understanding of supranational influence is at the heart of the emerging literature on the conditions determining when ECJ jurisprudence translates into concrete policy effects (see Slaughter *et al.* 1998; Alter 2000; Conant 2002).

Conclusion

In the late 1980s and 1990s, the Commission and the ECJ jointly and single-handedly shifted the gravity in EU enforcement toward greater reliance on decentralized, "fire-alarm" supervision, as opposed to centralized, "police-patrol" enforcement. The ECJ laid down enforcement-enhancing principles and requirements through its case law, while the Commission launched policy programs aimed at informational barriers in decentralized supervision. In this process, the ECJ enjoyed greater autonomy than the Commission, which is best explained by variation in monitoring mechanisms and means of rule creation. The potential implications of the Commission's actions were limited by participation-based monitoring, whereby governments forced the institution to withdraw contentious elements from its programs. By contrast, governments only possessed means of observation-based monitoring with regard to the ECJ, and sought in vain to influence the ECJ by signaling their preferences in case observations. Unable to prevent the ECJ from establishing and expanding the principle of state liability, member states took to *ex post* sanctions against perceived judicial activism. The ECJ managed to avoid the most threatening sanction, exploiting division among governments and the high institutional barriers involved in treaty revision. Recalcitrance at the national level functioned as an additional form of sanction, temporarily reducing the implications of the ECJ's actions in some member states.

7 Conclusion

This study departed from one of the most central points of contention in the study of European governance: are the EU's supranational institutions engines of integration that actively drive the process of integration, or simply obedient servants that passively fulfil the technical functions they have been delegated by member governments? At the heart of this debate are competing claims about the degree of independent causal influence exerted by the Commission, the ECJ, and the EP on the course of European integration. As opposed to existing research, which is heavily focused on the agenda-setting phase of EU policy-making, this book has examined the influence of the Commission and the ECJ in post-decisional compliance politics. EU decision-making is of little value *per se*, and does not result in actual policy results, unless member state compliance with EU rules can be secured. The extent to which the Commission and the ECJ can enforce compliance more strenuously than desired by member governments and originally intended is therefore pivotal to the understanding of European governance.

In this final chapter, I summarize the main results of the book and outline its implications for the study of European governance and international cooperation. The chapter is divided into three sections. In the first, I synthesize the empirical findings and assess the explanatory power of the P–S–A model. The second section isolates the implications of the study for research on European governance and the debate on supranational influence. I conclude by identifying the implications of the study for ongoing debates in IR theory on delegation to international institutions and determinants of state compliance.

Supranational influence in EU enforcement

The historical processes documented in this study suggests that the Commission and the ECJ are capable of exerting independent influence in EU enforcement, but that this capacity is conditioned by member states' means of monitoring and sanctioning the supranational institutions. Important parts of these historical developments were previously undocumented in the legal and political literature. By mapping the Commission's and the

ECJ's three parallel campaigns to strengthen EU enforcement, this study has served the dual purpose of closing empirical gaps in the historical record and generating new evidence on the theoretical question of supranational influence.

Confidence in these findings is secured by the methodological strategy of the study. The case-study format, combined with process-tracing and counterfactual analysis, allows for close analysis of actor interests and behavior, thus safeguarding the inferences against the problem of anticipated reactions. The reliability of the findings is further strengthened by the high dependency on primary rather than secondary sources.

In this section, the findings of the study are structured across the three areas where the P–S–A model generated specific expectations: the incentives for, scope for, and effects of supranational influence in EU enforcement.

Incentives for supranational influence

The P–S–A model generated specific expectations about the conditions that would lead the EU's supranational institutions to pursue independent agendas in conflict with government preferences. Given conflicting interests and information asymmetry, it was predicted that the EU's supranational institutions would engage in efforts to independently strengthen EU enforcement when delegated supervisory powers proved insufficient to ensure compliance. The Commission and the ECJ were seen as motivated by a desire to secure state adherence to EU rules – the equivalent of "more Europe" in the post-decisional phase.

The empirical analysis grants support to this basic hypothesis. The perception of growing compliance problems in the late 1980s, and the anticipation of a further aggravation in the 1990s, was the basic reason behind the supranational institutions' efforts to strengthen EU enforcement. Three forms of compliance problems were especially prominent and worrying: non-compliance in the legal transposition of directives, non-compliance in the application of EU rules on the ground, and non-compliance with ECJ judgments.

These compliance problems were considered particularly alarming in view of the internal market program – the most ambitious legislative project of the Community so far. If the internal market were to be realized, non-compliance would have to be attacked with all enforcement weapons available. Yet the instruments that existed in the late 1980s were perceived by the supranational institutions as limited in their capacity to ameliorate these compliance problems. The foremost instrument at the disposal of the institutions – the infringement procedure at the central EU level – was extremely time and resource consuming in nature. It was equally clear that the limits of this procedure would be even more exposed when the large body of internal market rules came up for implementation and application in the early 1990s.

The concrete steps taken by the supranational institutions in the late 1980s and early 1990s confirm their sensitivity to the capacity of existing means to effectively contain non-compliance. First, the Commission attempted to enhance the effectiveness of existing powers through a fivefold set of measures that improved the infringement procedure as an enforcement instrument. Second, the Commission sought to induce the delegation of new means of enforcement at the 1991 and 1996–7 IGCs; first the introduction of sanctions against non-complying states, and then more time and resource efficient procedures for the imposition of these sanctions. Third, the Commission and the ECJ took joint action to shift the center of gravity in EU enforcement toward greater reliance on decentralized supervision through national courts – a process that involved the creation of entirely new enforcement means.

Scope for supranational influence

The core hypotheses generated by the P–S–A model pertained to the scope for supranational influence in EU enforcement. Drawing on the most central elements of P–A theory, the model predicted that the Commission's and the ECJ's capacity to exert independent influence would be determined by member states' means for monitoring and sanctioning the actions of the institutions. In view of the existing mechanisms of control in EU enforcement, the model further predicted that the scope for supranational influence would be more extensive in the exercise of existing powers than at moments of treaty revision, that the ECJ would enjoy more room for maneuver than the Commission, and that unilateral sanctions would be more effective than collective sanctions as a means of state control.

The empirical record strongly supports the notion that member states' control mechanisms condition the ability of the supranational institutions to exert supranational influence. Where member states could readily observe, interpret, and intervene in supranational actions, and where unwanted behavior could be countered with sanctions, the Commission's and the ECJ's scope for supranational influence was highly limited, or even non-existent. By contrast, the supranational institutions enjoyed some capacity to introduce enforcement measures in conflict with government preferences, where few means existed to actively monitor their actions, and where sanctions were either lacking or difficult to apply effectively.

The three parallel strategies pursued by the supranational institutions effectively constituted three cases with an internal variation across key elements of the P–S–A relationship. Each conformed to one alternative way of exerting independent influence, involving specific conditions for government control:

1 exercising delegated powers contrary to the preferences of member governments;

2 inducing a delegation of powers that member governments would not have conferred in the absence of supranational maneuvering; and
3 single-handedly creating new means beyond the confines of the treaties.

As predicted, this variation in strategic context translated into a distinct variation in outcomes.

All five measures taken by the Commission to enhance the enforcement potential of the infringement procedure – the internal reforms streamlining the handling of cases, the shift to a firmer enforcement policy, the encouragement of complaints to the Commission, the development of a shaming strategy, and the intensification of compliance bargaining – in some way strengthened EU supervision. Yet none of these measures qualified as supranational influence, since governments were largely supportive of these actions. Unfortunately, this makes it impossible to evaluate strictly the Commission's scope for supranational influence within the infringement procedure; since governments did not oppose the Commission's actions, it cannot be assessed whether their control mechanisms were sufficient or inadequate to prevent supranational influence. That said, existing empirical patterns do suggest that the Commission operates with a significant degree of autonomy in relation to the infringement procedure. Anxious to secure credible commitments, governments have refrained from establishing control mechanisms that would allow them to interfere in the Commission's handling of infringement cases.

The Commission's attempts to induce the delegation of more far-reaching enforcement means at the 1991 and 1996–7 IGCs illustrate the limited capacity of the supranational institutions to exert independent influence at moments of treaty revision. Compared to everyday decision-making and enforcement in the EU, IGCs entail a high degree of agenda control for member governments. This agenda control generates a more even distribution of information about the consequences of supranational proposals and allows member states to present alternative solutions without involving the Commission, thus reducing the institutions' capacity to maneuver governments into accepting supranational proposals. At the 1991 IGC, the Commission sought to induce governments into accepting its preferred sanctioning mechanisms rather than the revision of Article 171 promoted by the UK, but failed, as the negative consequences for national sovereignty were fully observable to the member states. Similarly, the 1996–7 IGC entailed a rearguard battle for the Commission, which was forced to adapt its proposal for a more efficient and effective sanctioning procedure to governments' preferences in a number of consecutive steps. EU governments never showed any sign of failing to understand the consequences of the Commission's suggestion. Expressed in terms of alternative forms of monitoring, the IGC format on these occasions granted member states effective control through an extreme form of participation-based monitoring.

The Commission's and the ECJ's collective efforts to strengthen decentralized enforcement was, by contrast, a process which member states had great difficulty controlling, not least because of the pivotal role of the ECJ. Exploiting the discretion inherent in its competence to interpret Community law, the ECJ strengthened the remedies available to aggrieved parties in national courts – a process whose completion member states could do little but observe, save the option of sanctioning the ECJ and its actions. Two forms of sanctions were attempted and, whereas the sanction of treaty revision failed, the sanction of inaction at the national level partially and temporarily reduced the consequences of the ECJ's actions. The Commission, for its part, exerted limited supranational influence when launching policy programs that supplemented the ECJ's case law advances by reducing informational barriers. This joint reinforcement of decentralized supervision passes the counterfactual test that intergovernmentalist scholars recommend whenever an independent supranational effect on European integration is claimed. By any measure, it is highly unlikely that member states, in the absence of supranational action, would have stepped in to strengthen decentralized enforcement. It is simply unimaginable that national governments, somewhere between their 1991 rejection of state liability as a system of sanctions and their 1996–7 attempts to punish the ECJ for introducing this very sanction, would have decided to institutionalize this system themselves.

These empirical processes provide strong and unequivocal support for the notion that the ECJ is less constrained than the Commission. In general terms, attempts at supranational influence only succeeded where the ECJ was involved. Examinations of centralized enforcement, centered on the Commission and political processes, called for pessimistic conclusions as to the supranational institutions' ability to move EU enforcement beyond governments' preferences. By contrast, the tracing of developments in decentralized enforcement, centered on the ECJ and judicial processes, gave reason to question this verdict.

Variation in member states' control mechanisms provides a powerful explanation of the divergent records of the Commission and the ECJ. Consider, especially, the institutions' parallel attempts to enhance decentralized enforcement. Through a string of important decisions in the late 1980s and early 1990s, the ECJ laid down principles and requirements that strengthened the hand of individuals wishing to enforce their EU rights in national courts. The ECJ's capacity to introduce measures unwanted by member governments is best attributed to the latter's lack of means for intrusive, participation-based monitoring. The judicial independence inherent in the ECJ's position as legal supreme grants the institution an autonomy that makes it uniquely easy to introduce measures perceived to be in the interest of the EU and its judicial system. National governments may argue their cases before the ECJ, but cannot prevent it from handing down unwanted judgments. In effect, therefore, member states' only weapon against the ECJ are *ex post* sanctions. In the case of decentralized enforcement, the sanctions applied did not succeed in fully eliminating the effects of the ECJ actions.

In parallel, the Commission launched policy initiatives aimed at overcoming informational barriers in the existing structure of decentralized enforcement, thus reinforcing the measures introduced by the ECJ. As opposed to the ECJ, the Commission was far from relieved of oversight; the formulation of the Citizens First and Robert Schuman programs was monitored actively and intrusively by member governments. Irrespective of whether or not it was formally required, government consent was *de facto* necessary for the launching of both these programs, effectively facilitating control of the Commission's actions. Where the Commission did not adapt its proposals to government preferences *ex ante*, member states sanctioned the projects *ex post*, for instance, by opting out. While highly constrained, the Commission nevertheless exercised limited supranational influence when shielding these programs from wholesale rejection through the techniques of packaging, framing, and co-optive justification.

Finally, member states' attempts to sanction the ECJ for the introduction of state liability illustrate effectively the constraining capacity of unilateral sanctions compared to collective sanctions. Symptomatically, the UK-led attempt at the 1996–7 IGC to revise the ECJ's mandate and rewrite its enforcement-enhancing decisions was thwarted by the requirement for unanimous agreement, which could not be secured despite the support of powerful governments. The joint-decision trap proved impossible to overcome in the face of divergent government preferences and the most demanding decision rule. By contrast, available data suggest that inaction at the national level limited, at least partially and temporarily, the effects of the state liability principle. Rather than enthusiastically embracing the principle of state liability, some national governments and courts were reluctant to accept the full implications of the new case law.

Whereas the multilateral sanction of treaty revision could be applied only if all governments agreed, the unilateral sanction of inaction was merely contingent on the actions of a single government, or even a single official member state actor. Nor did it have to get over the hurdle of the domestic decision-making process to be effected, as it consisted of political and judicial inaction rather than action. This sanction is automatically executed whenever a national actor, whose active cooperation is required, prefers instead to maintain the status quo. In the particular case of state liability, it was clear that national courts held such a key position, and that some governments were fortunate enough to enjoy the support of national courts in their ambition of restricting the consequences of the principle. The major weakness of inaction as a sanction, compared to treaty revision, is that it cannot remove the basic cause of concern, but instead merely limits its effects, and perhaps only temporarily. Despite a recalcitrant reception at the national level, the principle of state liability remains a part of Community law that every now and then will remind governments of the hollowness of national sovereignty and the costs of non-compliance.

Effects of supranational influence

The P–S–A model generated specific expectations as to what kind of supervision the EU's supranational institutions were likely to promote. It was posited that the Commission and the ECJ would be sensitive to the relative resource efficiency of alternative forms of supervision, and therefore likely to favor the less resource demanding mode of decentralized enforcement over the highly resource intensive strategy of centralized enforcement. Since the costs of completely eradicating member state non-compliance would be prohibitively high, the supranational institutions would seek to shift from more to less resource intensive means in order to obtain as much enforcement as possible, given existing resources.

The striving for more resource efficient forms of supervision was a defining feature of all supranational action in EU enforcement during the period examined. All three aspects of the campaign to reinforce EU supervision testify to a well-developed resource-sensitivity among the supranational institutions, the Commission in particular. In the exercise of its delegated enforcement powers, the Commission consistently took steps or intensified practices that would make centralized enforcement more resource efficient, such as internal reforms and the extension of compliance bargaining. At the two IGCs, the Commission sought first to obtain sanctions that were relatively less resource demanding for the supranational institutions, and then to abolish any step in the new procedure that rendered it particularly time and resource consuming. Finally, in the quest to boost decentralized supervision, the Commission and the ECJ shifted the center of gravity in EU enforcement toward a form of supervision that was less resource intensive for the institutions.

The supranational institutions clearly appreciated the problem of resources in enforcement. Yet this is not the same as saying that the institutions were sensitive to the total resource requirements of various modes of supervision. The shift toward greater reliance on decentralized enforcement did not necessarily reduce the resources required as such; rather, it entailed that the costs of enforcement would increasingly have to be borne by individuals and national courts, instead of by the supranational institutions. Maximizing compliance and enforcement rather than competences, the Commission and the ECJ found it an attractive option to spread the cost and responsibility of supervision, as long as more enforcement and better compliance were likely to result.

Implications for the study of European governance

These findings carry two primary implications for the study of European governance. First, they challenge the prevailing understanding of the role, autonomy, and influence of the EU's supranational institutions. Second, they underline the merits of P–A analysis as a means of explaining the sources and effects of delegation in European governance.

The influence of the EU's supranational institutions

Existing scholarship on supranational influence has been heavily centered on the agenda-setting functions of the Commission, the ECJ, and the EP, paying little or no attention to the role of these institutions in post-decisional compliance politics. This study demonstrates the importance of integrating the enforcement of state compliance into our understanding of the supranational institutions' influence in European governance. Post-decisional compliance politics has the capacity to shift policy outcomes in EU policy-making. In the absence of implementation and compliance, EU rules are of little importance, as are the processes of agenda setting and bargaining that lead to the adoption of these rules. Furthermore, variation in compliance between states and sectors alters the terms on which European governments once entered into EU agreements.

This study demonstrates that the EU's supranational institutions play an important role in making states comply. Yet the Commission and the ECJ have not solely fulfilled the supervisory functions delegated to them by member governments. Historically, the EU's supranational institutions have exerted an independent influence on EU policy-making by moving the enforcement of state compliance beyond governments' original intentions when first delegating supervisory competences. The Commission and the ECJ are thus capable of transforming European governance, not only by introducing new issues to the policy agenda, but also by securing a higher degree of realization of the decisions that are indeed taken.

In fact, there is much to suggest that the Commission and the ECJ enjoy particularly extensive discretion in policy enforcement, as compared to their other functions in EU governance. This is best explained by the logic of credible commitments. The control mechanisms designed by member governments vary systematically depending on what functional problems the Commission and the ECJ have been set to mitigate or resolve (Tallberg 2002a). When enhancing the credibility of member state commitments by enforcing compliance and safeguarding the basic constitutional treaty, the supranational institutions are typically relieved of intrusive control mechanisms. When providing technical expertise or enhancing the efficiency of decision making by engaging in regulation, implementation, and policy interpretation, the Commission and the ECJ are subject to closer monitoring and a more credible threat of sanctions.

From the perspective of member governments, delegation of enforcement competences to supranational institutions constitutes a true dilemma. The very rationale of delegation is for member states to collectively tie their hands by conferring authority on actors that cannot be directly controlled. The act of self-commitment is only meaningful to the extent that supranational supervisors enjoy extensive discretion in the execution of their functions and do no face the immediate threat of having their decisions overturned by government principals. Monitoring of compliance is of limited value if those whose compliance is being monitored in turn control the monitor. Yet it is this discretion that permits the EU's supranational institutions to pursue independent agendas in the enforcement of state compliance. As demonstrated in this study, the EU's supranational institutions have not been hard pressed to exploit the additional discretion they enjoy in EU supervision. Delegation of supervisory competences thus carries certain logical and automatic side-effects that governments cannot protect themselves against without undermining the very purpose of delegation.

Furthermore, existing literature on supranational influence pays only limited attention to the question of variation between the Commission and the ECJ, and explicit comparative analyses are rare. This study has offered good conditions for controlled comparison between the two institutions, and it demonstrates how the Commission and the ECJ experienced distinctly different opportunities and constraints in the pursuit of the same supranational goal. Consider the Commission's and the ECJ's parallel attempts to achieve more effective sanctions through IGC maneuvering and treaty interpretation respectively.

These parallel campaigns illustrate how member states' control mechanisms and the institutions' means of influence condition the scope for autonomy, in this case by allowing the ECJ to introduce measures governments firmly opposed, while blocking the Commission's efforts in the same area. Subject to intrusive participation-based monitoring and the threat of government sanctions, the Commission failed to maneuver governments into creating effective sanctions. The ECJ, by contrast, exploited its power of interpretation and the absence of intrusive monitoring means for the purpose of developing a form of decentralized sanctions unwanted by member governments.

The source of this variation in supranational influence is the institutional functions of the Commission and the ECJ (Tallberg 2000a). The functions delegated to the two institutions shape the control mechanisms at governments' disposal and condition the supranational institutions' means of influence. This is particularly notable if we compare the Commission's core function of initiation and the ECJ's core function of interpretation. While the Commission participates in the political process of policy-making, whereby new legislation is adopted, the ECJ operates in the judicial process of interpretation, whereby already existing law is further explicated. The Commission's preparation and presentation of new legislative initiatives goes hand in hand with close government monitoring and credible sanctions, whereas the ECJ's interpretation of existing rules is relieved of intrusive monitoring and easily executed sanctions. This variation in control mechanisms translates into a systematically greater capacity for the ECJ to implement private agendas, compared to the Commission.

The ECJ has learned to exploit diverging member state positions for the purpose of pursuing agendas it knows governments cannot undo. To reverse the ECJ's treaty interpretations all EU governments must agree on the suggested revisions at an IGC and all member states must ratify the new treaty. Historically, no attempt to rewrite the ECJ's treaty interpretations, or to sanction the institution directly, has ever succeeded. In essence, the ECJ has learned to count on the support of at least one member state and, on this basis, developed techniques for introducing controversial doctrines that secure the institution against sanctions.

The Commission, by contrast, operates in a world with a more immediate and credible threat of sanctions. Rationally anticipating the risk of having its legislative proposals dismissed by the Council, or of having its executive decisions referred to the Council from the comitology committees, the Commission tends only to present proposals with a high likelihood of adoption. Interestingly, but hardly surprisingly, the Commission enjoys an unusual capacity to pursue private interests when drawing on the support of the less constrained ECJ.

The key elements of this stylised comparison between the two institutions are summarized in Table 7.1. Interpreting political relations in the EU through this lens, we find a strategic context comparatively more open to autonomous actions by the ECJ, which is more sheltered from intrusive government control than the Commission, and enjoys means of influence permitting more independent rule-creation. We are therefore more likely

Table 7.1 Sources of variation in supranational influence

Factors shaping autonomy	*European Commission*	*European Court of Justice*
Institutional function	Initiation of new rules, requiring member state mobilization	Interpretation of existing rules, not requiring mobilization
Member state monitoring	Participation-based monitoring, allowing member states to actively shape Commission proposals	Observation-based monitoring, relieving the ECJ from direct member state involvement
Member state sanctions (capacity to overturn supranational decisions)	Right to re-legislate through standard legislative procedures	Right to re-legislate when secondary law; treaty revision required when primary law
Institutional strategies for exercising autonomy	Strategies sensitive to the need for securing member state approval: packaging, framing, and co-optive justification	Strategies sensitive to the need for maintaining legitimacy: doctrinal anchoring and goal legitimization

Source: Tallberg 2000a: 850.

to find instances of supranational influence in the tracks of the pro-integrationist, but less restrained, ECJ. To quote Martin Shapiro: “To understand policymaking, one must hunt where the ducks are – even if they are in the deep thickets of the law” (1992: 124).

P–A analysis and the study of European governance

Derived from general P–A theory, the P–S–A model was construed to capture the problems of control inherent in the delegation of supervisory competences to supranational institutions. The empirical analysis in this study provides a firm endorsement of the model as a theoretical construct. Most fundamentally, the hypotheses generated by the model receive widespread support in the empirical findings. This is because the P–S–A model captures effectively the strategic context of EU enforcement: the configuration of actors, their preferences, their constraints, and their opportunities.

The extension of the generic P–A model into the triangular P–S–A model permitted a configuration of the key actors, which accords better with legal and political practice in EU enforcement. Higher explanatory and predictive capacity has been the substantive consequence of this reconfiguration and the dual role it confers on member states. The empirical examination offers extensive support for the actor preferences stipulated in the model. Member states are essentially torn between the threefold interests of securing compliance, safeguarding sovereignty, and retaining room for maneuver in the implementation of EU rules, each state conceiving the relative importance of these objectives slightly differently from the others. The supranational institutions, for their part, are steadfastly pursuing the objective of better compliance through more effective enforcement, which need not involve a maximization of their own competences. The empirical process covered in the study also testifies that monitoring and sanctions enable governments to better control the supranational institutions so that they work toward the objectives of the member states rather than pursue their own interests.

In broader terms, the study validates the advantages of P–A analysis as a tool for addressing delegation and autonomy in European governance. The neutral theoretical language of P–A analysis permits an open-ended assessment of the degree of independent influence exercised by agents, such as the EU’s supranational institutions, without discriminating between competing claims. Independent influence is treated as a question of empirical analysis rather than assumption, and empirical findings typically point to complex pictures of variation in agency.

Traditionally, the study of European integration has been preoccupied with delegation to supranational institutions. Yet, in today’s Europe, this is only one of many forms of delegation. One of the most powerful trends in European governance is the tendency for majoritarian bodies to delegate decision powers to non-majoritarian institutions, be they supranational institutions, central banks, or regulatory agencies (see Stone Sweet and

Thatcher 2002). Democratic politics in Europe has also been conceived as a chain of delegation from voters to elected representatives to the executive branch to civil servants (see Bergman *et al.* 2000). P–A theory offers an effective tool for analyzing and explaining the sources and effects of these processes of delegation in European governance. From a meta-theoretical perspective, the merits of P–A analysis as a general theoretical tool support the notion that the EU, while unique as political phenomenon, can in fact be adequately explained using general theories of political behavior.

Yet no theoretical approach is likely to capture all facets of a political phenomenon. P–A analysis does not constitute an exception in this respect, and this study points to two particular limits. First, in its original formulation, P–A theory places great emphasis on information asymmetry as the source of agent autonomy and influence. Only if the principal cannot fully monitor and correctly interpret the agent's actions is there scope for autonomous actions. However, various episodes in this study illustrate that principals may be fully aware of what an agent is doing, yet unable to prevent the agent from carrying through its plans. The best example is the ECJ's introduction of the principle of state liability in the face of vocal government opposition. This suggests that information asymmetry does not constitute a prerequisite for agent autonomy in political delegation.

Second, the dual position of national courts as integral parts of both the European and the national legal structures poses difficulties for P–A analysis, where the actors are assumed to be clearly delimited and mutually exclusive. This is a weakness that P–A analysis shares with many other theoretical conceptualizations of national, European, and international politics. As one legal scholar notes, existing political accounts of European legal integration simply do not "provide theoretical space for the fact that national courts are simultaneously both 'of' and 'not of' the national and European systems of governance" (Kilpatrick 1998: 145).

These weaknesses of P–A analysis reflect the downside of deductive models. What is gained in parsimony and logical inference may be partially lost in empirical comprehensiveness. The choice confronting scholars wishing to employ P–A analysis is therefore one of either relying entirely on the generic and theoretically coherent logic of the P–A model, while being aware that certain explanatory power may have to be sacrificed, or acknowledging a priori that the P–A relationship may be most useful as an imagery or general framework in which many forms of constraints and opportunities can be integrated.

Implications for the study of international cooperation

The EU is often described by students of European governance as *sui generis*, rendering comparisons with national and international forms of governance difficult. This pessimism is unjustified and contrary to standard methodological practices, which acknowledge that all cases in some way are unique, yet recognize the value of comparison for general theoretical inferences. This study generates implications for the debates in IR theory on delegation to international institutions and the determinants of state compliance.

Delegation to international institutions

The growth of governance beyond the nation-state is one of the most pronounced political trends in recent decades. To address problems that cannot be dealt with effectively at the national level, governments jointly develop international governance structures. Increasingly, the design of such structures involves the delegation of decision-making powers to institutions that are organisationally and, to varying extents, politically independent from the founding states. In this respect, the evolution of international governance reflects the previously noted general development in European governance: the delegation of political authority from representative organs to non-majoritarian institutions that are neither directly elected by the people nor directly managed by elected politicians.

Delegation to international institutions raises a set of questions of general relevance in political science: Why do elected politicians and sovereign member states freely give up some of their right to govern? Why do governments prefer certain forms of institutional design instead of others in the delegation of political authority? What are the consequences of delegation to international institutions for the problem-solving capacity and democratic legitimacy of international governance structures? In this book, I have addressed some of these themes with specific reference to the EU. It is now time to recognize that P–A theory may be equally relevant for addressing delegation and agency in international governance in general.

The EU is not the only case where governments have set up and delegated functions to international institutions, simultaneously creating potential control problems. Secretariats, courts, and dispute-settlement bodies of international organizations, such as the World Trade Organization (WTO), the International Monetary Fund (IMF), the UN, the International Atomic Energy Agency (IAEA), and the Council of Europe, generally enjoy certain duties of representation, initiation, execution, supervision, and rule interpretation. What makes the supranational institutions of the EU unique in this comparative perspective is the range of the powers delegated, not the act of delegation itself. The Commission and the ECJ perform functions they have in common with other secretariats, courts, and dispute-settlement bodies, but enjoy competences within these functions that exceed those of the other institutions.

Yet IR scholars have been slow to recognize the usefulness of P–A theory as a theoretical tool for understanding and explaining patterns of delegation in international governance. Though much thinking about international regimes and institutions originates from a functionalist understanding of international cooperation, P–A theory *per se* is only beginning to inform this literature (e.g. Alter 2002b; Kahler 2002; Martin 2002). While serious gaps in control are less likely to be found elsewhere, there is nothing inherent in P–A analysis that limits the use of this theoretical approach to the study of the EU. Rather, it may be employed to explain delegation decisions, design, and consequences whenever governments confer powers to international institutions. But P–A analysis may also generate important insights in cases where delegation does not take place, or only takes place gradually. As Andrew Moravcsik notes: "[G]overnments often refuse to assume the political risk of delegation, preferring instead imperfect enforcement and inefficient decision-making, to the surrender of sovereignty" (1993: 509).

The relationship between functional demands for delegation and concerns for national sovereignty is an area that begs further exploration. Process tracing of shifts over time in the underlying costs and benefits of alternative governance structures is likely to be particularly rewarding. Equally relevant are: cases where delegation never occurs despite strong functional demands; cases where entirely new supranational institutions are set up, such as the International Criminal Court (ICC); and cases that involve gradual extensions of delegation, such as the transformation of the GATT/WTO dispute-settlement mechanism.

Turning specifically to rule supervision – one of the classic functions of international organizations – this study suggests that the relationship between member states and international supervisory institutions can be captured effectively by the P–S–A configuration. In its stylized version, the P–S–A model expresses what standard P–A theory would consider as the typical problems, key factors, and logical consequences of conceptualizing member states and institutions as principals, supervisors, and agents. The model is not particular to EU enforcement as such, but generates the same expectations in all cases where states in an act of self-commitment delegate supervisory functions to international institutions.

By highlighting the dilemma of credible commitments, this study carries particular implications for the debate in IR on delegation to international courts, supervisory bodies, and dispute-settlement organs. For the reasons I have outlined above, delegation of supervisory competences, by necessity, involves the granting of certain discretion to international institutions, since monitoring, enforcement, and rule interpretation would be of little value if controlled by governments. It is therefore no coincidence that courts, such as the ECJ and the European Court of Human Rights (ECHR), are prominent among the examples of international institutions that demonstrably have acted independently in pursuit of private goals.

Again, what sets the EU apart from other international organizations is the range of the enforcement powers conferred on its institutions, not the delegation itself. One of the central trends in international relations today is the growing willingness of governments to equip international institutions with more far-reaching dispute-settlement powers. Yet few other international secretariats share the Commission's position as third-party prosecutor, and no other dispute-settlement bodies enjoy the same judicial authority as the ECJ.

> The common understanding of the role of international institutions is that they monitor the behavior of participants in cooperative agreements and paint "scarlet letters" on transgressors. The states themselves punish violations; all that the international institutions do is provide information that allows the states to further their own interests.
>
> (Garrett 1992: 535)

We had thus better conceive of international supervisory competences as a continuum, with a number of coexisting models involving varying degrees of delegation (see, e.g. Helfer and Slaughter 1997; Yarbrough and Yarbrough 1997; Keohane *et al.* 2000; Alter 2002a; Tallberg 2002b). P–A analysis offers effective theoretical tools for explaining this variation in delegation and its effects on the autonomy and influence of international institutions.

Paths to state compliance

In recent years, the question of what determines compliance with international regulatory agreements has gained an increasingly prominent position on the research agenda through the burgeoning literature on international regime effectiveness and international legal systems. The contemporary debate is framed in terms of two alternative perspectives on compliance: the enforcement approach and the management approach. The two perspectives present contending claims about the most effective means for addressing non-compliance in international cooperation.

The enforcement approach is firmly anchored in the political economy tradition of game theory and collective action theory (e.g. Olson 1965; Axelrod 1984; Axelrod and Keohane 1986; Yarbrough and Yarbrough 1992; Bayard and Elliott 1994; Downs *et al.* 1996; Dorn and Fulton 1997). States are conceived of as rational actors, which weigh the costs and benefits of alternative behavioral choices when making compliance decisions in cooperative situations. Both the sources of, and solutions to, non-compliance stem from the incentive structure. States choose to defect when confronted with an incentive structure in which the benefits of shirking exceed the costs of detection. Compliance problems are therefore best remedied by increasing the likelihood and costs of detection through monitoring and the threat of sanctions.

The management approach presents a perspective at odds with the claims of the enforcement school (e.g. Young 1992; Haas *et al.* 1993; Mitchell 1994; Chayes and Chayes 1995; Keohane and Levy 1996; Chayes *et al.* 1998). Drawing on qualitative case studies, managerial theorists stress states' general propensity to comply with international rules, owing to considerations of efficiency, interests, and norms. Non-compliance, when it occurs, is not the result of deliberate decisions to violate treaties, but an effect of capacity limitations and rule ambiguity. Consequently, non-compliance is best addressed through a problem-solving strategy of capacity building, rule interpretation, and transparency, rather than through coercive enforcement.

The two approaches are widely regarded as competing, both in theory and practice. Emphasize Kal Raustiala and David Victor: "The two schools of thought reflect different visions of how the international system works, the possibilities for governance with international law, and the policy tools that are available and should be used to handle implementation problems" (1998: 681). Similarly, a recent review of compliance theory concludes: "[The debate between management and enforcement theorists] has deep roots; at its heart it reflects a fundamental division about the nature of law that permeates domestic as well as international jurisprudence" (Raustiala and Slaughter 2002: 543).

The EU case, as described in this book, challenges this conception of enforcement and management as competing strategies for achieving compliance (Tallberg 2002b). The EU compliance system consists of both centralized, active, and direct "police-patrol" supervision, conducted by the EU's supranational institutions, and decentralized, reactive, and indirect "fire-alarm" supervision, where national courts and societal watchdogs are engaged to induce state compliance. At both these levels, the operation of the EU compliance system rests on a combination of enforcement and management mechanisms.

The combination of compliance mechanisms takes the form of a highly developed "management-enforcement ladder" – a twinning of cooperative and coercive measures that step by step improve states' capacity and incentives for compliance. Simplifying slightly, this ladder consists of four stages:

1 preventive capacity building and rule clarification that reduce the risk of violations due to incapacity or inadvertence;
2 forms of monitoring that enhance the transparency of state behavior and expose violators;
3 a legal system that permits cases to be brought against non-complying states and that further clarifies existing rules; and
4 deterrent sanctions as a final measure, in case states refuse to accept the rulings of the legal system.

This management-enforcement ladder makes the EU exceedingly effective in combating violations, thereby reducing non-compliance to temporal phenomenon.

The EU case thus suggests that enforcement and management mechanisms are most effective when combined. This conclusion is reinforced when the European experience is put in a comparative perspective, involving evidence from international regimes in the areas of trade, environment, and human rights (Tallberg 2002b: 632–9). Compliance systems that offer both forms of instrument tend to be particularly effective in securing rule conformance, whereas systems that only rely on one of the strategies often suffer in identifiable ways. By the same token, compliance systems that develop this complementarity over time demonstrate an enhanced capacity to handle non-compliance.

What is particular about the EU's combination of enforcement and management in this comparative perspective is the operation of these functions by independent supranational institutions and empowered societal interests. As opposed to most international regimes, where the signatories themselves play a central role in executing enforcement and management functions, the EU has supranational institutions in charge of capacity building, monitoring, rule interpretation, and sanctioning, with assistance from transnational societal interests. This organization has served the EU well, by facilitating effective inducement of state compliance, and by permitting the development of ever more constraining enforcement mechanisms over time.

Notes

1 Introduction

1 I refer to the EU by its current name, except where I speak of it in a particular historical context, when I use the historically correct term. The numbering of treaty articles follows that of the consolidated treaties after the Amsterdam treaty, with an article's former number in brackets the first time it is mentioned, except where I speak of the articles in a particular historical context, when I use the historically correct number.

2 The treaties are: the European Coal and Steel Community treaty (the ECSC treaty, the treaty of Paris), concluded 1951 and entered into force 1952; the European Economic Community treaty and the European Atomic Energy Community treaty (the EEC treaty and the Euratom treaty; the treaties of Rome), concluded 1957 and entered into force 1958; the Single European Act (SEA), concluded 1986 and entered into force 1987; the treaty on European Union (TEU, Maastricht treaty), concluded 1991 and entered into force 1993; the Amsterdam treaty, concluded 1997 and entered into force 1999, and the Nice treaty, concluded in 2000 and entered into force 2003.

3 In this review of the scholarly debate on supranational influence, I have therefore chosen to exclude important perspectives on European governance, most notably, the multilevel governance approach and constructivist approaches, since they do not coherently and systematically address the question of supranational influence. For works which depict the EU as a system of multi-level governance, see Marks 1993; Scharpf 1994; Peterson 1995; Hooghe 1996; Jachtenfuchs and Kohler-Koch 1996; Marks *et al.* 1996; Risse-Kappen 1996; Marks and Hooghe 2001. For good collections of constructivist contributions, see Jørgensen 1997; Christiansen *et al.* 2001.

4 Exceptions to this neglect are neofunctionalist, intergovernmentalist, and P–A interpretations of the ECJ's early transformation of the preliminary ruling procedure into an enforcement instrument (Garrett 1992; Burley and Mattli 1993; Alter 1998a). However, rather than enforcement *per se*, the key issue in this debate is legal integration. Enforcement is merely the domain affected by the ECJ decisions that first and most forcefully illustrated how its power of interpretation could be used to establish principles not previously acknowledged in the treaty.

5 Existing empirical literature in political science and law on the supranational institutions' enforcement tools can be divided into three strands: political analysis of the Commission's use of the infringement procedure (Mendrinou 1996; Jönsson and Tallberg 1998; Börzel 2001); legal analysis of the same infringement procedure (Cahier 1974; Evans 1979; Everling 1984; Audretsch 1986; Dashwood and White 1989; Snyder 1993); and legal scholarship on the ECJ's development of decentralized enforcement (e.g. Pescatore 1974, 1983;

Stein 1981; Rasmussen 1986; Weiler 1991, 1994; Craig 1993; Snyder 1993; Steiner 1993, 1995; Van Gerven 1995, 1996). These strands of literature fill important gaps in research on European governance, and in the empirical chapters of this study, I will draw on selected aspects of this literature. The limitations of this literature that justify the present study is the lack of attention to the analytical question of independent supranational influence, the absence of a comprehensive understanding of EU enforcement, and important blank spots in the coverage of the evolution of EU enforcement since the late 1970s.

2 Principals, supervisors, and agents in EU enforcement

1 The origin of rational choice institutionalism can be traced to the pioneering work of Kenneth Shepsle on the role of institutions in the US Congress (Shepsle 1979, 1986, 1989). Puzzled by the stability of majorities for legislation in Congress, Shepsle argued that this could be explained by the way in which congressional institutions, such as the committees, structured the choices and information available to members of Congress.

2 While the precise conception of what an institution is tends to shift within and between the three new institutionalisms, it should be noted that the term "institution" within all approaches generally is employed to denote something broader than formal institutions such as the Commission and the ECJ. Often, institutions are widely conceived of as formal or informal procedures, routines, norms, and conventions, or as Douglass North puts it, "any form of constraint that human beings devise to shape human interactions" (1990: 4). Consequently, the concept is taken to mean two things in this study depending on the context: formal organizations in the context of the supranational institutions of the EU, and the broader conception referred to above in the context of the new institutionalist approaches discussed here.

3 The new institutional economics arose in the 1970s in response to the failure of traditional neoclassical economics to recognize the importance of institutions for economic activity and exchange. Slightly simplified, the new institutional economics developed into three main branches: transaction cost theory, agency theory, and property rights theory. Seminal works in agency theory include Alchian and Demsetz 1972; Ross 1973; Jensen and Meckling 1976; Pratt and Zeckhauser 1985b.

4 This import was not restricted to P–A theory, but also included transaction cost theory. Important contributions include Shepsle 1979; Keohane 1984; Yarbrough and Yarbrough 1987, 1990, 1992; Weingast and Marshall 1988; Martin 1993; Simmons 1993.

5 In the economic P–A literature, the market is often stressed as an indirect, "fire-alarm" source of information on agent performance (e.g. Pratt and Zeckhauser 1985a: 5). The "decibel meter" is another term that is frequently used to denote the "fire-alarm" monitoring performed by constituency groups (e.g. Weingast 1984). On how administrative procedures create a "fire-alarm" system, see McCubbins *et al.* 1987; McCubbins and Page 1987. On how asymmetric "fire-alarm" signals can introduce a bias in regulatory outcomes, see Hopenhayn and Lohmann 1996.

6 Note that there is nothing in the P–A model that reduces incentive mechanisms to strictly monetary forms. Rewards and sanctions can be social in nature and can consist of, for instance, effects on an agent's reputation (e.g. Jensen and Meckling 1976: 351; Arrow 1985: 50; Pratt and Zeckhauser 1985a: 16–17).

7 The P–S–A model, in line with P–A theory in general, employs a conception of the actors as unified entities with a given set of preferences. Obviously, this is a simplification that does not recognize the degree of division inside the supra-

national institutions and the member states. However, as the purpose here is to model strategic interaction between these actors, rather than internal relations within, this assumption is quite helpful. Moreover, it should be noted that this conception accords with the legal status of these actors in the EU policy process; the *member states* agree to decisions in intergovernmental bodies, the *Commission* and the *ECJ* are delegated enforcement competences, and the *member states* are responsible for adequate implementation and compliance. For the sake of linguistic variation, however, I often use the terms "national governments," "member governments," and "EU governments" when I refer to member states as principals.

8 Note, however, that it is often acknowledged that the preferences of the supranational institutions, the Commission in particular, are less consistent and predictable on substantive issues, where internal political strife between the Commission's directorates-general (DGs) can cause the external position to shift from issue to issue.

9 The first and third preferences are firmly rooted in the literature on cooperation, e.g. collective action theory and game theory, and the third preference is also widely recognized in the public policy and implementation literature. The second preference is a cornerstone in all realist and statist theory.

3 The European market and state non-compliance

1 The sources of the internal market initiative and the SEA have been the object of an intense scientific exchange. See, in particular, Sandholtz and Zysman 1989; Moravcsik 1991; Cameron 1992; Garrett 1992; Garrett and Weingast 1993.

2 The deadline of December 31, 1992 should be interpreted as an expression of political will, and was not legally binding in the sense that it had certain legal consequences or created an automatic legal effect.

3 Note that this number of 300 measures has not remained constant over time, as some measures have been abandoned, become obsolete, or been merged, while others have been added. At an early stage in the process, the number dropped to about 280 measures, and since then it has hovered between 270 and 280.

4 It is often forgotten that about 100 of the measures were already before the Parliament and the Council when the internal market program was presented in June 1985. These were proposals that had been bogged down in the Council for years, but which also would have to be adopted if a truly unified internal market were to be created (Cockfield 1994: 82).

5 The Luxembourg compromise was the result of a prolonged crisis in 1965–6, when France refused to accept the introduction of majority voting in the Council as specified in the EEC treaty. The compromise, which granted a member state the right to veto proposals when "very important interests" were at stake, enabled France to resume normal business in the Council after a six-month long "empty chair" policy. The Luxembourg compromise greatly handicapped the work in the Council in areas where some form of majority voting should have been the case according to the treaty. Note, however, that proposals for directives aimed at harmonizing national policies for the purpose of establishing the common market in any case were subject to the requirement of unanimity (Article 100 EEC).

6 The measures that had not been adopted were primarily found in the areas of intellectual property rights, company law, VAT, and company taxation (European Commission 1994c: xi). Paradoxically, a very large portion of the measures that could have been adopted through QMV where in fact adopted by unanimity, as the identification of a sufficient majority made formal voting superfluous (Wallace and Young 1996: 137, 140; de Schoutheete 1997: 21).

7 Note that certain forms of NTBs, e.g. quantitative restrictions, had already been abolished in the EEC through the completion of the customs union.

8 The economic benefits that could result from a unified European market were assessed by the Commission in the "Costs of Non-Europe" project. For summaries, see Ceccini 1988; Emerson *et al.* 1988.

9 Note that students of European regulation have testified to the emergence of a particular European model of regulation as the internal market has been progressively completed. This model brings together different regulatory traditions, with the philosophy being guided by the Anglo-Saxon emphasis on free markets, while the instruments owe more to French and German regulatory styles. Through this model, the regulatory powers of the states are partly reinvented at the European level. See, for example Majone 1994, 1996; Begg 1996; McGowan and Wallace 1996.

10 ECJ judgments, which formally establish non-compliance, are a less useful indicator of actual compliance problems, since states often yield to Commission pressure during the course of proceedings, and do so to varying extents.

11 Austria, Finland, and Sweden are excluded because they joined the EU only in 1995.

4 Centralized enforcement through supranational institutions: the exploitation of existing powers

1 In view of the preliminary character of the letter of formal notice, press releases were restricted to the sending of reasoned opinions and the referral of cases to the ECJ, unless the letters of formal notice pertained to failures to comply with ECJ rulings or failures to notify national implementing measures.

2 This discretion is most notable with regard to three essential aspects of the infringement procedure: the decision of whether to initiate infringement proceedings, the decision on time limits for compliance before the Commission brings the case further in the procedure, and the decision of when and how to close formal infringement proceedings.

3 Note, however, that legal observers have suggested that the Commission, in cases of particular political sensitivity, has not always followed the instruction that it *shall* rather than *may* deliver a reasoned opinion, if it suspects infringements (e.g. Evans 1979; Audretsch 1986: 35–9). Yet this potential violation of the Commission's obligations in the infringement procedure weakens rather than strengthens the Commission's enforcement position.

5 Delegation of enforcement powers: the supranational quest for sanctioning authority

1 Note that Articles 169 and 171 EEC in this respect did not only differ from the ECSC treaty, but also from Articles 85 and 86 EEC, which conferred on the Commission the power to take authoritative decisions on compliance with the treaty's rules on competition (for a discussion, see Shaw 1993).

2 At the time, this declaration was described as the culmination of governments' concern with non-compliance (Snyder 1993: 21). Declaration 19 of the TEU reads as follows:

> The Conference stresses that it is central to the coherence and unity of the process of European construction that each Member state should fully and accurately transpose into national law the Community Directives addressed to it within the deadlines laid down therein. Moreover, the Conference, while recognizing that it must be for each Member State to determine how the

provisions of Community law can best be enforced in the light of its own particular institutions, legal system and other circumstances, but in any event in compliance with Article 189 of the Treaty establishing the European Community, considers it essential for the proper functioning of the Community that the measures taken by the different Member States should result in Community law being applied with the same effectiveness and rigour as in the application of their national law. The Conference calls on the Commission to ensure, in exercising its powers under Article 155 of this Treaty, that Member States fulfil their obligations. It asks the Commission to publish periodically a full report for the Member States and the European Parliament.

3 Article 228 (ex. Art. 171) today reads:

> 1. If the Court of Justice finds that a Member State has failed to fulfil an obligation under this Treaty, the State shall be required to take the necessary measures to comply with the judgment of the Court of Justice. 2. If the Commission considers that the Member State concerned has not taken such measures it shall, after giving that State the opportunity to submit its observations, issue a reasoned opinion specifying the points on which the Member State concerned has not complied with the judgment of the Court of Justice. If the Member State concerned fails to take the necessary measures to comply with the Court's judgment within the time-limit laid down by the Commission, the latter may bring the case before the Court of Justice. In so doing it shall specify the amount of the lump sum or penalty payment to be paid by the Member State concerned which it considers appropriate in the circumstances. If the Court finds that the Member State concerned has not complied with its judgment it may impose a lump sum or penalty payment on it. This procedure shall be without prejudice to Article 170.

4 Most notably, under the Belgian proposal (a) a second ECJ decision would still be required in cases where a member state and the Commission disputed whether or not the necessary measures to comply with the first judgment had been taken, and (b) the Commission would have to go through the time-consuming job of calculating penalties in each infringement case referred to the ECJ, including those where the member state then decided to comply with the ECJ's judgment.

5 It may be noted that the Commission, in its evaluation of this mechanism in 2001, found this instrument to have been too weak and ineffective to fulfill its purpose during the first years of use (European Commission 2001e).

6 Decentralized enforcement through national courts: the supranational creation of new powers

1 On the Commission's limited resources, see Ehlermann 1988: 146; Ludlow 1991: 94; European Commission 1993c: 18; From and Stava 1993: 64; interviews, Commission officials, September 25, 1996 and February 13, 1998.

2 As the Commission acknowledged in its 1993 Strategic Programme: "The scale of the problem is such that it merits a more detailed examination in order to identify the most efficient approaches to the task [of monitoring]" (1993c: 11).

3 In a 1991 talk, Ehlermann confirmed the solid anchoring of these thoughts within the Commission at the time: "Whatever views may have been held in the Commission regarding its own supervisory powers, for a number of years we in Brussels have been convinced that centralized supervision must increasingly be supplemented by decentralized enforcement" (1992: 225).

4 The relationship between the ECJ and national courts is the subject of a

substantial literature in political science and law. On the acceptance among national courts of the doctrines and principles handed down by the ECJ, see Weiler 1991, 1993; Burley and Mattli 1993; Golub 1996; Slaughter *et al.* 1998; Stone Sweet and Brunell 1998; Alter 2001. On the duties of national courts as EU courts, see Maher 1994; Temple Lang 1997. For critical evaluations of this literature, see Alter 1998b; Kilpatrick 1998.

5 These measures to induce state compliance by boosting decentralized enforcement paralleled simultaneous processes of decentralization in the enforcement of competition rules, in the establishment of regulatory standards, and in the administration and application of EU rules. On competition, see European Commission 1993a, 1995d. On regulation, see Majone 1996: ch. 3. On administrative cooperation, see European Commission 1994a, 1996a.

6 The principle of state liability has been the object of an enormous amount of legal attention and research. See, for example Bebr 1992; Duffy 1992; Szyszczak 1992; Tesauro 1992; Caranta 1993, 1995; Craig 1993, 1997; Ross 1993; Steiner 1993; Uecker 1994; Tagaras 1995; Emiliou 1996; Gardner 1996; Jarvis 1996; Simon 1996; Wooldridge and D'Sa 1996; Irmer and Wooldridge 1997; Lonbay and Biondi 1997; King 1997; Quitzow 1997; Wathelet and Van Raepenbusch 1997; Tridimas 2001.

7 Gardner advances a similar conclusion: "Although the Court has traditionally held that only national courts are free to determine what form of remedies to award for the infringement of EU law, it has eviscerated that principle in practice" (1996: 280).

8 Note, however, that this distinction between interpretation and application never has been fully respected by the ECJ. Particularly revealing is a description by ECJ judge Mancini of how the ECJ's respect for the division in principle was coupled with transgressions in practice:

> But having paid this lip service to the language of the Treaty and having clarified the meaning of the relevant Community measure, the Court usually went on to indicate to what extent a *certain type* of national legislation can be regarded as compatible with that measure. The national judge is thus led by the hand as far as the door; crossing the threshold is the judge's job, but now a job no harder than child's play.
>
> (Mancini 1991: 185)

See Kakouris 1997, for an article where another judge of the ECJ defends the court's actions by claiming that there really is no such thing as national procedural autonomy, thereby inadvertently explaining the ECJ's behavior in this area and confirming the fears of many legal observers.

9 For Commission documentation on the Citizens First initiative, see, for example European Commission 1995f: 2, 1997l: 2–3, 1997o: 4, 1997p: 4, 1997r: 2–3, 1998f: 4–5, 1998g: 4–5.

10 The effects of the UK's resistance are clearly traceable in the statistics on Citizens First inquiries. The UK was the country where the lowest share of people had seen, heard, or read about the first phase of the initiative, which directly contributed to making the UK the state with the lowest number of inquiries per 100,000 households (European Commission 1997k: 2–3).

11 The legal base is a common source of conflict between member governments and the Commission, illustrating the continued dispute between intergovernmentalism and supranationalism. For good discussions, see Emiliou 1994; Usher 1994.

12 Also the Spanish government was likely to have given its tacit approval as the Spanish general policy statement on the IGC proposed reducing the "law-creating" powers of the ECJ (internal Commission memo, no date).

13 Note, however, that toward the end of the IGC, when these proposals were laid to rest in the face of insufficient backing, the skeptic sentiments of certain member states were instead channeled into the negotiations on the ECJ's future role in the area of Justice and Home Affairs (JHA). In particular, the UK, Germany, France, and Spain criticized the ECJ and questioned whether it should really be given the same powers in JHA as it already held in the Community pillar. This time it was the skeptical governments that enjoyed the power to block any treaty revision, and these states subsequently succeeded in limiting the involvement of the ECJ in JHA (interview, Commission official, January 7, 1998; Alter 1998a: 141).

14 As the ECJ put it:

> [T]he substantive and procedural conditions for reparation of loss and damage laid down by the national law of the Member States must not be less favourable than those relating to similar domestic claims and must not be so framed as to make it virtually impossible or excessively difficult to obtain reparation.
>
> (*Francovich*, Joined Cases C-6 and 9/90, 1991, para. 43).

15 Carefulness is warranted, since it cannot be automatically inferred from a low number of cases that individuals have not been able to rely on the principle of state liability. A low number can also be interpreted as an indication that the legal situation has been clear, and that the government has chosen conciliation rather than court decision. Moreover, one case may function as a precedent allowing later claimants compensation without having their cases determined in court. In at least one of the cases noted above – Sweden's incorrect implementation of the wage guarantee directive – the decision has led to hundreds of people claiming and receiving compensation from the state on the basis of one decision (FIDE 1998: 398; interview, Swedish government official, April 16, 1998).

16 Note also that in *Factortame III*, where the UK Divisional Court found the state liable, the national court exploited its discretion to heavily restrict the damages awarded, denying the claimants exemplary damages.

17 It is no coincidence that this occurred in Italy, where mistrust toward the supremacy of Community law has been the leitmotif of the constitutional court during the last three decades (Laderchi 1998: 147).

18 Note, however, that the joint-decision trap and these key variables worked in the opposite direction as regards the extension of competence to the ECJ in the third pillar of JHA at the IGC. Since unanimity was required for the transfer of new policy areas into the domain of the ECJ, skeptical governments enjoyed the power to block the extension of the ECJ's involvement (Alter 1998a: 141–2).

Bibliography

Books and articles

Alchian, Armen A. and Demsetz, Harold (1972) "Production, information costs, and economic organization," *American Economic Review* 62: 777–95.

Alter, Karen J. (1996) "The European court's political power," *West European Politics* 19 (3): 458–87.

——(1998a) "Who are the 'masters of the treaty'?: European governments and the European Court of Justice," *International Organization* 52 (1): 121–47.

——(1998b) "Explaining national court acceptance of European court jurisprudence: a critical evaluation of theories of legal integration," in Anne-Marie Slaughter, Alec Stone Sweet, and Joseph H. H. Weiler (eds) *The European Courts and National Courts: Doctrine and Jurisprudence*, Oxford: Hart.

——(2000) "The European Union's legal system and domestic policy: spillover or backlash?," *International Organization* 54 (3): 489–518.

——(2001) *Establishing the Supremacy of European Law: The Making of an International Rule of Law in Europe*, Oxford: Oxford University Press.

——(2002a) "International legal systems, regime design, and the shadow of the law in international relations," paper presented at the Annual Meeting of the American Political Science Association, Boston, MA, August 26–September 1, 2002.

——(2002b) "Delegating to international courts: why, how, and problems in doing so," paper presented at the Conference on Delegation to International Organizations, Park City, UT, May 3–4, 2002.

Andersson, Torbjörn (1997) "Remedies for breach of EC law before Swedish courts," in Julian Lonbay and Andrea Biondi (eds) *Remedies for Breach of EC Law*, Chichester: John Wiley.

Armstrong, Kenneth and Bulmer, Simon (1998) *The Governance of the Single European Market*, Manchester: Manchester University Press.

Arrow, Kenneth J. (1985) "The economics of agency," in John W. Pratt and Richard J. Zeckhauser (eds) *Principals and Agents: The Structure of Business*, Boston, MA: Harvard Business School Press.

Aspinwall, Mark D. and Schneider, Gerald (2000) "Same menu, separate tables: the institutionalist turn in political science and the study of European integration," *European Journal of Political Research* 38: 1–36.

——(2001) "Institutional research on the European Union: mapping the field," in Gerald Schneider and Mark Aspinwall (eds) *The Rules of Integration: Institutionalist Approaches to the Study of Europe*, Manchester: Manchester University Press.

Audretsch, H. A. H. (1986) *Supervision in European Community Law*, 2nd edn, Amsterdam: North-Holland.

Axelrod, Robert (1984) *The Evolution of Cooperation*, London: Penguin.

Axelrod, Robert and Keohane, Robert O. (1986) "Achieving cooperation under anarchy: strategies and institutions," in Kenneth A. Oye (ed.) *Cooperation under Anarchy*, Princeton, NJ: Princeton University Press.

Azzi, Guiseppe Ciavarini (1988) "What is this new research into the implementation of Community legislation bringing us?," in Heinrich Siedentopf and Jacques Ziller (eds) *Making European Policies Work: The Implementation of Community Legislation in the Member States*, Vol. 1, Comparative Syntheses, London: Sage.

Balassa, Bela (1961) *The Theory of Economic Integration*, Homewood, IL: Richard D. Irwin.

Baldwin, Robert (1993) "The new protectionism: a response to shifts in national economic power," in Dominick Salvatore (ed.) *Protectionism and World Welfare*, Cambridge: Cambridge University Press.

Barav, Ami (1988) "Damages in the domestic courts for breach of Community law by national public authorities," in H. G. Schermers, T. Heukels, and P. Mead (eds) *Non-contractual Liability of the European Communities*, Dordrecht: Martinus Nijhoff.

Bayard, Thomas O. and Elliott, Kimberley (1994) *Reciprocity and Retaliation in US Trade Policy*, Washington DC: Institute of International Economics.

Bebr, Gerhard (1992) "Joined cases C-6/90 and C-9/90, *Francovich v. Italy, Bonifaci v. Italy*," *Common Market Law Review* 29: 557–84.

Begg, Iain (1996) "Introduction: regulation in the European Union," *Journal of European Public Policy* 3 (4): 525–35.

Bergman, Torbjörn (2000) "The European Union as the next step of delegation and accountability," *European Journal of Political Research* 37 (3): 415–29.

Bergman, Torbjörn, Müller, Wolfgang C., and Strøm, Kaare (2000) "Introduction: parliamentary democracy and the chain of delegation," *European Journal of Political Research* 37 (3): 255–60.

Bhagwati, Jagdish (1988) *Protectionism*, Cambridge, MA: MIT Press.

Biering, Peter (2000) "The application of EU law in Denmark," *Common Market Law Review* 37: 925–69.

Börzel, Tanja A. (2001) "Non-compliance in the European Union: pathology or statistical artefact?," *Journal of European Public Policy* 8 (5): 803–24.

Bronckers, Marco C. E. J. (1989) "Private enforcement of 1992: do trade and industry stand a chance against the member states?," *Common Market Law Review* 26: 513–33.

Burley, Anne-Marie and Mattli, Walter (1993) "Europe before the court: a political theory of legal integration," *International Organization* 47 (1): 41–76.

Cahier, P. (1967) "Le recours en constatation de manquements des états membres devant la Cour des Communautés européennes," *Cahiers de Droit Européen* 1967 (2): 123–59.

——(1974) "Les articles 169 et 171 du traité instituant la CEE à travers la pratique de la Commission et la jurisprudence de la Cour," *Cahiers de Droit Européen* 1974 (1): 3–38.

Cameron, David R. (1992) "The 1992 initiative: causes and consequences," in Alberta M. Sbragia (ed.) *Euro-Politics: Institutions and Policymaking in the "New" European Community*, Washington DC: The Brookings Institution.

Caporaso, James (1998) "Regional integration theory: understanding our past and anticipating our future," *Journal of European Public Policy* 5 (1): 1–16.

Caporaso, James A. and Keeler, John T. S. (1995) "The European Union and regional integration theory," in Carolyn Rhodes and Sonia Mazey (eds) *The State of the European Union*, Vol. 3, *Building a European Polity?*, Boulder, CO: Lynne Rienner.

Caranta, Roberto (1993) "Governmental liability after Francovich," *Cambridge Law Journal* 52 (2): 272–97.

——(1995) "Judicial protection against member states: a new *jus commune* takes shape," *Common Market Law Review* 32: 703–26.

Ceccini, Paolo (1988) *The European Challenge 1992: The Benefits of a Single Market*, Aldershot: Gower.

Chalmers, Damian (1997) "Judicial preferences and the Community legal order," *Modern Law Review* 60 (2): 164–99.

——(2000) "The application of Community law in the United Kingdom, 1994–1998," *Common Market Law Review* 37: 83–128.

Chayes, Abram and Chayes, Antonia Handler (1995) *The New Sovereignty: Compliance with International Regulatory Agreements*, Cambridge, MA: Harvard University Press.

Chayes, Abram, Chayes, Antonia Handler, and Mitchell, Ronald B. (1998) "Managing compliance: a comparative perspective," in Edith Brown Weiss and Harold K. Jacobson (eds) *Engaging Countries: Strengthening Compliance with International Environmental Accords*, Cambridge, MA: MIT Press.

Christiansen, Thomas, Jørgensen, Knud Erik, and Wiener, Antje (eds) (2001) *The Social Construction of Europe*, London: Sage.

Claes, Monica and de Witte, Bruno (1998) "Report on the Netherlands," in Anne-Marie Slaughter, Alec Stone Sweet, and Joseph H. H. Weiler (eds) *The European Court and National Courts: Doctrine and Jurisprudence*, Oxford: Hart.

Cockfield, Lord (1994) *The European Union: Creating the Single Market*, Chichester: John Wiley.

Conant, Lisa (2002) *Justice Contained: Law and Politics in the European Union*, Ithaca, NY: Cornell University Press.

Craig, P. P. (1993) "*Francovich*, remedies and the scope for damages liability," *Law Quarterly Review* 109: 595–621.

——(1997) "Once more unto the breach: the Community, the state and damages liability," *Law Quarterly Review* 113: 67–94.

Cram, Laura (1997) *Policy-Making in the EU: Conceptual Lenses and the Integration Process*, London: Routledge.

Dashwood, Alan and White, Robin (1989) "Enforcement actions under Articles 169 and 170 EEC," *European Law Review* 14: 388–413.

Deards, Elspeth (1997) "*Brasserie du Pêcheur*: snatching defeat from the jaws of victory?," *European Law Review* 22: 620–25.

Dehousse, Renaud (1998) *The European Court of Justice: The Politics of Judicial Integration*, London: Macmillan.

De Schoutheete, Philippe (1997) *Une Europe pour tous*, Paris: Editions Odile Jacob.

Dinan, Desmond (1997) "The Commission and the intergovernmental conferences," in Neill Nugent (ed.) *At the Heart of the Union: Studies of the European Commission*, Houndmills: Macmillan.

Dorn, A. Walter and Fulton, Andrew (1997) "Securing compliance with disarmament treaties: carrots, sticks, and the case of North Korea," *Global Governance* 3: 17–40.

Downs, George W., Rocke, David M., and Barsoon, Peter N. (1996) "Is the good news about compliance also good news about cooperation?," *International Organization* 50 (3): 379–406.

Duffy, Peter (1992) "Damages against the state: a new remedy for failure to implement Community obligations," *European Law Review* 17 (2): 133–8.

Egan, Michelle (1998) "Regulatory strategies, delegation and European market integration," *Journal of European Public Policy* 5 (3): 485–506.

Ehlermann, Claus-Dieter (1988) "Opening speech at the IVth Erenstein colloquium," in Heinrich Siedentopf and Jacques Ziller (eds) *Making European Policies Work: The Implementation of Community Legislation in the Member States*, Vol. 1, Comparative Syntheses, London: Sage.

——(1992) "The second Wilberforce lecture," *Common Market Law Review* 29: 213–27.

Emerson, Michael, Aujean, Michel, Catinat, Michel, Goybet, Philippe, and Jacquemin, Alexis (1988) *The Economics of 1992: The EC Commission's Assessment of the Economic Effects of Completing the Internal Market*, Oxford: Oxford University Press.

Emiliou, Nicholas (1994) "Opening Pandora's box: the legal basis of Community measures before the Court of Justice," *European Law Review* 19 (5): 488–507.

——(1996) "State liability under Community law: shedding more light on the *Francovich* principle?" *European Law Review* 21 (5): 399–411.

EOS Gallup Europe (1995) *Lawyers and the Community Law*, unpublished report, February 1995.

Epstein, David and O'Halloran, Sharyn (1999) *Delegating Powers: A Transaction Cost Politics Approach to Policy Making Under Separate Powers*, Cambridge: Cambridge University Press.

Evans, A. C. (1979) "The enforcement procedure of Article 169 EEC: Commission discretion," *European Law Review* 4 (6): 442–56.

Everling, Ulrich (1984) "The member states of the European Community before their Court of Justice," *European Law Review* 9 (4): 215–41.

Fearon, James D. (1991) "Counterfactuals and hypothesis testing in political science," *World Politics* 43: 169–95.

FIDE (1998) *Les Directives communautaires: effets, efficacité, justiciabilité*. Report from XVIII FIDE Congress, June 3–6, 1998, Stockholm.

Franchino, Fabio (2000) "Control of the Commission's executive functions: uncertainty, conflict, and decision rules," *European Union Politics* 1 (1): 63–92.

Friedman, Milton (1953) "The methodology of positive economics," in Milton Friedman *Essays in Positive Economics*, Chicago, IL: University of Chicago Press.

From, Johan and Stava, Per (1993) "Implementation of Community law: the last stronghold of national control?," in Svein S. Andersen and Kjell A. Eliassen (eds) *Making Policy in Europe: The Europeification of National Policy-Making*, London: Sage.

Gardner, Anthony (1996) "EU member state liability: a cure for Euro-sclerosis?," *European Competition Law Review* 17 (5): 275–82.

Garrett, Geoffrey (1992) "International cooperation and institutional choice: the European Community's internal market," *International Organization* 46 (2): 533–60.

——(1995 "The politics of legal integration in the European Union," *International Organization* 49 (1): 171–81.

Garrett, Geoffrey and Tsebelis, George (1996) "An institutional critique of intergovernmentalism," *International Organization* 50 (2): 269–99.

Garrett, Geoffrey and Weingast, Barry R. (1993) "Ideas, interests, and institutions: constructing the European Community's internal market," in Judith Goldstein and Robert O. Keohane (eds) *Ideas and Foreign Policy: Beliefs, Institutions, and Political Change*, Ithaca, NY: Cornell University Press.

Garrett, Geoffrey, Kelemen, R. Daniel and Schulz, Heiner (1998) "The European Court of Justice, national governments, and legal integration in the European Union," *International Organization* 52 (1): 149–76.

George, Alexander L. and McKeown, Timothy J. (1985) "Case studies and theories of organizational decision making," *Advances in Information Processing in Organizations* 2: 21–58.

Goebel, Roger J. (1997) "Achieving full effectiveness of Community law: The Court of Justice's third stage of enforcement rules," paper presented at the 91st Annual Meeting of the American Society of International Law, Washington DC, April 9–12, 1997.

Golub, Jonathan (1996) "The politics of judicial discretion: rethinking the interaction between national courts and the European Court of Justice," *West European Politics* 19 (2): 360–85.

——(1999) "In the shadow of the vote? Decision making in the European Community," *International Organization* 53 (4): 733–64.

Grant, Charles (1994) *Delors: Inside the House That Jacques Built*, London: Nicholas Brealey.

Greenaway, David (1983) *International Trade Policy: From Tariffs to the New Protectionism*, Houndmills: Macmillan.

Haas, Ernst B. (1958) *The Uniting of Europe: Political, Social and Economical Forces 1950–1957*, London: Stevens.

——(1964) *Beyond the Nation State: Functionalism and International Organization*, Stanford, CA: Stanford University Press.

——(1967) "*The Uniting of Europe* and the Uniting of Latin America," *Journal of Common Market Studies* 5: 315–44.

Haas, Peter M., Keohane, Robert O., and Levy, Marc A. (eds) (1993) *Institutions for the Earth: Sources of Effective International Environmental Protection*, Cambridge, MA: MIT Press.

Hall, Peter A. and Taylor, Rosemary C. R. (1996) "Political science and the three new institutionalisms," *Political Studies* 44: 936–57.

Hancher, Leigh (1996) "The regulatory role of the European Union," in Hussein Kassim and Anand Menon (eds) *The European Union and National Industrial Policy*, London: Routledge.

Hansen, Roger D. (1969) "Regional integration: reflections on a decade of theoretical efforts," *World Politics* 21: 242–71.

Hartley, T. C. (1994) *The Foundations of European Community Law. An Introduction to the Constitutional and Administrative Law of the European Community*, 3rd edn, Oxford: Clarendon Press.

Helfer, Laurence R. and Slaughter, Anne-Marie (1997) "Toward a theory of effective supranational adjudication," *Yale Law Journal* 107 (2): 273–391.

Hix, Simon (1994) "The study of the European Community: the challenge to comparative politics," *West European Politics* 17 (1): 1–30.
——(1998) "The study of the European Union II: the 'new governance' agenda and its rival," *Journal of European Public Policy* 5 (1): 38–65.
Hoffmann, Stanley (1966) "Obstinate or obsolete? The fate of the nation-state and the case of Western Europe," *Dædalus* 95 (3): 862–915.
——(1982) "Reflections on the nation-state in Western Europe today," *Journal of Common Market Studies* 21: 21–37.
Holmström, Bengt (1979) "Moral hazard and observability," *The Bell Journal of Economics* 10 (1): 74–91.
Holmström, Bengt and Tirole, Jean (1989) "The theory of the firm," in Richard Schmalensee and Robert D. Willig (eds) *Handbook of Industrial Organization*, Vol. 1, Amsterdam: North Holland.
Hooghe, Liesbet (ed.) (1996) *Cohesion Policy and European Integration: Building Multi-Level Governance*, Oxford: Oxford University Press.
Hooghe, Liesbet and Marks, Gary (2001) *Multi-level Governance and European Integration*, Lanham, MD: Rowman & Littlefield.
Hopenhayn, Hugo and Lohmann, Susanne (1996) "Fire-alarm signals and the political oversight of regulatory agencies," *Journal of Law, Economics, and Organization* 12 (1): 196–213.
Immergut, Ellen M. (1998) "The theoretical core of the new institutionalism, *Politics & Society* 26 (1): 5–34.
Irmer, Wolfram and Wooldridge, Frank (1997) "1996: The return of Francovich," *European Business Law Review* 8 (3): 67–74.
Jachtenfuchs, Markus and Kohler-Koch, Beate (1996) "Einleitung: regieren im dynamischen Mehrebenensystem," in Markus Jachtenfuchs and Beate Kohler-Koch (eds) *Europäische Integration*, Opladen: Leske and Budrich.
Jacobs, Francis G. (1997) "Enforcing Community rights and obligations in national courts: striking the balance," in Julian Lonbay and Andrea Biondi (eds) *Remedies for Breach of EC Law*, Chichester: John Wiley.
Jacobson, Harold K. and Brown Weiss, Edith (1998) "Assessing the record and designing strategies to engage countries," in Edith Brown Weiss and Harold K. Jacobson (eds) *Engaging Countries: Strengthening Compliance with International Environmental Accords*, Cambridge, MA: MIT Press.
Jarvis, Malcolm (1996) "The liability of member states for legislative omissions: a summary of conference proceedings," *European Business Law Review* 7 (10): 230–5.
Jensen, Michael C. and Meckling, William H. (1976) "Theory of the firm: managerial behavior, agency costs and ownership structure," *Journal of Financial Economics* 3: 305–59.
Jönsson, Christer and Tallberg, Jonas (1998) "Compliance and post-agreement bargaining," *European Journal of International Relations* 4 (4): 371–408.
Jørgensen, Knud Erik (ed.) (1997) *Reflective Approaches to European Governance*, London: Macmillan.
Kahler, Miles (1995) *International Institutions and the Political Economy of Integration*, Washington DC: The Brookings Institution.
——(2002) "Domestic politics and delegation to international organizations," paper presented at the Conference on Delegation to International Organizations, Park City, UT, May 3–4, 2002.

Kakouris, C. N. (1997) "Do the member states possess judicial procedural 'autonomy'?" *Common Market Law Review* 34: 1389–412.

Keohane, Robert O. (1984) *After Hegemony*, Princeton, NJ: Princeton University Press.

Keohane, Robert O. and Hoffmann, Stanley (1991) "Institutional change in Europe in the 1980s," in Robert O. Keohane and Stanley Hoffmann (eds) *The New European Community: Decisionmaking and Institutional Change*, Boulder, CO: Westview Press.

Keohane, Robert O. and Levy, Marc A. (eds) (1996) *Institutions for Environmental Aid*, Cambridge, MA: MIT Press.

Keohane, Robert O., Haas, Peter M., and Levy, Marc A. (1993) "The effectiveness of international environmental institutions," in Peter M. Haas, Robert O. Keohane, and Marc A. Levy (eds) *Institutions for the Earth: Sources of Effective International Environmental Protection*, Cambridge, MA: MIT Press.

Keohane, Robert O., Moravcsik, Andrew, and Slaughter, Anne-Marie (2000) "Legalized dispute resolution: interstate and transnational," *International Organization* 54 (3): 457–88.

Kiewiet, D. Roderick and McCubbins, Mathew D. (1991) *The Logic of Delegation: Congressional Parties and the Appropriation Process*, Chicago, IL: University of Chicago Press.

Kilpatrick, Claire (1998) "Community or communities of courts in European integration? Sex equality dialogues between UK Courts and the ECJ," *European Law Journal* 4 (2): 121–47.

King, Gary, Keohane, Robert O., and Verba, Sidney (1994) *Designing Social Inquiry: Scientific Inference in Qualitative Research*, Princeton, NJ: Princeton University Press.

King, Victoria (1997) "The fault issue in state liability: from Francovich to Dillenkofer," *European Competition Law Review* 18 (2): 110–13.

Kohler-Koch, Beate (1996) "The strengths of weakness: the transformation of governance in the EU," in Sverker Gustavsson and Leif Lewin (eds) *The Future of the Nation State*, Stockholm: Nerenius & Santérus.

Krauss, Melvyn B. (1979) *The New Protectionism, the Welfare State, and International Trade*, Oxford: Blackwell.

Krislov, Samuel, Ehlermann, Claus-Dieter, and Weiler, Joseph (1986) "The political organs and the decision-making process in the United States and the European Community," in Mauro Cappelletti, Monica Seccombe, and Joseph Weiler (eds) *Integration through Law*, Vol. 1, book 2, Berlin: De Gruyter.

Laderchi, P. Ruggeri (1998) "Report on Italy," in Anne-Marie Slaughter, Alec Stone Sweet, and Joseph H. H. Weiler (eds) *The European Court and National Courts: Doctrine and Jurisprudence*, Oxford: Hart.

Lindberg, Leon N. (1963) *The Political Dynamics of European Economic Integration*, Stanford, CA: Stanford University Press.

Lindberg, Leon N. and Scheingold, Stuart A. (1970) *Europe's Would-Be Polity: Patterns of Change in the European Community*, Englewood Cliffs, NJ: Prentice-Hall.

——(eds) (1971) *Regional Integration: Theory and Research*, Cambridge, MA: Harvard University Press.

Lonbay, Julian and Biondi, Andrea (eds) (1997) *Remedies for Breach of EC Law*, Chichester: John Wiley.

Ludlow, Peter (1991) "The European Commission," in Robert O. Keohane and Stanley Hoffmann (eds) *The New European Community: Decisionmaking and Institutional Change*, Boulder, CO: Westview Press.

McCubbins, Mathew D. and Page, Talbot (1987) "A theory of congressional delegation," in Mathew D. McCubbins and Terry Sullivan (eds) *Congress: Structure and Policy*, New York, NY: Cambridge University Press.

McCubbins, Mathew D. and Schwartz, Thomas (1984) "Congressional oversight overlooked: police patrols versus fire alarms," *American Journal of Political Science* 28 (1): 165–79.

McCubbins, Mathew D. and Sullivan, Terry (eds) (1987) *Congress: Structure and Policy*, New York, NY: Cambridge University Press.

McCubbins, Mathew D., Noll, Roger G. and Weingast, Barry R. (1987) "Administrative procedures as instruments of political control," *Journal of Law, Economics, and Organization* 3 (2): 243–77.

McCubbins, Mathew D., Noll, Roger G., and Weingast, Barry R. (1989) "Structure and process, policy and politics: administrative arrangements and the political control of agencies," *Virginia Law Review* 75: 431–82.

McGowan, Francis and Wallace, Helen (1996) "Towards a European Regulatory State," *Journal of European Public Policy* 3 (4): 560–76.

McNamara, Kathleen R. (2002) "Rational fictions: central bank independence and the social logic of delegation," *West European Politics* 25 (1): 47–76.

Maher, Imelda (1994) "National courts as European Community courts," *Legal Studies* 14 (2): 226–43.

Majone, Giandomenico (1994) "The rise of the regulatory state in Europe," *West European Politics* 17: 77–101.

——(1996) *Regulating Europe*, London: Routledge.

——(2001) "Two logics of delegation: agency and fudiciary relations in EU governance," *European Union Politics* 2 (1): 103–22.

Mancini, G. Federico (1991) "The making of a constitution for Europe," in Robert O. Keohane and Stanley Hoffmann (eds) *The New European Community: Decisionmaking and Institutional Change*, Boulder, CO: Westview Press.

Marks, Gary (1993) "Structural policy and multilevel governance in the EC," in Alan W. Cafruny and Glenda G. Rosenthal (eds) *The State of the European Community*, Vol. 2, Boulder, CO: Lynne Rienner.

Marks, Gary, Hooghe, Liesbet, and Blank, Kermit (1996) "European Integration from the 1980s," *Journal of Common Market Studies* 34 (3): 341–78.

Martin, Lisa L. (1993) "Credibility, costs, and institutions: cooperation on economic sanctions," *World Politics* 45 (3): 903–18.

——(2002) "Agency and delegation in IMF conditionality," paper presented at the Conference on Delegation to International Organizations, Park City, UT, May 3–4, 2002.

Mendrinou, Maria (1996) "Non-compliance and the European Commission's role in integration," *Journal of European Public Policy* 3 (1): 1–22.

Miller, Gary J. (1992) *Managerial Dilemmas: The Political Economy of Hierarchy*, Cambridge: Cambridge University Press.

Mitchell, Ronald B. (1994) *Intentional Oil Pollution at Sea: Environmental Policy and Treaty Compliance*, Cambridge, MA: MIT Press.

Moe, Terry M. (1984) "The new economics of organization," *American Journal of Political Science* 28: 739–77.

——(1987) "An assessment of the positive theory of 'congressional dominance'," *Legislative Studies Quarterly* 12 (4): 475–520.

——(1990) "The politics of structural choice: toward a theory of public bureaucracy," in Oliver Williamson (ed.) *Organization Theory: From Chester Barnard to the Present and Beyond*, New York, NY: Oxford University Press.

Moravcsik, Andrew (1991) "Negotiating the Single European Act," *International Organization* 45 (1): 651–88.

——(1993) "Preferences and power in the European Community: a liberal intergovernmentalist approach," *Journal of Common Market Studies* 31 (4): 473–524.

——(1995) "Liberal intergovernmentalism and integration: a rejoinder," *Journal of Common Market Studies* 33 (4): 611–28.

——(1998) *The Choice for Europe: Social Purpose and State Power from Messina to Maastricht*, Ithaca, NY: Cornell University Press.

——(1999) "A new statecraft? Supranational entrepreneurs and international cooperation," *International Organization* 53(2): 267–306.

Moravcsik, Andrew and Nicolaïdis, Kalypso (1999) "Explaining the Amsterdam treaty: interests, influence, institutions," *Journal of Common Market Studies* 37 (1): 59–85.

Neill, Patrick (1995) "The European Court of Justice: a case study in judicial activism," working paper, London: European Policy Forum.

North, Douglass C. (1990) *Institutions, Institutional Change and Economic Performance*, Cambridge: Cambridge University Press.

Nye, Joseph (1971) *Peace in Parts: Integration and Conflict in Regional Organization*, Boston, MA: Little, Brown.

Olson, Mancur (1965) *The Logic of Collective Action: Public Goods and the Theory of Groups*, Cambridge, MA: Harvard University Press.

Oye, Kenneth A. (ed.) (1986) *Cooperation under Anarchy*, Princeton, NJ: Princeton University Press.

Pescatore, Pierre (1974) *The Law of Integration: Emergence of a New Phenomenon in International Relations, Based on the Experience of the European Communities*, Leiden: A. W. Sijthoff.

——(1983) "The doctrine of 'direct effect': an infant disease of Community Law," *European Law Review* 8 (3): 155–77.

Peters, B. Guy (1992) "Bureaucratic politics and the institutions of the European Community," in Alberta M. Sbragia (ed.) *Euro-Politics: Institutions and Policy-making in the 'New' European Community*, Washington DC: The Brookings Institution.

——(1999) *Institutional Theory in Political Science*, London: Pinter.

Peterson, John (1995) "Decision-making in the European Union: towards a framework for analysis," *Journal of European Public Policy* 2 (1): 69–93.

Pierson, Paul (1996) "The path to European integration: a historical institutionalist analysis," *Comparative Political Studies* 29 (2): 123–63.

Pollack, Mark A. (1997) "Delegation, agency, and agenda-setting in the European Community," *International Organization* 51 (1): 99–134.

——(1998) "The engines of integration? Supranational autonomy and influence in the European Union," in Alec Stone Sweet and Wayne Sandholtz (eds) *European Integration and Supranational Governance*, Oxford: Oxford University Press.

——(1999) "Delegation, agency and agenda setting in the treaty of Amsterdam,

European Integration online Papers 3 (6). Available at http://eiop.or.at/eiop/texte/1999-006a.htm.

——(2002) "Learning from the Americanists (again): theory and method in the study of delegation," *West European Politics* 25 (1): 200–19.

——(2003) *The Engines of European Integration: Delegation, Agency, and Agenda Setting in the EU*, Oxford: Oxford University Press.

Pratt, John W. and Zeckhauser, Richard J. (1985a) "Principals and agents: an overview," in John W. Pratt and Richard J. Zeckhauser (eds) *Principals and Agents: The Structure of Business*, Boston, MA: Harvard Business School Press.

——(eds) (1985b) *Principals and Agents: The Structure of Business*, Boston, MA: Harvard Business School Press.

Prechal, Sacha (1997) "EC requirements for an effective remedy," in Julian Lonbay and Andrea Biondi (eds) *Remedies for Breach of EC Law*, Chichester: John Wiley.

Price, Victoria C. (1988) *1992: Europe's Last Chance?* London: Institute of Economic Affairs.

Puchala, Donald J. (1972) "Of blind men, elephants and international integration," *Journal of Common Market Studies* 10: 267–85.

——(1975) "Domestic politics and regional harmonization in the European Communities," *World Politics* 27 (4): 496–520.

Quitzow, Carl Michael (1997) "'Private enforcement' i EG-rätten: en studie av medlemsstaternas skadeståndsansvar i samband med överträdelser av gemenskapsregler," *Juridisk Tidskrift* 1997 (3): 682–700.

Rasmussen, Hjalte (1986) *On Law and Policy in the European Court of Justice: A Comparative Study in Judicial Policymaking*, Dordrecht: Martinus Nijhoff.

Raustiala, Kal and Slaughter, Anne-Marie (2002) "International law and compliance," in Walter Carlsnaes, Thomas Risse, and Beth Simmons (eds) *Handbook of International Relations*, London: Sage.

Raustiala, Kal and Victor, David G. (1998) "Conclusions," in David G. Victor, Kal Raustiala, and Eugene B. Skolnikoff (eds) *The Implementation and Effectiveness of International Environmental Commitments: Theory and Evidence*, Cambridge, MA: MIT Press.

Risse-Kappen, Thomas (1996) "Exploring the nature of the beast: international relations theory and comparative policy analysis meet the European Union," *Journal of Common Market Studies* 34 (1): 53–80.

Ross, George (1995) *Jacques Delors and European Integration*, Cambridge: Polity Press.

Ross, Malcolm (1993) "Beyond *Francovich*," *Modern Law Review* 56 (1): 55–73.

Ross, Stephen A. (1973) "The economic theory of agency: the principal's problem," *The American Economic Review* 63 (2): 134–9.

Sandholtz, Wayne (1992) "ESPRIT and the politics of international collective action," *Journal of Common Market Studies* 30 (1): 1–21.

——(1993) "Institutions and collective action: the new telecommunications in Western Europe," *World Politics* 45 (2): 242–70.

Sandholtz, Wayne and Zysman, John (1989) "1992: recasting the European bargain," *World Politics* 42 (1): 95–128.

Sappington, David E. M. (1991) "Incentives in principal–agent relationships," *Journal of Economic Perspectives* 5 (2): 45–66.

Scharpf, Fritz W. (1988) "The joint-decision trap: lessons from German federalism and European integration," *Public Administration* 66: 239–78.

——(1994) "Community and autonomy: multi-level policy-making in the European Union," *Journal of European Public Policy* 1 (2): 219–42.

Scheingold, Stuart A. (1965) *The Rule of Law in European Integration: The Path of the Schuman Plan*, New Haven, CT: Yale University Press.

Schmidt, Susanne K. (1998) "Commission activism: subsuming telecommunications and electricity under European competition law," *Journal of European Public Policy* 5 (1): 169–84.

——(2000) "Only an agenda setter? The European Commission's power over the Council of Ministers," *European Union Politics* 1 (1): 37–61.

Shackleton, Michael (1991) "The European Community between three ways of life: a cultural analysis," *Journal of Common Market Studies* 29 (6): 575–601.

Shapiro, Martin (1992) "The European Court of Justice," in Alberta M. Sbragia (ed.) *Euro-Politics: Institutions and Policymaking in the 'New' European Community*, Washington DC: The Brookings Institution.

Shaw, Josephine (1993) *European Community Law*, London: Macmillan.

Shepsle, Kenneth A. (1979) "Institutional arrangements and equilibrium in multi-dimensional voting models," *American Journal of Political Science* 23: 27–60.

——(1986) "Institutional equilibrium and equilibrium institutions," in Herbert Weisberg (ed.) *Political Science: The Science of Politics*, New York, NY: Agathon.

——(1989) "Studying institutions: some lessons from the rational choice approach," *Journal of Theoretical Politics* 1: 131–47.

Siedentopf, Heinrich and Hauschild, Christoph (1988) "The implementation of Community legislation by the member states: a comparative analysis," in Heinrich Siedentopf and Jacques Ziller (eds) *Making European Policies Work: The Implementation of Community Legislation in the Member States*, Vol. 1, Comparative Syntheses, London: Sage.

Siedentopf, Heinrich and Ziller, Jacques (eds) (1988) *Making European Policies Work. The Implementation of Community Legislation in the Member States*, Vol. 1, Comparative Syntheses, London: Sage.

Simmons, Beth A. (1993) "Why innovate? Founding the Bank for International Settlements," *World Politics* 45: 361–405.

Simon, Denys (1996) "La responsabilité de l'état saisie par le droit communautaire," *L'Actualité Juridique – Droit Administratif* 7–8: 489–99.

Simon, Denys and Barav, Ami (1987) "La responsabilité de l'administration nationale en cas de violation du droit communautaire," *Revue du Marché Commun* no. 305: 165–74.

Slaughter, Anne-Marie, Stone Sweet, Alec and Weiler, Joseph H. H. (eds) (1998) *The European Court and National Courts: Doctrine and Jurisprudence*, Oxford: Hart.

Snidal, Duncan (1986) "The game *theory* of international politics," in Kenneth A. Oye (ed.) *Cooperation under Anarchy*, Princeton, NJ: Princeton University Press.

Snyder, Francis (1993) "The effectiveness of European Community law: institutions, processes, tools and techniques," *Modern Law Review* 56 (1): 19–54.

Stein, Eric (1981) "Lawyers, judges, and the making of a transnational constitution," *American Journal of International Law* 75: 1–27.

Steiner, Josephine (1987) "How to make the action suit the case: domestic remedies for breach of EEC law," *European Law Review* 12: 102–22.

——(1993) "From direct effects to *Francovich*: shifting means of enforcement of Community law," *European Law Review* 18 (1): 3–22.

——(1995) *Enforcing EC Law*, London: Blackstone Press.

Steiner, Josephine and Woods, Lorna (1996) *Textbook on EC Law*, London: Blackstone Press.

Stone Sweet, Alec (2002) "Constitutional courts and parliamentary democracy," *West European Politics* 25 (1): 77–100.

Stone Sweet, Alec and Brunell, Thomas L. (1998) "The European court and the national courts: a statistical analysis of preliminary references, 1961–95," *Journal of European Public Policy* 5 (1): 66–97.

Stone Sweet, Alec and Caporaso, James A. (1998) "From free trade to supranational polity: the European court and integration," in Alec Stone Sweet and Wayne Sandholtz (eds) *European Integration and Supranational Governance*, Oxford: Oxford University Press.

Stone Sweet, Alec and Sandholtz, Wayne (1997) "European integration and supranational governance," *Journal of European Public Policy* 4 (3): 297–317.

Stone Sweet, Alec and Thatcher, Mark (2002) The politics of delegation: non-majoritarian institutions in Europe," special issue of *West European Politics* 25 (1): 1–22.

Swann, Dennis (1995) *The Economics of the Common Market: Integration in the European Union*, 8th edn, London: Penguin.

Szyszczak, Erika (1992) "European Community law: new remedies, new directions? Joined cases C-6/90 and C-9/90, *Francovich and Bonifaci v Italy*," *Modern Law Review* 55 (5): 690–7.

Tagaras, Haris (1995) "La responsabilité étatique pour les dommages causés aux particuliers du fait de violations du droit communautaire," *Revue Hellenique de Droit International* 48: 147–63.

Tallberg, Jonas (2000a) "The anatomy of autonomy: an institutional account of variation in supranational influence," *Journal of Common Market Studies* 38 (5): 843–64.

——(2000b) "Supranational influence in EU enforcement: the ECJ and the principle of state liability," *Journal of European Public Policy* 7 (1): 104–21.

——(2002a) "Delegation to supranational institutions: why, how, and with what consequences?" *West European Politics* 25 (1): 23–46.

——(2002b) "Paths to compliance: enforcement, management, and the European Union," *International Organization* 56 (3): 609–43.

Tallberg, Jonas and Jönsson, Christer (2001) "Compliance bargaining in the European Union," paper prepared for presentation at ECSA 7th Biennial International Conference, May 31–June 2, 2001, Madison.

Temple Lang, John (1997) "The duties of national courts under Community constitutional law," *European Law Review* 22 (1): 3–18.

Tesauro, Guiseppe (1992) "La sanction des infractions au droit communautaire," *Rivisita di Diritto Europeo* 32 (3): 477–509.

Tetlock, Philip E. and Belkin, Aaron (eds) (1996) *Counterfactual Thought Experiments in World Politics: Logical, Methodological, and Psychological Perspectives*, Princeton, NJ: Princeton University Press.

Thatcher, Mark (2001) "The Commission and national governments as partners: EC regulatory expansion in telecommunications 1979–2000," *Journal of European Public Policy* 8 (4): 558–84.

——(2002) "Delegation to independent regulatory agencies: pressures, functions and contextual mediation," *West European Politics* 25 (1): 125–47.

Thatcher, Mark and Stone Sweet, Alec (2002) "Theory and practice of delegation to non-majoritarian institutions," *West European Politics* 25 (1): 1–22.

Tirole, Jean (1986) "Hierarchies and bureaucracies: on the role of collusion in organizations," *Journal of Law, Economics, and Organization* 2 (2): 181–214.

Tridimas, Takis (1996) "The Court of Justice and judicial activism," *European Law Review* 21 (3): 199–210.

——(2001) "Liability for breach of Community law: growing up and mellowing down?," *Common Market Law Review* 38: 301–22.

Tsebelis, George and Garrett, Geoffrey (2001) "The institutional foundations of intergovernmentalism and supranationalism in the European Union," *International Organization* 55 (2): 357–90.

Tsoukalis, Loukas (1997) *The New European Economy Revisited*, Oxford: Oxford University Press.

Uecker, Rolf (1994) "*Francovich* and beyond: a German perspective," *European Business Law Review* 5 (12): 286–91.

Usher, John A. (1994) "The Commission and the law," in Geoffrey Edwards and David Spence (eds) *The European Commission*, London: Cartermill.

Van Gerven, Walter (1995) "Bridging the gap between Community and national laws: towards a principle of homogeneity in the field of legal remedies," *Common Market Law Review* 32: 679–702.

——(1996) "Bridging the unbridgeable: Community and national tort laws after *Francovich* and *Brasserie*," *International and Comparative Law Quarterly* 45 (3): 507–44.

Varian, Hal R. (1990) "Monitoring agents with other agents," *Journal of Institutional and Theoretical Economics* 146 (1): 85–105.

Wallace, Helen and Young, Alasdair R. (1996) "The Single Market," in Helen Wallace and William Wallace (eds) *Policy-Making in the European Union*, 3rd edn, Oxford: Oxford University Press.

Wathelet, Melchior and Van Raepenbusch, Sean (1997) "La responsabilité des états membres en cas de violation du droit communautaire: vers un alignement de la responsabilité de l'état sur celle de la Communauté ou l'inverse?," *Cahiers de Droit Europeen* 1–2: 13–65.

Weatherill, Stephen and Beaumont, Paul (1995) *EC Law: The Essential Guide to the Legal Workings of the European Community*, 2nd edn, London: Penguin.

Weiler, J. H. H. (1991) "The transformation of Europe," *Yale Law Journal* 100: 2403–83.

——(1993) "Journey to an unknown destination: a retrospective and prospective of the European Court of Justice in the arena of political integration," *Journal of Common Market Studies* 31 (4): 417–46.

——(1994) "A quiet revolution: the European Court of Justice and its interlocutors," *Comparative Political Studies* 26 (4): 510–34.

Weingast, Barry R. (1984) "The congressional-bureaucratic system: a principal–agent perspective (with applications to the SEC)," *Public Choice* 44: 147–91.

Weingast, Barry R. and Marshall, William J. (1988) "The industrial organization of Congress: or why legislatures, like firms, are not organized as markets," *Journal of Political Economy* 96: 132–63.

Weingast, Barry R. and Moran, Mark J. (1982) "The myth of runaway bureaucracy," *Regulation* 6: 33–8.

——(1983) "Bureaucratic discretion or congressional control: regulatory policy-making by the Federal Trade Commission," *Journal of Political Economy* 91: 765–800.

Wilks, Stephen with Bartle, Ian (2002) "The unanticipated consequences of creating independent competition agencies," *West European Politics* 25 (1): 148–72.

Williams, Allan M. (1991) *The European Community*, Oxford: Blackwell.

Williamson, Oliver E. (1995) "Transaction cost economics and organization theory," in Oliver E. Williamson (ed.) *Organization Theory: From Chester Barnard to the Present and Beyond*, New York, NY: Oxford University Press.

Wooldridge, Frank (1996) "The United Kingdom memorandum on the European Court of Justice," *European Business Law Review* 7 (12): 279–84.

Wooldridge, Frank and D'Sa, Rose M. (1996) "ECJ decides Factortame (No. 3) and Brasserie du Pêcheur," *European Business Law Review* 7 (7): 161–7.

Yarbrough, Beth V. and Yarbrough, Robert M. (1987) "Cooperation in the liberalization of international trade: after hegemony, what?," *International Organization* 41 (1): 1–26.

——(1990) "International institutions and the new economics of organization." *International Organization* 44 (2): 235–60.

——(1992) *Cooperation and Governance in International Trade: The Strategic Organizational Approach*, Princeton, NJ: Princeton University Press.

——(1997) "Dispute settlement in international trade: regionalism and procedural coordination," in Edward D. Mansfield and Helen V. Milner (eds) *The Political Economy of Regionalism*, New York, NY: Columbia University Press.

Young, Oran R. (1992) "The effectiveness of international institutions: hard cases and critical variables," in James N. Rosenau and Ernst-Otto Czempiel (eds) *Governance without Government: Order and Change in World Politics*, Cambridge: Cambridge University Press.

Official documents

CEN (1994) *The New Approach: Legislation and Standards on the Free Movement of Goods in Europe*, Brussels: CEN.

Davis, David (1995) *1996 Inter-Governmental Conference: European Court of Justice*. Letter to Carlos Westendorp, chairman of the Reflection Group, September 25, 1995.

European Commission (1984) *First Annual Report to the European Parliament on Commission Monitoring of the Application of Community Law (1983)*. COM (84) 181 Final. 11.4.1984.

——(1985a) *Second Annual Report to the European Parliament on Commission Monitoring of the Application of Community Law (1984)*. COM (85) 149 Final. 6.5.1985.

——(1985b) *Completing the Internal Market: White Paper from the Commission to the European Council (Milan, 28 and 29 June 1985)*. COM (85) 310 Final. 14.6.1985.

——(1986a) *Third Annual Report to the European Parliament on Commission Monitoring of the Application of Community Law (1986)*. COM (86) 204 Final. 3.6.1986.

——(1986b) *First Report from the Commission to the Council and the European Parliament on the Implementation of the Commission's White Paper on Completing the Internal Market*. COM (86) 300 Final. 26.5.1986.

——(1987a) *Second Report from the Commission to the Council and the European Parliament on the Implementation of the Commission's White Paper on Completing the Internal Market*. COM (87) 203 Final. 11.5.1987.

——(1987b) *Fourth Annual Report to the European Parliament on Commission Monitoring of the Application of Community Law (1987)*. COM (87) 250 Final. 16.12.1987.

——(1988a) *Third Report from the Commission to the Council and the European Parliament on the Implementation of the Commission's White Paper on Completing the Internal Market*. COM (88) 134 Final. 21.3.1988.

——(1988b) *Fifth Annual Report to the European Parliament on Commission Monitoring of the Application of Community Law (1987)*. COM (88) 425 Final. 3.10.1988.

——(1988c) *Completing the Internal Market: An Area without Internal Frontiers. The Progress Report Required by Article 8b of the Treaty*. COM (88) 650 Final. 17.11.1988.

——(1989a) "Complaint to the Commission of the European Communities for failure to comply with Community law," *Official Journal*, No. C/26/6–7. 1.2.1989.

——(1989b) *Fourth Progress Report of the Commission to the Council and the European Parliament Concerning the Implementation of the Commission's White Paper on the Completion of the Internal Market*. COM (89) 311 Final. 20.6.1989.

——(1989c) *Communication from the Commission on Implementation of the Legal Acts Required to Build the Single Market*. COM (89) 422 Final. 7.9.1989.

——(1989d) *Sixth Annual Report to the European Parliament on Commission Monitoring of the Application of Community Law (1988)*. COM (89) 411 Final. 21.12.1989.

——(1990a) *Seventh Annual Report to the European Parliament on Commission Monitoring of the Application of Community Law (1989)*. COM (90) 288 Final. 22.5.1990.

——(1990b) *Commission Opinion of 21 October 1990 on the Proposal for Amendment of the Treaty Establishing the European Economic Community with a View to Political Union*. COM (90) 600 Final. 23.10.1990.

——(1990c) *Completing the Internal Market: An Area without Internal Frontiers. Progress Report Required by Article 8b of the Treaty*. COM (90) 552 Final. 23.11.1990.

——(1991a) *Initial Contributions by the Commission to the Intergovernmental Conference on Political Union: Composite Working Paper*. SEC (91) 500. 15.5.1991.

——(1991b) *Sixth Report of the Commission to the Council and the European Parliament Concerning the Implementation of the White Paper on the Completion of the Internal Market*. COM (91) 237 Final. 19.5.1991.

——(1991c) *Eighth Annual Report to the European Parliament on Commission Monitoring of the Application of Community Law (1990)*. COM (91) 321 Final. 16.10.1991.

——(1992a) *Ninth Annual Report on Commission Monitoring of the Application of Community Law (1991)*. COM (92) 136 Final. 12.5.1992.

——(1992b) *Seventh Report of the Commission to the Council and the European Parliament Concerning the Implementation of the White Paper on the Completion of the Internal Market*. COM (92) 383 Final. 2.9.1992.

——(1992c) *The Internal Market After 1992: Meeting the Challenge. Report to the EEC Commission by the High Level Group on the Operation of the Internal Market*. Brussels, October 1992.
——(1993a) "Notice on cooperation between national courts and the Commission in applying Article 85 and 86 of the EEC treaty," *Official Journal*, No. C 39/6–12. 13.2.1993.
——(1993b) *Tenth Annual Report on the Monitoring of the Application of Community Law (1992)*. COM (93) 320 Final. 28.4.1993.
——(1993c) *Making the Most of the Internal Market: Strategic Programme. Communication from the Commission to the Council*. COM (93) 632 Final. 22.12.1993.
——(1994a) *Communication from the Commission to the Council and the European Parliament on the Development of Administrative Cooperation in the Implementation and Enforcement of Community Legislation in the Internal Market*. COM (94) 29 Final. 16.2.1994.
——(1994b) *Eleventh Annual Report on Monitoring the Application of Community Law (1993)*. COM (94) 500 Final. 29.3.1994.
——(1994c) *The Community Internal Market: 1993 Report*. Luxembourg: Office for Official Publications of the European Communities.
——(1995a) *Communication from the Commission to the Council and the European Parliament on the Role of Penalties in Implementing Community Internal Market Legislation*. COM (95) 162 Final. 3.5.1995.
——(1995b) *Twelfth Annual Report on Monitoring the Application of Community Law (1994)*. COM (95) 500 Final. 7.6.1995.
——(1995c) *The Single Market in 1994: Report from the Commission to the Council and the European Parliament*. COM (95) 238 Final. 15.6.1995.
——(1995d) "Notice on cooperation between national courts and the Commission in the state aid field," *Official Journal*, No. C 312/8–13. 23.11. 1995.
——(1995e) *Commission Report for the Reflection Group*, Luxembourg: Office for Official Publications of the European Communities.
——(1995f) "Initiative: 'Les citoyens d'abord'. Informer les citoyens de leurs droits," *Single Market News* 1: 2.
——(1996a) *Cooperation between Administrations for Enforcement of Internal Market Law: A Progress Report. Report from the Commission to the Council and the European Parliament*. COM (96) 20 Final. 29.1.1996.
——(1996b) *The Single Market in 1995: Report from the Commission to the Council and the European Parliament*. COM (96) 51 Final. 20.2.1996.
——(1996c) *Reinforcing Political Union and Preparing for Enlargement: Commission Opinion*. COM (96) 90 Final. 28.2.1996.
——(1996d) *Thirteenth Annual Report on Monitoring the Application of Community Law (1995)*. COM (96) 600 Final. 29.5.1996.
——(1996e) "Memorandum on applying Article 171 of the EC treaty," *Official Journal*, No. C 242/6–8. 21.8.1996.
——(1996f) *The Impact and Effectiveness of the Single Market: Communication from the Commission to the European Parliament and the Council*. COM (96) 520 Final. 30.10.1996.
——(1996g) *Proposal for a European Parliament and Council Decision Establishing an Action Programme to Improve Awareness of Community Law for the Legal Professions (Robert Schuman Project)*. COM (96) 580 Final. 15.11.1996.

——(1996h) *The Single Market and Tomorrow's Europe: A Progress Report from the European Commission*, Luxembourg: Office for Official Publications of the European Communities.
——(1996i) "Economic evaluation of the internal market," *European Economy* 4, Luxembourg: Office for Official Publications of the European Communities.
——(1996j) *Living in Another Country of the European Union*, information brochure, Citizens First initiative.
——(1996k) *Internal Market: Action Programme to Improve the Application of Community Law*. Press Release IP/96/1069.
——(1997a) *The Commission for the First Time Seeks Financial Penalties against Non-compliance with European Court Judgements*. Press Release IP/97/63. 29.1.1997.
——(1997b) "Method of calculating the penalty payments provided for pursuant to Article 171 of the EC treaty," *Official Journal*, No. C 63/2–4. 28.2.1997.
——(1997c) *Single Market: Overview of Compliance Problems in 1996*. Press Release IP/97/362. 29.4.1997.
——(1997d) *Fourteenth Annual Report on Monitoring the Application of Community Law (1996)*. COM (97) 299 Final. 29.5.1997.
——(1997e) *Amended Proposal for a European Parliament and Council Decision Establishing an Action Programme to Improve Awareness of Community Law for the Legal Professions (Robert Schuman Project)*. COM (97) 596 Final. 7.11.1997.
——(1997f) *Proposal for a Council Regulation (EC) Creating a Mechanism whereby the Commission Can Intervene in Order to Remove Certain Obstacles to Trade*. COM (97) 619 Final. 18.11.1997.
——(1997g) *The Commission Proposes an Intervention Mechanism to Safeguard Free Trade in the Single Market*. Press Release IP/97/1016. 19.11.1997.
——(1997h) *Citizens First: EU Rights on Equal Opportunities, Buying Goods and Services and Travelling*. Press Release IP/97/1035. 25.11.1997.
——(1997i) *Towards Greater Efficiency in Obtaining and Enforcing Judgements in the European Union: Proposal for a Council Act Establishing the Convention on Jurisdiction and the Recognition of Judgements in Civil and Commercial Matters in the Member States of the European Union. Commission Communication to the Council and the European Parliament*. COM (97) 609 Final. 26.11.1997.
——(1997j) *Single Market Scoreboard*. No. 1. November 1997.
——(1997k) *Evaluation of Phase 1 of Citizens First*.
——(1997l) "Citoyens d'Europe: mieux faire connaître leurs droits aux habitants de l'Union," *Single Market News* 6: 2–3.
——(1997m) "Help desk on complaints procedure," *Single Market News* 6: 25.
——(1997n) "Transposition: state of implementation of the White Paper measures," *Single Market News* 7: 2.
——(1997o) "Citizens First: 450,000 people have now contacted Citizens First," *Single Market News* 7: 4.
——(1997p) "Citizens First: the next phase will be launched in November," *Single Market News* 9: 4.
——(1997q) "Strengths and weaknesses of the Single Market," special dossier in *Single Market News* 10.
——(1997r) "Initiative 'Citoyens d'Europe': une deuxième phase aussi ambitieuse que la première," *Single Market News* 10: 2–3.

——(1998a) *Citizens First Signpost Service: Analysis of Enquiries, November 1996–July 1997*. 18.5.1998.
——(1998b) *Listening to Citizens: The Difficulties that People Face in Exercising their Rights within the Single European Market. A Report Drafted by the Signpost Service as Part of the "Citizens First" Initiative*. 18.5. 1998.
——(1998c) *Fifteenth Annual Report on Monitoring the Application of Community Law (1997)*. COM (98) 317 Final. 19.5.1998.
——(1998d) *Single Market Scoreboard*. No. 2. May 1998.
——(1998e) *Informal Meeting of Internal Market Ministers, Cambridge, 13–14 February*. Available at http://europa.eu.int/comm/dg15/en/index.htm
——(1998f) "Citizens First – phase 2: new dialogues with citizens and business," *Single Market News* 11: 4–5.
——(1998g) "Citizens First update: results of phase II for all member states," *Single Market News* 12: 4–5.
——(1998h) "Pour éliminer certains obstacles aux échanges: instauration d'un double mécanisme d'intervention rapide," *Single Market News* 13: 11.
——(1998i) "Dialogue with citizens and business: encouraging awareness of opportunities in the single market," *Single Market News* 13: 2–3.
——(1998j) "Action Robert Schuman: sensibiliser les juristes au droit communautaire," *Single Market News* 15: 5.
——(1999a) *Sixteenth Annual Report on Monitoring the Application of Community Law (1998)*. COM (1999) 301 Final. 9.7.1999.
——(1999b) *Single Market Scoreboard*. No. 5. November 1999.
——(2000a) *Seventeenth Annual Report on Monitoring the Application of Community Law (1999)*. COM (2000) 92 Final. 23.6.2000.
——(2000b) *Enforcing your Rights in the Single European Market*, information guide, Dialogue with Citizens and Business initiative. Available at http://europa.eu.int/citizens
——(2001a) *Internal Market Scoreboard*. No. 9. November 2001.
——(2001b) *Interactive Policy Making. Communication from the Commission*. C (2001) 1014. 3.4.2001.
——(2001c) *Eighteenth Annual Report on Monitoring the Application of Community Law (2000)*. COM (2001) 309 Final. 16.7.2001.
——(2001d) "Interactive policy making through the Internet," *Single Market News* 26: 2–3.
——(2001e) "Mécanisme d'intervention en cas de blocages routiers: rapport après deux ans d'application," *Single Market News* 26: 10.
——(2002a) *Dix-neuvième Rapport annuel sur le contrôle de l'application du droit communautaire (2001)*. COM (2002) 324 Provisoire. 28.6.2002.
——(2002b) *Report to the European Parliament, the Council, the Economic and Social Committee and the Committee of the Regions on the Implementation of the Robert Schuman Project 1999–2001*. SEC (2002) 157. 7.2.2002.
European Council (1997) "Amsterdam European Council: Conclusions of the Presidency," *Bulletin of the European Union* 1997 (6): 8–22.
European Court of Justice (1975) "Suggestions of the Court of Justice on European Union," *Bulletin of the EC*, Supplement 9/75: 17–21.
——(1995) *Report of the Court of Justice on Certain Aspects of the Application of the Treaty on European Union*, Luxembourg: European Court of Justice.
European Parliament (1983a) *Report Drawn up on Behalf of the Legal Affairs*

Committee on the Responsibility of Member States for the Application of Community Law. PE 77.275/fin. 10.1.1983.
——(1983b) “Resolution on the responsibility of the member states for the application of and compliance with Community law,” *Official Journal*, No. C 68/32–4. 14.3.1983.
——(1988) *Report Drawn up on Behalf of the Committee on Legal Affairs and Citizens' Rights on the Fourth Annual Report to the European Parliament on Commission Monitoring of the Application of Community Law – 1986*. PE 119.095/fin. 22.2.1988.
IGC (1996a) *Position du gouvernement italien sur la conférence intergouvernementale pour la révision des traités*. CONF/3839/96.
——(1996b) *Note from the Presidency: The Institutions of a More Democratic and More Effective Union*. CONF 3849/96.
——(1996c) *Memorandum by the United Kingdom on the European Court of Justice*. CONF/3883/96.
——(1996d) *Création de la possibilité de transférer au Tribunal de Première Instance les procédures relatives aux questions préjudicielles: Note de transmission, délégation allemande*. CONF/3962/96.
——(1997a) *Proposition d'amendement de la délégation française sur la Cour de Justice*. CONF/3853/97.
——(1997b) *Pour une application uniforme et efficace des disposition relatives au marché intérieur: Note de transmission de la délégation italienne, transmise par M. Silvio Fagiolo, représentant à la conférence intergouvernementale, à M. Jürgen Trumpf, secrétaire général du Conseil de l'Union européenne*. CONF/3913/97.
Mogg, John (1996) “Editorial,” *Single Market News* 5: 1.
——(1998) “Editorial,” *Single Market News* 13: 1.
Monti, Mario (1997) *Making the Single Market Work: The Next Steps*. Speech, March 7, 1997, Brussels.
Reflection Group (1995) *Reflection Group's Report*. Brussels, 5.12.1995.
SOU (1997) *Det allmännas skadeståndsansvar vid överträdelse av EG-regler: Betänkande av utredningen om det allmännas skadeståndsansvar vid överträdelse av EG-rätten*. Statens offentliga utredningar, SOU 1997: 194.

Judgments by the European Court of Justice

Andersson and Wåkerås-Andersson *v*. Swedish State, Case C-321/97, ECR 1999 (I): 3551.
Brasserie du Pêcheur SA *v*. Germany, and Factortame and Others *v*. the UK, Joined Cases C-46 and 48/93 (Factortame III), ECR 1996 (I): 1029.
Brinkmann Tabakfabriken GmbH *v*. Skatteministeriet, Case C-319/96, ECR 1998 (I): 5255.
British Telecommunications *v*. the UK, Case C-392/93, ECR 1996 (I): 1631.
Costa *v*. ENEL, Case 6/64, ECR 1964: 585.
Dillenkofer and Others *v*. Germany, Joined Cases C-178, 179, 188, 189, and 190/94, ECR 1996 (I): 4845.
Emmott *v*. Minister for Social Welfare, Case C-208/90, ECR 1991 (I): 4269.
Factortame *v*. Secretary of State for Transport, Case C-213/89 (Factortame I), ECR 1990: 2433.

Francovich and Others *v*. Italy, Joined Cases C-6 and 9/90, ECR 1991 (I): 5357.
Haim *v*. Kassenzahnärtzliche Vereinigung Nordrhein (Haim II), Case C-424/97, ECR 2000 (I): 5123.
Hedley Lomas *v*. the UK, Case C-5/94, ECR 1996 (I): 2553.
Konle *v*. Republic of Austria, Case C-302/97, ECR 1999 (I): 3099.
Marshall *v*. Southampton and South West Hampshire Health Authority, Case C-271/91 (Marshall II), ECR 1993 (I): 4367.
Norbrook Laboratories Limited *v*. Ministry of Agriculture, Case C-127/95, ECR 1998 (I): 1531.
Rechberger and Greindl *v*. Austria, Case C-140/97, ECR 1999 (I): 3499.
Rewe-Zentral AG *v*. Bundesmonopolverwaltung für Branntwein, Case 120/78 (Cassis de Dijon), ECR 1979: 649.
Rewe-Zentralfinanz *v*. Landwirtschaftskammer, Case 33/76, ECR 1976: 1989.
Van Gend & Loos *v*. Nederlandse Administratie der Belastingen, Case 26/62, European Court Reports (ECR) 1963: 1.
Von Colson and Kamann *v*. Land Nordrhein-Westfalen, Case 14/83, ECR 1984: 1891.
Zuckerfabrik Süderdithmarschen AG *v*. Hauptzollamt Itzehoe, Joined Cases C-143/88 and C-92/89, ECR 1991 (I): 415.

Index